Long and Winding Road

Adolescents *and* Youth in Canada Today

Vappu Tyyskä

Canadian Scholars' Press Inc.

Long and Winding Road:
Adolescents and Youth in Canada Today
Vappu Tyyskä

First published in 2001 by
Canadian Scholars' Press Inc.
180 Bloor Street West, Suite 1202
Toronto, Ontario
M5S 2V6

www.cspi.org

Canadian Scholars' Press gratefully acknowledges financial assistance for our publishing activities from the Ontario Arts Council, The Canada Council for the Arts, and the Government of Canada through the Book Publishing Industry Development Program.

Every reasonable effort has been made to identify copyright holders. CSPI would be pleased to have any errors or omissions brought to its attention.

Canadian Cataloguing in Publication Data

National Library of Canada Cataloguing in Publication Data

Tyyskä, Vappu, 1956-
    Long and winding road : adolescents and youth in Canada today

Includes bibliographical references.
ISBN 1-55130-194-6

1. Adolescence—Canada. 2. Teenagers—Canada. I. Title.

HQ799.C3T99 2001   305.235'0971   C2001-902005-8

Managing Editor: Ruth Bradley-St-Cyr
Production Editor: Rebecka Sheffield
Proofreading: Linda Bissinger
Page Layout: Brad Horning
Cover Design: Rebecka Sheffield
Cover Images: roB Breadner, Rebecka Sheffield
Interior Images: Vincenzo Pietropaolo

01   02   03   04   05   06   07   7   6   5   4   3   2   1

Printed and bound in Canada by AGMV Marquis

Publisher's Acknowledgements

Material from *Canada's Teens: Today, Yesterday and Tomorrow* copyright © 2001 by Reginald Bibby. Reprinted by permission of Stoddart Publishing Co. Limited.

Excerpt from *The Sociology of Education in Canada: Critical Perspectives* by Terry Wotherspoon. Copyright © Oxford University Press Canada 1998.

Excerpt from *Enter at Your Own Risk: Canadian Youth and the Labour Market* copyright © 1998 by Richard Marquardt. Reprinted by permission of Between the Lines.

Excerpt from *How Teens Got The Power: Gen Y has cash, the cool – and a burgeoning consumer culture* copyright © 1999 by Andrew Clark. Reprinted by permission of Maclean's.

Excerpt from *Rave Fever: raves are all the rage, but drugs are casting a pall over their sunny peace-and-love ethos* copyright © 2000 by Susan Oh. Reprinted by permission of Maclean's.

Excerpt from *Wild Ones Through the Ages: Some of the Youth Movements that have Captivated Kids – and in most cases, scandalized parents – over the past 60 years* copyright © 2000 by Maclean's. Reprinted by permission of Maclean's.

Excerpt from *Immigrant Youth in Canada* copyright © 2000 by the Canadian Council on Social Development. Reprinted with permission from the Canadian Council on Social Development.

Excerpt from *Cool: The Signs and Meanings of Adolescence* copyright © 1994 by Marcel Danesi. Reprinted with permission of University of Toronto Press, Inc.

Excerpt from *Girl Talk: Adolescent Magazines and Their Readers* copyright © 1999 by D. Currie. Reprinted with permission from University of Toronto Press, Inc.

Contents

List of Figures and Tables

Preface

In the winter of 1998/99 I began teaching a course entitled *Youth and Society* at Ryerson University. I discovered that, although a lot has been written about the lives of adolescents, there were no suitable undergraduate textbooks about the lives of Canadian juveniles.

Most studies and books on the topic are either American or European, and many of them offer either psychologically-based or uncritical views of the issues faced by young people. Further, some studies treat the category "youth" as a homogeneous entity, without regard to differences based on social class, gender, sexual orientation, race, or ethnicity.

While there is no lack of good Canadian studies and books on youth (for example, Côté and Allahar, 1994; Marquardt, 1998; Livingstone, 1999; Bell, 1999; Wong and Checkland, 1999; James, 1998; O'Grady et al., 1998), they tend to be overspecialized (youth crime, education, and employment being the most popular subjects), each giving a picture rich in detail but clearly limited in its scope. The strength that a number of these Canadian works about young people offers is a critical perspective on the challenging conditions that youth struggle with, whether in education, employment, the legal system, family, or other institutions. However, what is required is to bring together the separate strands of Canadian youth research and present a comprehensive picture of this diverse population at the beginning of the new millennium. This book is my response to that challenge.

In the process of writing this book, I relied on the help of many institutions and individuals.

I would like to thank the editorial staff of Canadian Scholars' Press, especially Jack Wayne, Ruth Bradley-St-Cyr, Rebecka Sheffield, and Chris Doda, for their help and encouragement in leading me through the publication process.

It would have been impossible to write this book without financial assistance. I thank the Office of Research Services at Ryerson University for making it possible to hire two intelligent and energetic Ryerson students as research assistants at various stages of the research and writing process. Both Carolyn Deegan and Fiona Whittington-Walsh assisted with the literature process. Additional thanks to Carolyn for her help with the writing of the sections on legal and illegal drug use; and to Fiona, both for assisting with the writing of the chapter on youth culture, and for being a good friend.

I owe special thanks to my colleagues in the Department of Sociology at Ryerson University for their generous support and for creating a pleasant and productive working environment. I am particularly grateful to the departmental chair, Murray Pomerance, for facilitating the book-writing process in many ways: by finding ways to ease my other university duties and by funding a production assistant, Bryan Dale, at the final stages of the process. I thank Bryan for creating the tables and figures in this book.

My love and thanks to my partner, Allen, and my son, Mikko, for everything.

Mikko — this one is for (and about) you!

Toronto, June 19, 2001
Vappu Tyyskä

1 | *Introduction*

Adults do not realize the stressfulness of being eighteen, and that it's not just one big party. I find that I don't have time to worry about things like the federal deficit while worrying about obtaining a job, school, boyfriend, social life, and dealing with my emotions, problems, and pressures of everyday life. (Female, Grade twelve, in Bibby, 2001: 34)

Today's youth are intelligent but some adults don't seem to think so. We are people too. Youths are discriminated against and that's not right. To get through to young people, you have to listen to them, trust them, and respect them. The way I look and the music I listen to does not make me a "bad" person. I am my own person (Fifteen-year-old from Montreal, in Bibby, 2001: 70).

I have not only personally experienced the dehumanizing of black youth, but also witnessed it.

It was a typical Wednesday afternoon during rush hour at the Dundas subway station. Everyone was hurrying toward the northbound train, including a braided black teen in baggy jeans.

As I walked through the turnstiles and turned to my left, I saw two male TTC employees yelling at this young man for showing a wrong transfer. He stopped and paid the correct fare, but the verbal abuse continued.

One of the employees shouted: "Do you need a father to teach you how to take the TTC, or are you just stupid, boy?'"Now, showing a wrong transfer does not give anyone the right to verbally assault a young black person. The language the TTC employee used was a sickening reminder of our racist past when even gray-haired black men were called "boy."

The young man who had been so humiliated in front of a huge group of people walked away, enraged and embarrassed, to stand alone at the back of the platform. I imagined that I knew exactly how he felt.

I asked myself, "Why did these two adults feel the need to make us feel so discouraged?".... (Kirk Moss, age twenty-one)

What is Wrong with Young People Today?

Every day, we are bombarded with the problems of youth. We get anecdotes about problematic adolescents from family members and acquaintances. Media feed us a daily dose of stories about young people in trouble. The range of issues includes concern over the economic futures of youth amidst high unemployment, matters related to education with questions about school-to-work transitions and whether the education system is serving our youth adequately, and family pressures, including divorces and violence. At the same time, fear is expressed that different social pressures, combined with poor parental supervision, result in delinquency and crime. Other areas identified include social problems associated with young people's withdrawal from communities, manifested in poor health, stress, suicides, drug abuse, poverty, life on the streets, teenage pregnancies, and sexually transmitted diseases.

While pointing to these and many other legitimate concerns about young people's lives, there is an unfortunate tendency in the media and among the general public either to vilify youth or to blame them and/or their families for their plight. The voices of young people themselves are frequently missing. When youthful views are presented, they are used to show how unconcerned adolescents and people in their twenties are with their communities, to witness their passivity in politics, and their preoccupation with trivial pursuits presented by the leisure industry. Where young people are associated with action, it tends to be negative. Slanted coverage of youth crime, street youth, gangs, and other delinquent or criminal forms of activity gives the impression of young people run amok in their homes, on the streets, and in our communities. Witness the most recent reports about the "rave" phenomenon or about the violence in large youth-driven demonstrations against the power of global corporations and the international financial machinery. The views presented in media both shape and reflect generally accepted public opinions.

While some of the concerns outlined above have a real and factual basis, many of the popular notions about youth are based on misreading of studies and statistics or a misdirection of attention. Many misconceptions will be presented, discussed, and criticized in the substantive chapters of this book. For now we can note, for example, that the real problem of the education system is not with the individuals who drop out, but conditions in the system itself that result in high-school dropouts or stalled post-secondary education, including gender and race discrimination and a lack of resources. Problems of youth employment have less to do with a lack of skills among young people and more with the ways in which the labour market is becoming governed by jobs requiring low skill and offering poor wages and working conditions. And rather than living on the streets as a lifestyle choice, some young people's family lives are subject to abuse and neglect that leave them little choice but to get away. Lacking alternatives, they end up on the streets and become targets of public fear and prejudice. While alone they may garner some sympathy, but in groups they are labelled as gangs with the expectation that they engage in deviant and criminal acts. This is also true for other youth who represent a specific brand of youth culture, such as the recent phenomenon of raves. While actual youth gangs do exist, there is an unfortunate impression that young people in groups have to be watched, especially if they happen to be visible minorities. There are widespread misconceptions about increasing levels of youth crime and violence and about the juvenile justice system. One most common is that youth sentencing is too lenient. In fact, sentences for young people are often harsher than for adults convicted of the same crimes. With all the factors in place, an atmosphere exists where young people are likely to be viewed negatively, subjected to increasing controls, and given little or positive feedback at a stage of life supposedly full of hope and promise.

The popular anecdotal, misleading, and negative views about young people need to be taken apart. We need to systematically analyze the root causes of different ideologies and theories related to youth. The main task of this book is this: move away from dealing with youth as the problem to addressing the social, economic, and political circumstances of their lives that are problematic.

Taking a critical approach, this book deals with the overlapping power relationships of capitalism, patriarchy, and racism that shape the lives of all people, but have special relevance to youth in societies in which age is yet another significant basis for power differences.

The different strands in the history of adolescence and youth point to an ongoing social construction of these age categories that has emerged in a specific form out of the development of industrial capitalism. What unites young people are the expectations of education and a tenuous link to the labour force. Overall, they are subject to an age division in which their parents wield the most power due to their connection to full-time employment and political participation. What divides young people are distinct educational and employment histories based on their social class, gender, race, and ethnicity. These similarities and differences are manifested in social institutions, including not only work and education, but families, peers, the legal system, and the state.

In this chapter, I will begin with a segment that outlines the meaning of youth categories as we understand them today and as they are used in this book. Next, I will outline the general theories and ideologies that drive both research and public views about young people, some of which view young people as a problem to be dealt with. In contrast to this, I will present a critical view which questions the environment that young people occupy as the problem.

Second, in order to understand the meanings of contemporary youth categories, I will outline some of the Canadian history of pre-adults, particularly as it relates to education and employment of young men and women. To illustrate the divisions based on race in the Canadian context, I will present some of the history of Aboriginal and Black youth populations in Canada. The historical focus will be on education and employment and, to some degree the justice system. Most of what we know about young people's lives is through their contact with these major social institutions.

Out of the historical developments arises a picture of youth prolonged, or a "generation on hold" (Côté and Allahar, 1994). Adolescence and youth are ever longer time periods, stamped by a suspension of full social, economic, and political rights to this age group. Young people's dependency or semi-dependency on adult-led institutions provides a foundation for a multitude of situations of conflict based on age. Power is held by adults in positions of economic and political importance while young people's lives are held in an ever lengthening period of suspension.

The historical account will help us understand the age parameters of contemporary youth categories in society and the ways in which these categories are used in this book. Further, this social construction of youthful age categories in history will lay the groundwork for a more detailed discussion of different social, economic, and political aspects of young people's lives in contemporary Canada.

Defining Adolescence and Youth Today

There are numerous and competing definitions about pre-adult age categories that prevail both among the public and among scholars. One view is that youth is "not a particular age range; it is a social status," characterized by a period of life in which a person is either partly or fully dependent on others, usually family, for material support (Marquardt, 1998: 7). This generalization reflects the difficulties in maintaining consistency when discussing the category youth, because of the enormous variety of definitions used. Our difficulties in pinpointing the exact year markers for younger age groups reflect their continuing social construction. Age-related terms are fluid, subject to alteration in response to changing times and circumstances. This is easily illustrated by the ongoing debates between those who see young people at an adult-like stage of maturity earlier and those who would like to raise the bar for this presumed maturity. Examples of the maturity debate are easy to find and include disagreements over the acceptable age range for juvenile criminal offenders, historic shifts in the acceptable minimum age for consensual sexual activity, the proper voting age, or the variance in the legal drinking age across Canadian provinces and territories.

Similarly, scholarly and everyday usage varies to some degree. For example, according to Galambos and Kolaric (1994), young people fall between the ages 10–24. Within this category, they distinguish between "young adolescents"(10–14), "teens" (15–19), and "young adults" (20–24). They also use the term "youth" to refer to those aged 15–24. In the everyday usage of contemporary North America, the term adolescent is used synonymously with the word teenager (13–19) (e.g. Danesi, 1994: 6), whereas for a long time the term "adolescent" was used of a wider age category, those between fifteen and twenty-four years of age (Ambrose, 1999: 338). The term "tweens," first introduced by the advertizing industry in the 1990s, is also increasingly used for those who are aged 10–12.

The categories and dividing lines are further confounded by official definitions. During the International Year of the Youth, in 1985, the United Nations defined youth as those between fifteen and twenty-five years of age (Brown, 1990: 62). This corresponds to Statistics Canada's use of five-year age clusters, e.g. 10–14, 15–19, 20–24 (see Table 1.1). This makes it difficult to isolate "teens" as a separate category, because the age group 10–14 includes both "tweens" and teens. In this sense, government statistics are in conflict with our general understanding of socially significant age categories.

However, if we follow Marquardt's (1998) use of dependence or semi-dependence as the sole criterion to define youth, we could just as easily fit other large segments of the population into this category, including stay-at-home mothers and most co-dependent wage-earners. Therefore, we need to set some age limits for the category of youth as we understand them in today's society. Noting the various official and everyday usages, and recognizing that the category of youth is socially constructed, the term youth or young people is used here primarily in reference to people who are in their adolescence (13–19) and in their early- to mid-twenties (20–24).

According to the 1996 Census, forty-three percent of the Canadian population is under the age of twenty-five. Of this, approximately thirteen percent are in the age group 15–24. Chui (1999: 9) reports that men outnumber women in all age categories from birth to age thirty-nine, while the reverse is true of all age groups older than that. Table 1.1 shows a more detailed breakdown of age groups, by sex, as of 1999.

Because of low fertility and mortality rates, there is a general trend toward the aging of the Canadian population. This is particularly marked as the baby boomer cohort makes its way through the population pyramid: there is a smaller proportion of young people as compared with older people. As the boomers reached 18–24 years of age, there was a peak population of 3.5 million in 1982. Subsequent populations of this age group are smaller, in line with the "baby bust," with a slight increase expected again between 2016 and 2041. Similarly, because of the relatively large numbers in the baby boom cohort, the comparatively larger population of their offspring ("Gen-Xers" or the "echo" cohort) exerted an upward pressure on the numbers of young people under eighteen years of age until 1995, reaching 7.2 million, or twenty-four percent of the population. This is expected to drop to approximately twenty percent by 2016, and to nineteen percent by 2041 (Chui, 1999: 9; also see Galambos and Kolaric, 1994). The fluidity of age categories, from teens to the mid-twenties, addressed here will be shown through this book.

Table 1.1. Population by Sex and Age (1999):
% of Total Population

All Ages	100%*	Male	Female
0–4	5.99	6.20	5.78
5–9	6.76	7.00	6.53
10–14	6.65	6.89	6.41
15–19	6.76	7.00	6.52
20–24	6.75	6.96	6.54
25–29	6.94	7.08	6.79
30–34	7.68	7.83	7.54
35–39	8.88	9.03	8.73
40–44	8.42	8.51	8.34
45–49	7.38	7.43	7.33
50–54	6.42	6.46	6.38
55–59	4.90	4.90	4.91
60–64	4.04	4.00	4.09
65–69	3.74	3.63	3.85
70–74	3.24	2.95	3.52
75–79	2.58	2.15	3.00
80–84	1.561	1.171	1.94
85–89	0.878	0.572	1.178
90+	0.416	0.218	0.610

Source: Statistics Canada, CANSIM, Matrix 6367.
* N=30,567,962

Theories and Ideologies of Youth

To a large degree the information we receive about the state of young people in our society conflicts with our general imagery and ideology about youth. There is a general belief that youth is the most carefree stage of our lives, a time to gradually learn about who we are, how and where we fit into society around us, and explore our options. These ideals form the dominant view of Western nation-states, Canada included, as liberal democracies that offer the best opportunities in life for everyone. Therefore, the thinking goes, if problems exist they have to do with the individuals' or groups' inability to adapt to normal conditions. Such an approach is uncritical and conservative and focuses on the biological and social development of human beings, most frequently expressed in socio-biology, or developmental and life-stage theories. These views are popularized, among other things, in imagery of young people enslaved to their "hormonal hurricanes," and requiring firm regulation so that they will learn to modify their behaviour and act in accordance with mainstream rules and norms.

Conservative Theories: Conformity

Many contemporary conservative theories are rooted in Social Darwinism, which flourished from the nineteenth century onward, premised on the evolutionary theories of Charles Darwin, who wrote *The Origin of the Species by Means of Natural Selection* (1859) and *The Descent of Man* (1871). In these books, he outlined a theory of adaptation and natural selection, a process of selecting biological traits of adaptive value that were most likely to appear in the successive generations. The biological analogy is extended to society by structural-functionalists (see below), who propose that different elements in society are present because they serve some beneficial purpose to the system as a whole. Any possible problems have to be addressed by society to ensure the continuity of the system over time.

The biological and structural-functionalist theories are linked in their application to the emergence of adolescence and youth. The development of age strata has a direct and adaptive biological basis, particularly as a new stage of youth developed out of specific biological imperatives of maturation. This developmental stage involves biologically driven disruptive elements, often identified as "hormonal hurricanes," as young people learn to adapt to their environment. In order for society not to suffer from the negative outbursts of youthful rebellion, youth need to be subjected to a number of control mechanisms, including education, which are often presented as natural parts of preparation for adult life.

To elaborate, age strata, such as adolescence or youth are seen to be a beneficial adaptation to new environmental conditions. As explained by Côté and Allahar (1994: 16–19), structural-functionalist theories of youth see it as a necessary stage of life, characterized by preparation to meet diverse societal needs. For example, industrialization is seen to have created a need for a longer stage of preparation for adulthood. With the onset of industrial labour and gradual improvements in the standard of living of working people, the labour of young people was no longer required and their stage of total or partial dependence on parents was prolonged. As the service economy expanded, "youth" became entrenched as a stage for education and preparation for the demands of the new economy.

It is generally accepted in structural-functionalist theory that prolonged education is necessary in order to prepare for adult life, including a full participation in the economy. It is equally accepted that this requires postponement of other aspects of life, including having sufficient income to live independently, and delaying marriage and family formation. This theory promotes the notion that youth is a stage for instilling conformity within the requirements of prevailing economic and social conditions. This conservative script calls for mechanisms of control on youth to ensure a smooth functioning of society, while conflict is seen to be detrimental to the system as a whole (e.g. Eisenstadt, in O'Donnell, 1985: 5–8).

Not all structural-functionalists promote the doing away with conflict through institutional measures, but all of them promote the idea of common good over narrower group interests, which are seen to disrupt the orderly development of societies (O'Donnell, 1985: 7–8). Little attention is paid either to the problems that youth may face through this stage of the suspension of their rights or to any active role that young people may play in changing the ground rules.

The earliest structural-functionalist contribution to theories of youth comes from G. Stanley Hall who, in 1904, proposed that human development from birth to death mirrored the evolutionary path of the human race. Fuelled by Darwinism, Hall developed his recapitulation theory, proposing that *ha ha ha*

adolescence was a stage of savagery, a period of "Sturm und Drang" (storm and stress) (Danesi, 1994 7; Côté and Allahar, 1994: 6–7). His theory proposed that, like human evolution, individual development and maturation was a gradual process in which each stage was crucial in laying the stepping stones for the next. In adolescence, as the physical, cognitive, and social development reached its peak, young people were also subject to biologically driven storm and stress. Because of this, their path toward adulthood and a higher stage of development is a stormy one, as they learn to subject their instincts to their environment (Grinder, 1973: 22–32).

Hall's contemporary, Sigmund Freud developed his psychoanalytic theory, which was likewise rooted in Darwinism and strongly supported the "Sturm und Drang" approach. He proposed that at each stage of human development, the narcissistic tendencies of the human being are gradually subjected to controls. However, the central drive toward maturity in Freud's theory, unlike in Hall's theory, is laden with psychosexual energies, which become particularly important in adolescence. The onset of puberty drives the adolescent toward the conflicting forces of dependence and independence. The crisis is solved as new codes of societal conduct are internalized by the individual as a means of self-control (Grinder, 1973: 32–36).

In the mid-to-late twentieth century, the views of two other developmental stage theorists, Erik Erikson and Jean Piaget, emerged as dominant. Both proposed a sequence of life stages in human development, driven by biology and leading toward a fully developed, mature human being. The stage of adolescence is seen as particularly crucial for the development of a sense of self, or identity (Danesi, 1994: 7–10; Grinder, 1973: 4–6). For Erikson, successful identity formation in adolescence is a process through which a person gradually internalizes societal expectations. An unsuccessful integration of individual and society would lead to "prolonged identity confusion" (Grinder, 1973: 5; Howe and Bukowski, 1996: 189–190). The common strand going through the stage theories is the view that unless a person learns to conform to the mainstream in adolescence, he is not likely to be a fully integrated, individuated being.

Alongside theories aimed at understanding the socio-biological drive toward maturity and self-awareness, attention has been paid to the role of physiological changes in adolescence. The psycho-social changes that take place in adolescence are linked to the biological and bodily changes accompanying puberty. Changes that signify a transition toward adulthood are seen to create a need to bond with others in the same stage of development, amidst a heightened awareness of the physiological and cognitive changes young people are going through (Danesi, 1994: 11–12; Offer and Offer, 1972).

Very few scholars and academics today would endorse a purely biologically based theory of human life stages. Most would see a combination of biological and environmental influences behind the transition toward adulthood, by virtue of the power of cross-cultural and historical studies that show the diverse ways of signifying human life stages (Danesi, 1994: 12–14). Among others, Canadian youth researchers Côté and Allahar (1994: 13–15) are critical of the "nature approaches" which place too much stress on the significance of biological factors in puberty. The theories show a profound misunderstanding of the correspondence between biological and social variables because there simply is no one-to-one correspondence between genetic, hormonal, or physiological developments and human social behaviour.

Furthermore, and most importantly, these theories can be criticized for putting pressure on young people to adapt to society rather than changing societies to accommodate them. Essentially they endorse the prevailing social order, unlike theories that pay attention to society from a more critical perspective that is sensitive to power differences.

Critical Theories: Age and Stratification
Critical theories focus on the constraints set by society on the opportunities for youth. Close attention is paid to the problems and inequities that prevail in society, despite the ideology of equality of opportunity embedded in Western democracies. Especially in the last two decades, Canadian studies and reports point to the many problems that young

people face and are finding difficult to confront and change due to rules and boundaries set by adult-led social institutions, including the family, the economy, and the state (e.g. Marquardt, 1998: 4–6; Smandych, 2001; Carrigan, 1998).

In contrast to conservative theories, critical theorists point to the institutionalized powerlessness of youth. It is noted by Côté and Allahar (1998: 121) that the idea of youth as a state of powerlessness (or disenfranchisement) is not necessarily easily accepted. Witness the indifferent or negative reactions by their academic colleagues to *Generation on Hold* (1994), where they outline the educational and employment experiences of young people at the end of the twentieth century. They argue that employers and the state have created, over more than a century, a system in which youth are deprived of full access to economic and political rights. They are processed through an education system that creates credentials that young people are made to believe they need in order to succeed but do not match with the reality of low-level jobs. Rather than having access to economic institutions, youth are exploited as an underpaid working mass and form a convenient "target market" for goods sold to them as part of a ready-made package of corporate-driven youth culture.

Côté and Allahar's theory typifies a Marxist or political economy approach. When applied to different social positions by age, it is a type of age stratification theory. There are several varieties of this theory (Dowd, 1981; O'Rand, 1990), but in its Marxist variant, economic inequalities are linked to age inequalities because of specific features in a capitalist economy. To exploit the work force to the fullest, different age categories of workers are granted different types of work, allowing for the exploitation of the young, as the weakest segment of the working population. At the same time, these age categories provide useful divided groupings of workers whose interests differ. Workers are prevented from the realization of their common interests by employers' "divide and conquer" methods. An added element in this mechanism of control are the ideological forces utilized by the capitalist class. The education system and media provide a form of control and ongoing indoctrination of people into the expectations of the economic system.

Even if we are to acknowledge the power of age stratification theory in explaining the emergence of and the present condition of youth, we are still left with only a partial picture of the lives of young people. Adolescence and youth are age strata, but they are also age strata differentiated along other dimensions.

Especially in the 1990s, there are numerous diversity and equity theorists who have documented the relative disadvantage in the general population of those who are not white middle- or upper- class males in their prime adult years and living in major urban centres (Naiman, 2000; Allahar and Côté, 1998). There are different types of these theories, but what holds them together is a critical approach to the patterns of allocation of societal goods and rewards based, not only on social class, but also gender, race and ethnic inequality, geography, or region. These patterns are not seen to be coincidental or due to some inherent differences between the different categories of populations. Rather, they are seen to be manifestations of different power structures created and sustained through social institutions.

The patterns that emerge in Canadian society show women as generally disadvantaged through a gender division of labour that delegates them to work that is either unpaid or underpaid. Similarly, members of ethnic and racial minorities face challenges to their economic and social participation due to discriminatory practices and attitudes. Both gender and ethno-racial inequality are proven to contribute to the lower-social-class status of members of visible minorities and women.

When age stratification is further added to this equation, a picture emerges that is both complex and somewhat predictable. Young people, as defined in this book, are disadvantaged in relation to the older population in the wage-earning categories. Meanwhile, the lives of youths are differentiated by their social class, gender, race, and ethnicity. To understand how these intersect today, we need to examine some of the ways in which these emerged and were shaped in Canadian history.

Race, Ethnicity, and Immigrant Status

Overall, the youth population of Canada is becoming more ethnically and racially diverse. Prior to 1961, most of the immigrants arriving to Canada were white Europeans or Americans. This changed dramatically, beginning with an influx of Caribbean, South American, and Asian immigrants from the 1960s onward. By the mid-1970s, immigration from Third World regions accounted for forty percent of all immigrants (Thomson, 1979: 105). While immigration from Europe and the United States declined dramatically between 1961 and 1996, there has been an increase in immigration from Central and South America (peaked in 1981–1990), the Caribbean and Bermuda (peaking in 1971–1980), West-Central Asia, and the Middle East (growing since 1981). Immigration from Asia and Africa is steadily growing.

Generally, this brings to Canada both youth who are immigrants themselves, and immigrants who will bear children, adding to the Canadian youth population. A growing number of Canadian children and youth were born outside the country. The number of immigrant children grew by twenty-six percent and the number of immigrant youth (15–24 years of age) grew by seven percent between 1991 and 1996. In Toronto and Vancouver, over one quarter of youth in this age group were born outside Canada (Canadian Council on Social Development, 1998). Of the estimated 200,000 immigrants who arrive in Canada annually, approximately one third are under age twenty-five. For example, of the 174,100 immigrants in 1998, about 65,140 were under the age of twenty-five (Canadian Council on Social Development, 2000).

There are traditionally significant differences in the age structure of Aboriginal communities. According to Statistics Canada, the proportions of young people among the North American Indian population exceed the national average by ten percent, with fifty-four percent of the population in the age category under twenty-five. Among the Métis and the Inuit, the percentages are forty-nine and sixty, respectively.

In later chapters, specific issues related to the lives of minority youth will be taken up, including their experiences of racism and discrimination in education and employment, relationships with the police and the legal system, intergenerational relationships between immigrant parents and their Canadian-born children, and the cultural manifestations of youth. These will show that, both historically and in contemporary Canada, the lives of young people are differentiated by race, ethnicity, and immigrant status.

Given the wide variety of ethnic and racial minorities in Canada, it is impossible to deal exhaustively with all of them. Therefore, amidst general information about many immigrant, ethnic, and racial groups throughout this book, I will pay particular attention to the experiences of Native and Black youth.

A Short History of Native Youth

In pre-colonial Native communities everyone made an economic contribution as soon as they were able. Children and young people were gradually integrated into adult activities, which were generally divided by gender. Members of the community were responsible for the education of the young in their daily practices, aimed at ensuring material and cultural survival (Wotherspoon, 1998: 47). Further, as Bradbury (e.g. 1996) has documented extensively, old Jesuit records of Huron life show that children were treated with kindness and harsh punishment was not generally used.

Serious disruption brought on by colonization resulted in significant changes in the lives of young people. As Canada was colonized by the French and the English from the seventeenth century onward, Native communities were gradually pushed out of the way, and many died out as a result of disease, war, or deliberate extermination by the settlers. Most of the settlers and colonizers were men, most of them single. The solution to their wifeless state was found through marriages to Native women. In general, men greatly outnumbered women in the colonies, which meant in some cases that the age of marriage for young girls was as low as twelve, and husbands were a great deal older than wives (Bradbury, 1996).

Young Native people were pulled into missionary schools or boarding schools, aimed at assimilating Native peoples into the now-dominant English culture. The residential school system became official government policy in the 1870s (Wotherspoon, 1998: 48; also see Marquardt, 1998: 23) and was launched in a systematic way in 1908 as a part of a paternalistic and racist attempt by the Canadian government to assimilate the Native population. Most of these schools closed in the 1960s, and by the time the last school closed in 1988, there had been losses of life due to poor conditions, malnourishment and disease. There was a denigration of culture and destruction and torment imposed on countless Native families whose children were denied access to their families and culture under the thin disguise of "civilization" and "education." It is estimated that there were no educational benefits to at least half the children who went through the residential school system (Henry, Tator, Mattis and Rees, 2000: 125–127). This "education" consisted of harsh discipline for offences such as speaking their own language, and students saw their family members only a few times a year (Wotherspoon, 1998: 48). Resulting cultural isolation meant that generations of young people were lost to their families even though residing in their original communities, and patterns of livelihood were disrupted as young boys and girls were taught the ways of the colonizers (Fiske and Johnny, 1996: 230–232). Lois Gus (Wotherspoon, 1998: 49) recalls:

> Normally, in a Native family, a child is allowed to learn by trial and error, with love and support being freely given. My experiences in residential school were a sharp contrast to this. There, our natural curiosity was impeded by the outlook of nuns, who had no experience in life and no experience as a parent. Even the natural curiosity of the opposite sex was discouraged and one was made to feel ashamed for even having had such curiosities.
>
> There were very few times you could enjoy life as it was so regimented. There was no freedom of thought or expression allowed. Everyone had to conform to a rigid set of standard rules: pray, learn, pray, obey, pray, eat, pray. Up

at 6:30 a.m., Mass at 7:00 a.m., breakfast at 8:00 a.m., class
at 9:00 a.m., lunch at 12:00 noon, class at 1:00 p.m., sewing
and mending at 4:00 p.m., supper at 6:00 p.m., bed at 9:00
p.m. The next day it started again.

Even our bodily functions were regimented; there were
certain times to go to the washroom, and castor oil was
administered once a year. We had a bath once a week, and
laundry duty every Saturday. We attended church once a
day and twice on Sunday. On Sundays we had a few hours of
free time but we were unaccustomed to such freedom, so
we usually looked to an older student to organize our
activities.

The treatment of Natives in the residential system is
presently before the courts as more and more survivors of this
repressive system come forth and reveal the extensive abuse
they suffered in these institutions. Meanwhile, social problems
continue in Native communities, manifested in high rates of
illiteracy, poverty, unemployment, poor health, substance
abuse, and suicides, particularly among the youth.

A Short History of Black Youth

As colonizers arrived in North America, so did the first
slaves. The first African slave landed at Quebec in 1628
(Walker, 1985: 8). He is reported to have been from Madagascar
and was named Olivier Le Jeune, after the Jesuit missionary
who was his teacher. Although, at this time slavery was
officially illegal in colonial New France, it was upheld by both
the French and the English until the early 1800s. In the late
1700s, almost all Canadian blacks were slaves, mostly in
domestic service to white colonizers (Walker, 1985: 8; Thomson,
1979: 17–18; 96). In 1760, there were approximately 4,000
black and Indian slaves in Quebec (Thomson, 1979: 96).

Slaves were generally subjected to harsh treatment,
including public whippings and death, for misdemeanours or
attempts to flee (Thompson, 1979: 18–19). They were mostly
illiterate (Winks, 1997: 364). Even as slavery was abolished in

the British Empire in 1833, the general image of servitude remained, and there were still cases of indentured service after this, including a twelve-year-old girl by the name of Maria Walker reported to be a slave in New Brunswick (Thomson, 1979: 19, 98; Walker, 1985: 80–90), and two eleven-year-old slaves sold by public auction in Halifax in 1852 (Thomson, 1979: 18).

As the practice of slavery gradually disappeared, more black people arrived in Canada, ostensibly free but, in reality, running away from slavery in the United States. Several thousand black people (the so-called Black Loyalists) arrived in Canada in the century before Confederation (1867). They settled in Nova Scotia, New Brunswick, and Ontario, where they engaged in labour on farms and in industry, constructed roads, and cleared land (Walker, 1985: 8–11; Thomson, 1979: 89). Another group of some 700 black people arrived on Vancouver Island in 1858–59 (Walker, 1985: 11–12).

Canadians cannot claim much pride in their treatment of black people, despite such well-known phenomena as the underground railroad, which secretly brought fugitive slaves to safety in Canada. Although conditions for black people in Canada improved gradually, racism and colour barriers prevailed. White immigration to Canada was welcomed while blacks continued to be segregated into the lowest paying jobs, despite economic expansion. One such story is that of Harry Gairey, a well-known figure in the Toronto Black community, who immigrated from Cuba at age sixteen, just before World War One began (Hill, 1981: 7):

> There was a cigar factory on Front Street, between Yonge and Bay, by the name of Androse, I can remember well. They wanted a cigar maker, and I was one, I learned back home. I saw this sign in the window, "Help Wanted," and then I saw it in the paper. When I went into the factory, it didn't take me long to see that it was all white there. But I applied. They says, "No, we have no job for coloured people." Then I saw a job advertised for one of the boats. For help. I went down to the employment place, where the people phone in for help. They phoned up and then said, "No, they don't

want you." That was in the early twenties. And when I got
the job on the road, I never turned anywhere else. Never
bothered, because I knew I was blocked everywhere I went;
it was no use to butt my head against a stone wall; I'd have
a railroad job and I'd make the best of it.

The time period between Confederation and World War Two
was characterized by the return of large numbers of fugitive
slaves to the slavery-free northern United States, or their
movement to Sierra Leone or Trinidad, reflecting an
unwelcoming Canadian public opinion (Walker, 1985: 8–9;
Thomson, 1979: 98). Racist ideologies promoting the natural
biological superiority of white people fell on receptive ears,
and black people's presumed inferiority gained public
acceptance (Walker, 1985: 12–14; Thomson, 1979: 21–22). This
is evident in the open segregation practiced in the emerging
public school system. School segregation existed by law and in
practice in Ontario and Nova Scotia (Thomson, 1979: 20, 99–
106; Wilks, 1997: 367–370). From the early 1800s onward,
resistance by white parents to the presence of black children
in schools led to the creation of separate schools for blacks,
run by churches and by black communities themselves, despite
the fact that the majority of blacks paid public school taxes
and wished access to public schools (Wilks, 1997: 365–366).
Accumulating anti-black prejudice in the 1850s was
manifested in the seating of black children on separate benches
in mostly white schools and the withdrawal of white children
by their parents from mixed schools. Meanwhile separate
schools for blacks had poor resources, poor teachers, and poor
attendance; most had no library and attendance was irregular.
Toward the end of the 1800s, protests against segregation led
to a gradual integration of black students into public schools
(Wilks, 1997: 371–380).

Racist practices prevail in the twentieth century, with
regard to the black population. While black people were blatantly
excluded from mainstream activity in the early twentieth
century, they continued to collectively resist the colour divide,
as they had with regard to the segregated school system. Yet
segregation in all aspects of life persisted. During World War

One, young black men, mainly from Nova Scotia and New Brunswick, were recruited into a separate battalion to provide auxiliary services to white troops (Walker, 1985: 15–17), even though numerous black organizations across Canada raised money toward the war effort (Thomson, 1979: 102).

In the school system, the official segregation of black students was gradually abandoned. All but one separate school had closed in Ontario by 1900, although a single separate black school existed in Alberta until the 1960s. In Nova Scotia, the last separate school is reported to have closed in 1917, but de facto segregation of black students continued well into the twentieth century through barring of black students to some schools and by not operating school buses for black communities. It took until the 1960s for Ontario and Nova Scotia to revise their legislation and practices related to separate schooling for black children. By this time there were disastrous consequences for black children's education, manifested in high rates of illiteracy (Wilks, 1997: 371–389; also see Kelly, 1998: 33–47).

Racial discrimination in employment and community life continued during the inter-war years despite the fact that by 1921, nearly seventy-five percent of the black population was Canadian-born (Thomson, 1979: 103). The hostility of the inter-war climate toward blacks was fueled by the entry of the Ku Klux Klan into Canada in the 1920s and 1930s, mostly concentrated in the four Western provinces and Ontario (Thomson, 1979: 103–104).

I didn't know!!

In the aftermath of the horrors of Nazi concentration camps following World War Two, there was an increased activation by black communities as they moved to challenge discriminatory legislation related to employment, accommodation, and public facilities. In the 1960s, human rights legislation federally and provincially began to emerge to refute limitations based on race, sex, or religion (Walker, 1985: 16–18). This also reflects the gradual revitalization of the black community through immigration. West Indian immigration to Canada began in 1960 (Thomson, 1979: 105) and the population grew from 12,000 in 1961 to 200,000 in 1981. An additional 50,000 blacks had arrived from Africa in the same time frame. The indigenous

Canadian black community, the descendants of the arrivals from the previous centuries, numbered around 40,000, or fifteen percent of all black people in Canada (Walker, 1985: 17–19).

Youth in the White Mainstream

In Canada's colonial period, young people's economic and social independence emerged amidst strict codes of filial obligation and parental (particularly paternal) power over children's lives, including the right to mete out harsh physical punishment. The major social institutions, including families, communities, churches, and schools, were based on the notion that young people needed a firm guiding hand. The transition from childhood to adulthood was abrupt in that children were expected to participate in adult activities as soon as they were physically able. This meant that children as young as six began training for different work through apprenticeship or home-based vocational training (Mandell, 1988: 53–54). Apprentice programs were not as common as in continental Europe but some youth, more commonly boys, entered into a period of semi-independence as they lived away from home while learning a trade (Bradbury, 1996; Mandell, 1988: 53–59, 66).

There were different pathways for boys and girls, marked by social class differences. Boys would follow the occupational and status positions of their fathers, specializing in trades or professions. There were fewer choices for girls, who were expected to learn domestic skills toward their future as wives and mothers or their future in domestic service for wealthy households (Mandell, 1988: 53–56).

Children of the upper classes had more time on their hands, and they were subjected to other types of control over their time and behaviour, including religious training and schooling. In Europe, schools for the children of the upper classes existed from the end of the seventeenth century onward. Although they was mainly meant for male children, some upper-class girls were also given general instruction in basic literacy. For this privileged group there was a gradual lengthening of childhood through education. This was gradually introduced to the lower classes and girls (Mandell, 1988: 59).

As the colonizers began to form permanent settlements, standard work patterns emerged within their families, with the labours of all family members, including children and youth, needed to make a living. Working-class boys would generally leave home by age fifteen to work in lumber camps, fishing boats, or jobs in the town. Girls more commonly entered into domestic service and learned wifely domestic duties, such as making clothes (Bradbury, 1996: 62; Baker, 1989: 35; Marquardst, 1998: 15–20). Parr (1980: 82–83, in Mandell, 1988: 64) describes a typical farm work setting as follows:

> Young boys of eight fetched wood and water, gathered eggs, fed and herded animals. As they grew older, boys chopped wood, hoed potatoes, dug turnips and helped with the haying. Fourteen year old boys worked like men, ploughing in the spring and fall, threshing and husking corn in the winter, cutting wood...Girls from age six on, participated in the household chores by babysitting, cleaning, cooking and sewing and they helped the men outdoors. Their responsibilities increased as they grew older. Hired girls between fourteen and eighteen did more heavy housework and helped in the cash-earning dairy and poultry enterprises on the farm.

The great changes in economic organization that ushered in capitalism also marked the continuity of child labour for the vast majority of the population. Marquardt (1998: 20) notes that the employment of youth was not only important to the financial survival of their families, but also to the "business strategies of early industrial capitalists." That there was need for child labour was demonstrated in the importation of British children between 1867 and 1919, when approximately 73,000 children immigrated to enter into work as labourers and servants. Children under nine years of age were adopted, but those between nine and eighteen years of age became indentured labourers. Under contract, they got room and board, clothing, and literacy in exchange for performing household chores that freed adults for heavy farm tasks (Mandell, 1988: 66).

Social reformers worked hard to combat the negative effects that child labour had on the development or even survival of young people. For example, city children regularly worked sixty-hour weeks (Mandell, 1988: 66). It was not until 1887 that child-labour laws in Canada limited the labour of children under the age of six. From the 1880s onward, the legal age limits were gradually raised, first to twelve for boys and fourteen for girls in 1886, and to fourteen for both sexes in 1895 (Baker, 1989: 35). This was not only a result of actions by well-meaning child protectionists but coincided with economic recessions that led to adult male protectionism in work areas where child labour was seen to threaten their employment (Mandell, 1988: 67).

Both women and children were regularly paid lower wages, on the assumption that they were not as productive or that they were not required to support a family (Baker, 1989: 35). Fewer girls than boys worked in industries and the participation of young women tended to diminish proportionally as they got older, reflecting the practice of women stopping to work for wages as they got married or had children (Bloomfield and Bloomfield, 1991: 31). As Canada became industrialised, the gender divide gradually hardened as boys and young men had a range of jobs to choose from and girls' and young women's choices were limited (Bradbury, 1996: 69).

It was expected that marriage was possible once you were economically self-sufficient. Given the poor availability of work and the low wages offered in the industrializing economy, young people in the mid- and late-nineteenth century stayed dependent on their families for a lengthened time period. The age of marriage was delayed and more young people continued living at home for longer periods of time. Men would typically marry in their late twenties and women in their early twenties. At that time, women would leave the paid labour market (Marquardt, 1998: 17). This prolonged stay in the parental home also meant that youth were increasingly under parental supervision (Mandell, 1988: 65). In southern and eastern Ontario, factory work was a preferred form of work over farm work or personal service work by young people because the former offered comparatively higher wages, shorter work days, and more personal autonomy (Baker, 1989: 35).

Idleness and Morality

The entry of young working people into industrial centres was accompanied by concerns about vagabond and delinquent youngsters on city streets. For example, Katz (1975, in Marquardt, 1998: 16) reports that in mid-nineteenth century Hamilton, Ontario, there were large numbers of "idle" young people whose presence and possible tendencies toward negative pursuits caused a great deal of concern to social reformers. At that time, almost half of young people aged 11–15 and approximately a quarter of 16–20-year-olds were neither employed full-time nor attending school.

Particularly, the entry of women into industrial centres, such as Toronto, was also accompanied by concerns of "urban perils" which may lead young women to "sin" and a neglect of their domestic responsibilities once they had tasted the freedom brought by wage earning. This preoccupation with the morality of young women was reflective of the trend, by the mid- to late-nineteenth century, of a shift in women's employment from domestic service to industrial work. New work opportunities, created by industrialization and paid labour, took young women away from the supposedly safe confines of their own family or the families of strangers that they worked for (Strange, 1997: 8–9).

Young working women lived either with their own families, in boarding houses, or in their employers' homes. The latter setting made them particularly vulnerable to sexual exploitation. For example, Bailey's (1991: 8) study of Upper Canada in the early- to mid-1800s tells of the special vulnerability of servant girls to sexual abuse by their masters, who were immune from prosecution. In 1837, the Seduction Act was passed which permitted a girl's parents (mostly the father) to sue the master and get support for any illegitimate children.

The concern over morality in the new industrial centres had a double edge, portraying young women either as hapless victims of urban vice or as "brazen" sin-filled beings. Both images were based on the increased freedoms of young working women who wanted to participate in the amusements offered in a big city. Increased social controls on women, brought on by morality-minded reform, were evident in the increased presence of female police officers, women's courts, and longer terms for female morals offenders. In extreme cases, young women who defied convention were also sent to psychiatric clinics and diagnosed as mentally unfit for wanting to do what they pleased (Strange, 1995; Strange, 1997: 11–13).

That young women's freedoms were seen as a threat is not unusual during a time period when their futures were defined in terms of motherhood. Exemplifying this, in Quebec of 1880–1940, girls were expected to act like "petites mères" or look after their younger siblings while participating in occasional work with the wages going to their parents. There is little evidence of education other than for a small number of girls (Lemieux and Mercier, in Bradbury, 1993: 162). A similar trend toward domesticity is noted in English Canada by Strong-Boag (in Bradbury, 1993: 162) and Davies (1995), who report differential schooling for boys and girls, with the latter being groomed for motherhood and homemaking through domestic science classes and moral education.

The Prolongation of Adolescence and Youth

During the nineteenth century we see the first references to adolescence as a distinct life stage, marked by semi-independence while getting educated or while engaging in some form of wage labour. Adolescence emerged first among the middle and upper classes, where mortality and fertility rates dropped earlier and where apprentice programs gave way to formal public education. This pattern gradually spread to the working class, where adolescence was, for a longer time, characterized by wage work participation.

The emergence of adolescence is a direct reflection of the prolongation of youth. Within the working class, adolescence was intricately connected to the decline of the working family as a unit of production. As industrial wage labour became the way of life for increasing masses, wage work was the main way toward a livelihood. Adolescence became a time of preparation for work through prolonged education and the removal of children from the labour market. As explained above, Côté and Allahar (1994: 17) call this process the "disenfranchisement of youth." During the advancement of industrialization, families began to rely less on the labour of the young. The youth population started to move from economic assets to economic liabilities. In urban areas, education formed the basis for adolescence among working-class youngsters as the standard of living rose to the point where the wage work of all family members was no longer needed.

With the resulting "partial idleness" (Marquardt, 1998:16) of youth and the rise of vocational training, educational reformers extended compulsory school to the age of sixteen. Gradually, in the mid- to late- 1800s, public school systems emerged for all of the population to add to the private schools available to privileged families (Baker, 1989: 37; see also Bradbury, 1996: 67; Marquardt, 1998: 21–23, 28).

The first public schools were aimed not only at creating a literate population, but at raising a patriotic citizenry and instilling into "idle youth" habits valuable in the workforce, such as obedience and punctuality (Marquardt, 1998: 21–23; Côté and Allahar, 1994: 40, 120–124; also see Mandell, 1988: 72), while reproducing the social order based on divisions of social class, race, and gender. For example, in the early twentieth century, working class youth tended to leave school sooner to take up jobs, while their middle-class counterparts continued their education (Marquardt, 1998: 27–31; Strong-Boag, in Bradbury, 1993: 162; Bradbury, 1996: 69). Indeed, the time period for education has gotten ever longer since the 1960s, when federal and provincial governments started investing in all levels of the educational system, including universities and community colleges (Marquardt, 1998: 42).

In general, Côté and Allahar (1994: 40; also see Bradbury, 1996: 69) argue that in the twentieth century, mass education has prolonged youth and made young people more vulnerable to capitalist exploitation, both as students working part-time and as graduates who cannot find work that corresponds to their level of education. The concern over the general deteriorating quality of jobs available to youth (Marquardt, 1998: 43) continues in the era of the "McDonaldization" of the labour market (Ritzer, 1993) and the "McJob." Since World War Two, while engaging in education, youth were generally found employed in either: 1) large secondary firms (for minimum wage): security businesses, grocery stores, cleaning services, and construction companies; 2) small businesses (low-paid casual work): bakers, news stands, restaurants, gas stations, or convenience stores, or in rural areas: farm work, wood cutting, and menial jobs in the primary sector; 3) under the table (one-off opportunities, usually neighbourhood based): babysitting, shovelling snow, painting houses, repairing cars, or some construction (Marquardt, 1998: 39–40).

Conclusions

As will be seen in the chapters to follow, there is a continuity of these historical patterns still today. An examination of young people's lives in relation to different social institutions will reveal the age hierarchy of Canadian society where today's youth are allowed to reach a full, independent adult status much later than in any previous period in Canadian history. Youth today are unable to gain full access to socially valued goods and services which were taken for granted by their parents at same age. For the luckiest among youth, this prolonged dependence causes continued economic hardship, extends education way beyond the actual skill requirements of the labour market, and delays relationship and family formation. Less fortunate youth are cast adrift in society, through no fault of their own, to become casualties seen in the statistics of high school dropouts, homelessness, and crime. All young people have to constantly mediate between different adult-led institutions that offer them few options amidst a tide of negative media and popular imagery, a situation all the more daunting for young people who are not part of the mainstream.

2 | Education

I can't afford it any more. I'm twenty grand in debt. I just can't keep going into debt...that's the reality...I don't want to graduate with a forty-odd-thousand debt load, with a mortgage and no house. (Rich Whyman, twenty-seven, in Galt, 1999: A16)

Rising Levels of Education

A long period of education is an expected part of being young. As much as adolescence is synonymous with finishing high school, it is seen increasingly necessary for young people to devote their early twenties to getting post-secondary education.

There is no question that the Canadian population is more educated than ever before. The median years of schooling for the population aged 25–44 have increased from 7.7 in 1941 to 13.2 in 1991 (Nakamura and Wong, 1998: 9). The 1996 Census (Statistics Canada, 1998a) showed the trend of attaining higher levels of education which has been observed since the early 1950s.

As seen in Chapter One, the system of public education emerged partly as a solution to the problem of "idle youth." While waiting for full entry into the labour market, young people are being prepared for the labour force, not only in terms of requisite skills, but in terms of discipline and attitudes required by the work environment. This chapter will outline young people's experiences in relation to education, including secondary schools and post-secondary educational institutions. While education is valued for its own sake and young people understand the importance of education, not all adolescents and young adults are equally equipped to get into educational institutions or complete their education. Many fall between the cracks due to institutionalized constraints based on social class, gender, race, and ethnicity. The uneven results are manifested in high school dropout rates, debt loads, and the general school experience which still favours those in the higher socio-economic groups who are male, white, and Canadian-born.

Secondary Schools

The increased association of youth with education is seen in the increased school attendance of young people aged 5–19 from 51.1 percent in 1901 to 90.8 percent in 1986. There was a period of particularly rapid increase between 1950 and 1970, with the post-war baby boom cohort making its way through the school system (Baker, 1989: 37–38). The Census of 1996 (Statistics Canada, 1998a) found that only thirty-five percent of the population aged fifteen and over had not completed high school, compared with forty-eight percent in 1981.

Secondary school attendance has become an expected part of young people's lives. In 1996, 295,937 Canadians graduated from secondary school, an increase of over 30,000 graduates since 1991. The province with the greatest increase in the number of people graduating was Quebec, where the number of graduates increased by 18,693 people between 1991 and 1996. Newfoundland and New Brunswick were the only two provinces that documented a decrease in the number of secondary school graduates between the years of 1991 and 1996 (Statistics Canada, 1991–1996).

Dropping Out

Not all young people make it through high school. Although in 1996, more people over the age of fifteen completed high school than in 1981 (Statistics Canada, 1998a), the school dropout problem is one of the most important issues in Canadian education. In international comparisons, Canada has one of the highest high-school dropout rates among advanced industrial nations. Depending on measurement techniques, somewhere between twenty and thirty percent of students do not finish high school (Dei, 1993). The most common age range for school dropouts is 16–18 (Wall, Covell, and MacIntyre, 1999). Internationally, a link has been made with legislation regarding compulsory school age. The dropout rate is lower in countries where the legal age for leaving school (currently sixteen in all Canadian provinces) is higher (Human Resources Development Canada, 1999c: 18). In addition, studies indicate that dropout rates vary depending on other considerations. Anisef (1998, in Anisef and Kilbride, 2000: 22) stresses that it is important to understand dropping out as a process involving many factors and not as a single event. There are multiple reasons for dropping out, having to do with the school, family, the community, labour markets, and government policy.

There is a definite link with students' social class background and the dropout rate, in that those in the lower socio-economic categories are more likely to leave school (Anisef et al., 1980; see also Davies, 1994: 345). Crysdale (1991) studied high-school dropout rates among youth in the economically depressed downtown Toronto core. He found that there was a sixty percent school dropout rate in this geographic area, twice the national average. The dropout rate generally is higher among low-income families (twenty-three percent) than among youth in higher income groups. Further, those in lower socio-economic groups are more likely to enroll in basic or general level programs. Based on Ontario data, Tanner (1990) reports that the dropout rates for general level programs are much higher, compared with those for advanced programs.

Some recent analyses suggest that dropping out is related to combining work and schooling, which is increasingly common among young people. Dropping out is more likely if the student works over ten hours a week or when the minimum wage is higher. This has led to suggestions that there be two levels of minimum wage, one for those aged over seventeen or eighteen and another for younger persons to encourage them to stay in school longer (Human Resources Development Canada, 1999c: 18-19; Taylor, 1997). Studies in 1980s Ontario also show that over ninety percent of all high-school dropouts were white, Canadian-born youth, while the rates for immigrants and minorities were lower. There were two exceptions to this rule: recent immigrants of visible minority background who had been in Canada less than four years; and aboriginal youth, whose dropout rates were over twice the national average (Davies and Guppy, 1998: 135).

Gender differences are also apparent. The dropout rate is somewhat higher for males than females (Côté and Allahar, 1994: 41–42, 173; Tanner, 1990). In the 1996 Census (Statistics Canada, 1998a), the proportion of men aged 20–29 without a high school diploma was twenty-one percent, a reduction from thirty-one percent in 1981. The comparable percentages for women were sixteen percent and twenty-eight percent, respectively. Davies (1994) also found a gender difference in predictors of dropping out. Young women put more emphasis on domestic issues than young men do. Davies argues that dropping out of school may be a realistic response by girls whose school success will not allow them to get themselves well situated in the labour market or in future education.

Interestingly, a survey of adolescent women by the Canadian Advisory Council on the Status of Women (Holmes and Silverman, 1992: 42–45) found that although by far the most of the teenage respondents thought that staying in school is important, only sixty-six percent of the young women and fifty-two percent of the young men said they actually liked school. Many respondents indicated that school performance is a concern for a lot of young women, including stress, competition, and pressure from parents. Some cited poor relationships with teachers, and some pointed to the whole school system being flawed. This conclusion is supported by Julian Tanner's (1990) study of 168 high-school dropouts in Edmonton, Alberta. One of the main reported factors were school-based reasons, including teachers, subjects, or peers. School failure was not among significant reasons, however, as only about one third reported poor grades as their reason for leaving. Similarly, paternal occupation seemed to have little effect. Some indicated that their dropping out was more a case of having been kicked out due to poor attendance or behaviour problems. Thus, leaving is not always purely voluntary, and schools, including teachers and guidance counsellors, may play a more active role in the process than is thought.

Tanner interprets this trend as indicative of the adolescent's antipathy toward the school environment, which the respondents reported to be authoritarian and denying them freedom and autonomy because they are young. Another major concern was fitting in and getting access to peer groups or disapproving of the peer culture. This argument has been extended by Davies (1994: 345), who found that school dropouts are more likely to form a subculture of students who "expend less effort than graduates, engage in more disruptive behaviour, experience greater difficulties with school, and have friends who are also dropouts," leading them to "disengage themselves from the culture of schooling, and learn to prefer the 'real world' of employment over 'irrelevant' schooling."

Tanner's (1990) study found that dropping out was an "ambiguous experience" for most young people. They reported a range of short-term positive consequences, such as freedom and making some money, but they were also aware of long-term problems dropping out might create. Although most of the respondents (seventy percent) were definitely in favour of getting more education, only thirty-six percent of the females and twenty-seven percent of the males indicated they would like to return to finish their high school education. Education was seen as a central value by the majority of the high-school dropouts in his study.

Colleges and Universities

One of the major developments in education from the 1870s to the 1960s is the growth in universities. Particularly with the expansion of the post-secondary education system in the 1960s and the 1970s, there was an influx of students from a wider socio-economic background (Baker, 1989: 41). There were only seventeen degree-granting institutions in 1871, with just over 1,500 students across Canada. By 1971, there were 316,000 full-time students in fifty such institutions (Axelrod and Reid, 1987: xiii). Putting it differently, while only six percent of those aged 18–24 were attending college or university in 1951, this increased to 25.5 percent by 1986–87. These figures partly reflect the expansion of education for women.

The 1996 Census (Statistics Canada, 1998a) found that over one third of post-secondary graduates held a university degree at bachelor's level or higher. Of the population fifteen and over, sixteen percent held university degrees, compared with ten percent in 1981. During the 1997/98 school year there were 573,099 people who enrolled in a university on a full-time basis, an increase of over 1,000 students from 1993–1994. However, there was a decrease of almost 50,000 within the same time span among part-time students, whose numbers had fallen to a quarter million in 1997–1998, from the over 300,000 in 1993–1994 (Statistics Canada, 1993-1998).

Community college enrollments have increased dramatically, in measure with the decline in part-time university numbers. While close to 370,000 people were enrolled full-time in community college programs in 1993/94, the number rose to over 395,000 in 1996/97. These statistics indicate a change in society's perception of education. There seems to be something of a return to the mentality of the era before mass education, whereby young people entered into apprenticeship in order to get a job (Statistics Canada, 1993–1997). This is supported by a report of the Council of Ministers on Education (1999). While gaining knowledge and developing individual potentials are valued in their own right, education is primarily seen to serve the needs of the economy and to help shape a cohesive society. Colleges are seen to be more rooted in their communities than universities are and to be more responsive to the needs of business, industry, and the public sector. At the same time, they are seen to be stepping stones toward university.

Student Loans

In 1988/89, full-time tuition fees for attending an Ontario university were just over $1,400 (Baker, 1989: 42). Tuition fees skyrocketed between the early and late 1990s, to nearly $3,400 per year, an increase of close to 126 percent (Naiman, 2000: 180–181; Fine, 2000: A8). This 1999/2000 rate is more than double the rate from 1990/91 (Fine, 2000: A8; Galt, 1999a). Because of the rising cost of education, more young people accumulate enormous debts in order to finance their education. At the same time, more students are compelled to work part-time and seasonally to finance their education (Baker, 1989: 43).

One credit counsellor reported to the *Globe and Mail Report on Business* that it is not unusual to see debt loads of $20,000 for young graduates who are earning $12,000–$15,000 a year (Read, 1996). Other sources (Elton and Brearton, 1997; Bailey, 1999) report that the average debt load for a graduate with a first degree from a university or college in 1996 was $17,000, up from around $8,000 in 1990. This means that most graduates will have difficulty paying back their loans, since eighty-five percent of those aged 18–24 earn less than $21,000 per year. There were approximately 35,000 university and college graduates who declared bankruptcy between 1990 and 1997 before reaching age thirty. Declaring bankruptcy on student loans is now only possible after a ten-year period. Moreover, the government turned over the management of student loans to the five big banks who are less hesitant about using drastic measures to collect their monies from graduates. By the end of 1997, over $36.9 million was recovered through collection agencies (*Globe and Mail*, 1999). At the same time, government per capita funding of post-secondary institutions has fallen thirty percent (Galt, 1999a).

According to one recent report by Human Resources Development Canada (1999b: 12), the increase in debt level of those seeking to obtain post-secondary education does not seem to be discouraging youth from pursuing further education because they have come to recognize the importance of education in a knowledge-based economy. However, if the costs of education continue to increase, it will become financially impossible for some youth to obtain an education. Parental financial support is important even though most students rely on earnings from summer and part-time work (Anisef et al., 1980). This is hardly surprising, considering that the average cost of one year of post-secondary education (including living costs) was $15,000 in 1997, while a full-time minimum wage job earned on average just under $4,000. It is also not surprising that there are higher proportions of students who have to borrow money to finance their education. The conclusion from these trends is that social class will increasingly be linked to one's educational achievement "in the face of rising educational costs and reduced services and financial support for students" (Wotherspoon, 1998: 184-185).

Inequality in Education

Despite general perceptions that past inequalities in education have been remedied, numerous studies from the 1980s and beyond (summarized in Maxwell and Maxwell, 1994; also see Anisef et al., 1980; Livingston, 1999: 57; Guttman and Alice, 1991; Baker, 1985; Anisef, 1994; Willms, 1999; Willms, 1997; Wotherspoon, 1998) have documented that social class, gender, and ethnicity have a significant effect on educational aspirations and attainment.

A major part of the reason for the continuation of these unequal patterns of education lies in the institutionalization of racism and sexism and the pro-middle-class mentality in the educational system. These are often captured under the general term "hidden curriculum" (Deem, 1980, in Mandell and Crysdale, 1993: 33). The term includes a range of dominant attitudes, values, norms, and practices by educators and administrators that create a cultural and social ethos in the academic institution that prevent the full and equal participation of subdominant groups (Henry and Tator, 1994). Among these are: course streaming (or "tracking"), invisibility of one's group in educational materials and among faculty and students, discriminatory practices by guidance counsellors and lack of teachers' positive attention and encouragement, as well as generally discriminatory attitudes by educators, administrators, and peers (Côté and Allahar, 1994: 89; Russell, 1987; Mandell and Crysdale, 1993; Anisef, 1994: 9–12; Henry and Tator, 1994; Anisef and Kilbride, 2000; Dei, 1993). Thus, youth who live in poverty, or who are women or members of racial or ethnic minority groups, are finding that their educational experience is qualitatively different from that of youth who come from dominant backgrounds (e.g. Anisef, 1994: 10–11; Wotherspoon, 1998: 182–185; African Heritage Educators' Network and Ontario Women's Directorate, 1996: 3).

Social Class

Generally, it has been found that academic attainment and ultimately occupational attainment are largely dependent on family origins and educational experiences. Children from privileged backgrounds have better access to quality education and are more likely to benefit from better finances and access to goods and services that enhance the general education experience. They are also more likely to accumulate "cultural capital," which refers to dominant forms of communication and organization that are a part of the privileged milieu; or "social capital" associated with one's social skills. These all amount to "human capital" or skills and cumulative learning (Willms, 1999: 9; also see Wotherspoon, 1998: 179–185). Children who live in poverty have to battle with teacher and parental discrimination and expectations of failure, leading toward low self-esteem and low motivation to excel (Anisef, 1994: 10–11; Wotherspoon, 1998: 182–185).

It is true that a lot of negative stereotyping accompanies poverty. In some neighbourhoods, such as Toronto's Parkdale, students and teachers are fighting back the ill effects of this negative imagery by encouraging community participation. Among the most recent contributions is a book produced by students at the Parkdale Collegiate Institute. Entitled *Not Poor in Spirit*, it contains contributions from members of the community and school outlining the efforts they make amidst difficult circumstances (Galt, 1999b).

Although these community-based efforts help to remove some of the stigma, we cannot erase the real and observable consequences of living in low-income neighbourhoods. Canada-wide, youth from advantaged family backgrounds fare well in tests of literacy, whereas youth from disadvantaged backgrounds fare uniformly poorly (Willms, 1997: 25). Young people who live in poverty are faced with additional challenges that those with more advantages cannot even think of, including the ill effects of hunger and sickness, housing conditions that make it difficult to do homework, limited access to educational materials such as books or computers, and lowered educational aspirations in the family environment (Anisef, 1994: 10–11; Wotherspoon, 1998: 182–185).

These disadvantages are likely to be perpetuated from parents to their children. Research from the 1990s has shown that educational inequality is reproduced across generations. A study by Clark (1991, in Wotherspoon, 1998: 180) showed that educational backgrounds of parents of post-secondary graduates were much higher than those of trade/vocational graduates. Along these lines, Siedule (1992, in Wotherspoon, 1998: 180) has shown that those with favourable backgrounds in terms of family income, family structure, province, and ethnicity had up to five years of educational advantage over those from less favourable conditions.

Based on the findings of the 1994 General Social Survey, Frederick and Boyd (1998: 13) report that family structure is linked to high school completion rates:

> Among Canadian-born adults aged twenty to forty-four, more than eighty percent of those from two-parent biological families completed high school, compared with about seventy-one percent of those from lone-parent families. Those who lived in blended or step-parent families at age fifteen also reported a seventy percent graduation rate, meaning they were just as likely as those from lone-parent families to have an incomplete education.

Further, those who have two biological parents who have finished high school have the highest rate for finishing high school. Meanwhile the rate drops if only one of the parents has a high school diploma and drops further if the lone-parent has a high school diploma. They are followed by the children of two parents without high school diplomas, and the least successful are the children of single parents who did not complete high school (Frederick and Boyd, 1998).

Frederick and Boyd (1998: 13–14) suggest that while low parental levels of education disadvantage children, this is even more pronounced in cases of marital breakup or where there is a single parent. Further, the poor material conditions of children in single-parent families result in poor educational outcomes. In 1996, nearly fifteen percent of families were lone-parent families but they made up over a half of families in poverty. In Canada, patterns of educational achievement are also linked to provincial and territorial differences, through regional disparities. Poorer regions, including Atlantic Canada, Quebec, Manitoba, Saskatchewan, and Northwest Territories, all have lower levels of educational attainment than the national average (Wotherspoon, 1998: 187–191).

Gender

There is no denying that women have entered educational institutions en masse. The main trends in the 1980s and 1990s are that men and women are equally likely to graduate from high school. Further, there has been a female majority among university entrants and those who receive bachelor's degrees since the early 1980s. As indicated in Figure 2.1, the present trend reflects a proportional representation of male and female students in the education system. In fact, females gain higher grades in high school, are more likely to graduate from high school and are more likely to attend post-secondary institutions (Mandell and Crysdale, 1993: 21; Normand, 2000: 73–77).

The 1996 Census (Statistics Canada, 1998a), found that fifty-one percent of women in the age group 20–29 held a degree or a diploma, compared with forty-two percent of men. This shows a significant change from 1981, when thirty-seven

Figure 2.1.   Proportion of young men and women attending school, 1921-1991

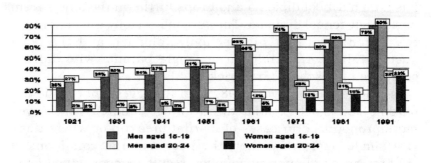

1 From 1971 to 1991, full-time attendance was used to best
  approximate the concepts used in earlier years.
Data from 1921 to 1961 exclude Newfoundland, and the Yukon and
  Northwest Territories.
Source: Statistics Canada, 1961 Census of Canada, Vol.7, Part and
  Catalogues 92-742, 92-743, 92-914 and 93-328. (from Normand
  'Education of Women in Canada' in Canadian Social Trends 3, 2000,
  p.76)

percent of both men and women held post-graduate degrees.
These trends hold for universities, as twenty-one percent of
the women aged 20–29 and sixteen percent of men 20–29 held
a university degree, compared with eleven percent and twelve
percent in 1981, respectively.

However, as shown in Table 2.1, mass education has not
served girls and young women as well as it could have. Women
are still under-represented in graduate programs and among
those with more advanced degrees and over-represented in
part-time studies. Further, gender divisions persist in the
choice of field of study. Women in secondary and post-secondary
education continue to be over-represented in traditionally
female fields, like education, nursing, social work, humanities,
or social sciences. They remain under-represented in areas
such as engineering, math, physical sciences, and computer
science, as well as dentistry, medicine, or law (Organization
for Economic Co-Operation and Development, 1986; Mandell
and Crysdale, 1993; Normand, 2000). Even academically gifted

school girls are less likely to choose careers in traditionally male-dominated areas (Guttman and Alice, 1991). These trends hold in the 1996 Census (Statistics Canada, 1998a). And as is shown in Table 2.1, women drop below fifty percent of enrolment at the doctoral level in almost all fields.

**Table 2.1. Women as a proportion
of full-time enrolment by level, 1992–93**

Field of study	Undergraduate	Master's %	Doctoral
Health professions	68	62	43
Education	67	66	60
Fine and applied arts	62	59	46
Humanities	61	56	46
Agriculture/ biological sciences	59	50	33
Social sciences	54	47	45
Mathematics/ physical sciences	30	27	19
Engineering/ applied sciences	19	18	11

Source: Statistics Canada, Education, Culture and Tourism Division (from Normand 'Education of Women in Canada' in Canadian Social Trends 3, 2000, p.75)

In 1994 seven countries, including Canada, collaborated on the first International Adult Literacy Survey. In reporting the survey's results related to the youth population aged sixteen to twenty-five, Willms (1997: 24–25) notes that nation wide, males and females scored equally well. However, there were notable province-based variations. Whereas females substantially outperformed males in New Brunswick and British Columbia, the reverse was true for Ontario and Manitoba. This is explained by informal streaming mechanisms that prevail in some provinces but not others. For example, Ontario youth in this study would have come from "streamed schools," where presumably boys would be more likely to enroll in academic programs than girls. On the other hand, New Brunswick has more girls enrolled in French immersion programs than boys. On average, French immersion students do better in reading and writing assessments.

It has been found that early socialization and sex-role stereotyping are responsible for the maintenance of traditional career choice patterns (Guttman and Alice, 1991; Organization for Economic Co-Operation and Development, 1986; Maxwell and Maxwell, 1994: 147). Young women continue to put a higher priority on marriage and family life than young men and consistently choose traditional educational and career patterns (Guttman and Alice, 1991). This type of "gender tracking" (Mandell and Crysdale, 1993) prepares young men and women for different paths in relation to education, work, and family.

Gender and Educational Aspirations and Expectations

Young women may not be aware of the challenges they face at all stages of schooling. Overall, young women do well but realization of the consequences of gender-based streaming processes in education may come much later. One survey of adolescent women (Holmes and Silverman, 1992: 45–46) found awareness of gender discrimination increases with age. For example, about ninety-six percent of thirteen-year-old boys and girls agreed that there are equal chances for success in schools for both sexes. This decreased by seven percent for women and two percent for men by the time they were sixteen years of age.

Studies have noted a persistent gap between the aspirations and expectations of young females (Nelson and Robinson, 1999: 174–175; Wall, Covell, and MacIntyre, 1999). Although a majority of young women as well as men aspire toward a good education and prestigious and well-paid occupations, only young women show a gap between their plans and what they actually expect to achieve. At a young age, females learn to anticipate their career plans will not work out and that they will be best gearing toward marriage and

[handwritten margin note: That's cause the older we get the more we're told, in school, that there is inequality.]

motherhood. Meanwhile, young men are more certain that their careers will match their expectations. This gender difference is telling of the persistence of traditional patterns whereby men do not expect marriage and parenthood to stop them from achieving their dreams. In contrast, young women are prepared for the barriers that family life will pose for the fulfillment of their professional plans. There are some signs that girls' educational and professional aspirations have risen toward the 1990s compared with the previous decades. Some reports note that the educational and life aspirations of young women and men are increasingly similar (Tanner 1990: 88–89; Bibby and Posterski, 1985, in Maxwell and Maxwell, 1994: 144).

It is a general finding (Wall, Covell, and MacIntyre, 1999; Mandell and Crysdale, 1993) that parental support is particularly important in adolescents' educational pathways. Wall, Covell, and MacIntyre (1999) summarize research that shows social supports to be as important in that they influence the level of aspirations and expectations of students. A supportive school environment is particularly important for youth's aspirations and expectations if familial support is missing. In their own study of 260 students aged 15–18 in Atlantic Canada, Wall, Covell, and MacIntyre found support for research showing that females perceive more social supports than male students. For boys' perceived opportunities family support was seen as crucial because they did not perceive as many peer or school supports as girls did. This translates to higher perceived opportunities by girls as well as higher expectations for education and career, and higher educational aspirations than their male peers. This study may indicate a shift in young women's perception of opportunities and aspirations even as gender divisions in education persist.

There is evidence that the attitudes and behaviours of parents regarding gender roles and gender equality have a role to play in young people's decisions about education and careers. Traditionally, parents have been more likely to encourage education of their sons than their daughters and promote gender-typed career and family-related choices for their children (Nelson and Robinson, 1999: 132).

For example, Mandell and Crysdale's (1993) study of 324 Ontario youth in their mid-twenties, regarding their experiences in the school-to-work transition found eighteen percent were traditional in their expectations while fifteen percent were labeled egalitarian. The majority of the parents were found to hold "quasi-egalitarian" views, supporting egalitarianism in some areas but not in others. This means that there is support for some combination of wage and domestic labour for both men and women, but this is characterized by "somewhat equal responsibility for children, a little sharing of housework, and equal educational and occupational aspirations for women and men, provided no financial problems or other hardships are involved" (Mandell and Crysdale, 1993: 26). In practice, this results in differential parental aspirations for sons than daughters, which in turn leads to differential labour market outcomes.

As well, social class differences shape educational and career outcomes. A recent study by Higginbotham and Weber (1992, in Nelson and Robinson, 1999: 132) of 200 career women from a working-class background indicated that parental support toward careers and postponement of marriage had been crucial in shaping their views and future success. Maxwell and Maxwell (1994) also found that both male and female students attending private schools have higher than average educational aspirations. The affect is more marked for girls who aspire to achieve a higher level of education than even their fathers did and a significantly higher level than their mothers. They also plan to work even after getting married. Thus, private schools are an avenue through which a select group of women can gain entry into the national elite. However, this will only perpetuate the existing class hierarchies and will do nothing for those students who are still battling against general structural barriers.

Gender Tracking

High school guidance counselling has been specifically identified as highly problematic in the way this process sustains and promotes traditional career choices based on gender (Russell, 1987; Cassie et al., 1981, in Guttman and

Alice, 1991). It has been suggested that counselling processes limit young women in several ways: by not having female counsellors available for female students; not having an appropriate range of career information available for women; not having ready access to career programs designed for women; not providing support for nontraditional careers for women. New innovations in the career counselling programs have begun to address these problems in the last decade (Cassie et al., 1981, in Guttman and Alice, 1991).

In the educational system, girls and young women get the message that they are not welcome and that they do not matter as much as boys and young men do. For example, Susan Russell (1987) has shown that there is pressure from male peers and teachers that creates an unwelcoming class room and school environment. This unwelcoming character of educational institutions and of traditionally male disciplines in particular carries the name "chilly climate" (Mandell and Crysdale, 1993: 21; Reynolds, 1998: 237). It is typical that in classrooms, males get more attention and approval and help from teachers than females do (Larkin, 1994: 49–53; Reynolds, 1998: 237). In universities particularly, women who enrol in traditional male bastions of physical sciences and engineering face a hostile setting that is antithetical to learning. Women students tend to receive less attention and less feedback than male students from the predominantly male faculty. They are also more likely to face disparaging comments about their work or their commitment to studies or comments that focus on their appearance rather than performance. Young women are likely to be counselled into lower career goals than men. As graduates, they are less likely to get faculty support, such as co-publications. Further, women who interrupt their studies or attend part-time while raising children are not taken seriously.

Sexual Harassment

A study by June Larkin (1994; also see Nelson and Robinson, 1999: 171–172) reports a range of male behaviours aimed at girls, including comments on their body or appearance, sexual innuendo, and unwelcome touching. These are part of a behaviour pattern aimed at putting girls "in their place." The consequences are negative to adolescent girls' self-esteem and their sense of power in the education setting. In Ontario, Larkin's and other studies (reported in Orton, 1999: 132) have found that eighty percent of female secondary school students reported having been subject to sexual harassment at school, versus thirty percent of males who reported being afraid of harassment by other males. Although it is possible that young men are less likely to report or admit fear, the results indicate that harassment is not seen as a serious issue by young men compared to women.

While sexual harassment of males does occur, it is not as prevalent as harassment of females. Further, based on traditional gender-based expectations, sexual harassment of females in high schools is more likely to be perceived as either "natural or as a threat," whereas females' harassment of males is more likely to seen as an "invitation" (Larkin, 1994: 35).

A part of sexual and gender harassment is directed at young males and females who are gay, lesbian, or bisexual. They are likely to be targets to disparaging behaviour and taunts. Also, their attentions toward same-sex individuals are more likely to cause discomfort and thus may be more likely to be interpreted as harassment (Larkin, 1994: 72–75).

Harassment can also contain elements based on one's social class or on minority status. Sexually and racially laced epithets and slurs are a part of the high school environment and can leave a serious mark on a person's self-esteem (Larkin, 1994: 28-29). One high school respondent in Larkin's (1994: 92) study told this story:

> The guys would play this game. They would all have...a number and [they would score] girls who passed by them in the hallway. If it was a pretty girl they'd say, "Ten, right on, you've got her!" If a Black girl walked by they'd go "Oh my God, she's got such a big ass..." They'd give her a low score.

The end result of sexual harassment is that girls and young women get discouraged. They tend to underestimate their academic abilities and experience a decline in their academic aspirations (Côté and Allahar, 1994; Larkin, 1994: 101–115). There is a large body of research documenting that girls' self-esteem takes a significant plunge during late childhood and early adolescence. Additionally, academic performance, particularly in traditional male subjects tends to decline (Nelson and Robinson, 1999: 170–171).

However, young women do not remain completely passive victims. Although they are silenced in their fear, they also develop some tactics to cope with and retaliate against harassment, including confrontation and public humiliation of the perpetrators. In Larkin's study (1994: 120) one young woman explained:

> Before I would just keep walking. Now I'll say some sort of comment back, but nothing to provoke them. But I'll say something to shut them up ... I guess they're surprised that I actually say something ... I was in the hall once and this Chinese guy goes, "Oh, I love you." And I said, "Are you that hard up? You don't even know me?" His friends are all, "Whoa!" I saw him the next day and nothing...nothing at all.

Ethnic and Race Minorities and Education

The race and ethnic patterns of education from the 1980s show that most minorities achieved higher levels of schooling than average Canadians (Li, 1989, in Davies and Guppy, 1998: 135). The 1996 Census (Statistics Canada, 1998a) notes that recent immigrants (arrived between 1991 and 1996) have higher levels of education than the Canadian-born population. Not only are there proportionally more university graduates among recent arrivals but the proportion without high school diplomas is lower. In 1996, thirty-four percent of all recent immigrants aged 25–44 were post-secondary graduates, compared with nineteen percent of the Canadian population. However, there is significant variation by the place of origin, with those born in United States most likely to have completed university, followed by the Philippines, Taiwan, The People's Republic of China, and India. Furthermore, there were more graduates in the fields of science and technology, both among men and women.

These trends indicate levels of education that were not necessarily gained while in Canada but are a result of Canada's immigration policies, which select those with higher levels of education. Therefore, it is important to look at the specifically Canadian educational experiences of race and ethnic minorities.

Anisef (1994: 8–9) reports that generally (with the exception of Asian students), visible minority students perform more poorly in the school system. It has been found in Ontario that visible minority students are more likely to be streamed into non-university tracks in high school, put in special education classes, or to be suspended. They are also more likely to drop out of school (Anisef and Kilbride, 2000; Dei, 1993).

Aboriginal youth have made some modest gains from the mid-1980s to the mid-1990s. More of them complete high school and more attend and complete post-secondary education. However, as indicated in Table 2.2, the gaps between Aboriginal and other Canadians are still grave. Based on 1996 Census data, Aboriginal people were 2.6 times more likely to not have completed high school than the non-Aboriginal population. There was some slight improvement at the post-secondary level where Aboriginal people aged 20–29 were fifty percent less likely to complete their education in 1986 than the same age group of average Canadians, compared with sixty percent less likely in 1986. At twenty-one percent, Aboriginal women have a slightly higher college completion rate than men, nineteen percent of whom have completed a college degree. These rates were slightly more favourable among the Métis than among North American Indians or the Inuit, who are more likely to live in remote or Northern communities and thus have less access to post-secondary education. Generally, those in urban areas are more likely to have higher educational levels than those living in rural areas (Tait, 1999: 6–9; Tait, 2000: 258–259; see also Statistics Canada, 1998a; Van Wert, 1997).

Black students continue to face difficult educational circumstances. Sherwood (1993) reports that in the late 1980s, seventy-six percent of Asian students in grade nine were in advanced programs, whereas the comparative figure is sixty-five percent of white students and forty-five percent for Black

Table 2.2. Education by Highest Level of Schooling Completed, Ages 15-49, Aboriginal Peoples and Total Canadian Population

Highest Level of Education	Total Population	Total Aboriginal Ancestry	North American Indian	On-reserve	Off-reserve	Métis	Inuit
Less than grade 9	4.9%	16.8%	16.5%	28.1%	10.5%	12.4%	37.6%
Secondary school	42.6	49.6	49.5	46.1	51.2	53.1	35.8
Some post-secondary	31.7	13.0	14.2	11.1	15.8	13.7	11.3
Certificate/diploma	9.4	16.5	16.6	12.9	18.5	17.3	14.1
University degree	11.4	2.7	2.7	1.0	3.6	3.1	0.6
Not specified	n/a	0.5	0.5	0.9	0.3	0.4	0.5
Total	21,304,740	325,460	241,115	81,965	159,145	70,610	17,590

Source: Calculated from Statistics Canada, Schooling, Work and Related Activities, Income, Expenses and Mobility: 1991 Aboriginal Peoples' Survey (Ottawa: Minister of Industry, Science and Technology, 1993), cat. No. 89-534 from Wotherspoon, 1998, p.174.

students. Meanwhile, twenty-one percent of the black students, nine percent of whites and three percent of Asians were enrolled in basic level programs. Similar results were reported in the mid-1980s in the North York Board of Education in Toronto. While fifty-five percent of the white children were enrolled in advanced programs and only fifteen percent in basic or vocational programs, the corresponding figures for black students were four percent and sixty percent respectively (Christensen and Weinfeld, 1993: 31). In their analysis of the 1986 Census results, Christensen and Weinfeld (1993: 34) found that both male and female blacks in the age group 15–24 have lower than average high school graduation, college entrance, and bachelor's degree completion rates. The particularly difficult situation of young black female students has been noted (African Heritage Educators' Network and Ontario Women's Directorate, 1996: 3).

The problems black and Aboriginal students face relate to poverty and lack of access to employment opportunities (Van Wert, 1997; African Heritage Educators' Network and Ontario Women's Directorate, 1996: 3; Davies and Guppy, 1998: 135). Poverty is particularly prevalent in minority families in general. Black children are 2.5 to three times more likely than the Canadian average to be living in a lone-parent household, characterised by low incomes. This is even more pronounced among Canadian-born blacks than foreign-born blacks (Christensen and Weinfeld, 1993: 41).

It has also been found that "thirty percent of all immigrant children live in families whose total income falls below the official poverty line" (Beiser et al., 1999, in Anisef and Kilbride, 2000: 13). There is a strong link between negative and marginalized employment experiences of parents and pressure to drop out of school. Therefore, it is suggested that it is not enough to offer language classes to newcomer youth; closer links are needed between home and school, and the education system itself must accommodate the diverse needs better. Difficulties in school also stand in the way of successful employment of minority youth. Some studies suggest that educational programs devised to aid the transition from school to employment may, in fact, unnecessarily label minority youth "at risk," which suppresses employers' willingness to engage them (Anisef and Kilbride, 2000: 25–26).

According to the Canadian Council on Social Development (2000), immigrant youth in the age group 15–19 are as likely, as Canadian-born youth to stay in school. However, those in the age group 20–24 are more likely than Canadian-born youth to be in school. More recent immigrant youth in this age group are more likely to be enrolled in educational institutions than Canadian-born youth.

However, we have to note the range of ethnic groups and racial minorities embedded in the more general group of "immigrant youth." In a recent analysis of the 1996 Census in relation to Toronto, Ornstein (2000: 51) notes that there are other ethnic and race groups with low chances of dropping out, including Caribbeans and Indo-Asians, Japanese, Koreans, West Asians and Europeans, Germans, Ukranians, and Jews. There were also some groups for whom high-school non-completion was a particular problem. Central Americans and Portuguese stand out, with nearly thirty percent of young people without high school diplomas, or not in full-time school attendance.

The low educational rates of Portuguese-Canadian youth have long been subject to concern. This lack of progress has been explained by the eagerness of Portuguese parents to have economic success, to be obtained by every family member's participation in wage work. Thus children's schooling is sacrificed to their early entry into the labour force. Furthermore, parents have a problem communicating with schools due to a lack of proficiency in English. However, these patterns were more prevalent in the 1970s and have begun to change, at least in Vancouver, where Portuguese parents have shown high educational aspirations for their children (Arruda, 1993: 16–18).

Institutionalized Racism in Education

Interestingly, unlike gender discrimination, race and ethnic discrimination are identified by young people themselves. In a Canadian Advisory Council on the Status of Women survey (Holmes and Silverman, 1992: 45), only a minority of young men and women identified gender discrimination as a problem, whereas discrimination based on race and ethnicity were recognized more readily. For example, black students reported (African Heritage Educators' Network and Ontario Women's Directorate, 1996: 3) the following experiences:

> "I told my teacher that I wanted to be a lawyer but she said that I should be a cook because the food I prepared for the school event was good."

> "I was pushed into sports and my school work suffered."

> "I told my teacher that I was interested in law but she said I should be an actor."

> "I was counselled to drop math without being told how it would affect my chances to go to university."

> "My guidance counsellor told me that I should be a hairdresser."

In the late 1990s, the Canadian Council on Social Development (2000) ran focus groups of a total of fifty immigrant youth aged 15–24 in Toronto, Montreal, and Vancouver. The study found that most of the participants, and almost all of those who were of visible minorities, had experienced bigotry and racism in Canada:

> The issue of racism was raised spontaneously in all of the focus groups. Often it arose as part of the discussions about negative aspects of Canada. Younger participants in particular felt that...teachers could be racists. Even participants who did not raise the issue themselves and those who had not faced racism from teachers agreed that certain teachers and school administrators seemed to single out certain students or groups of students for harsher treatment based on their ethnicity. "I have a teacher who hates the Hispanic kids." "Teachers don't like me because I'm Greek." "I had a teacher who deducted twenty points

from an oral presentation I gave because of my accent. She said that she marked everyone on their diction and she was going to treat me just like the others because it was the only way I was ever going to learn." "If a white kid does something and I do the same thing, there is no question that I'm going to get into worse trouble. In fact, teachers don't even bother with me. I go to the principal's office for the slightest offence."

Some youth are fighting back. In Chapter 1, the long history of racial discrimination in the Nova Scotia education system was outlined. In reaction to the persistent racism in Nova Scotia, black high-school youth organized themselves into the Cultural Awareness Youth Group (CAYG) in 1979. Most of the participants are high-school students aged 15–19, the majority are female and most come from communities where segregation, accompanied by unemployment, lack of recreation, and isolation are major problems. Since its foundation, the CAYG has organized a number of events for black youth and the wider community in schools and other venues. Some of them are annual and focus on black history and culture, as well as contemporary issues faced by black people (Woods, 1988). In the words of Shingai, a member of CAYG:

There has been a black community in Nova Scotia for over three hundred years, but you wouldn't know it by the history books. You won't find our faces on the post cards, you won't find our statues in the parks. The only time white people seem to notice us is when they want to call us "nigger" and say we've got an attitude. Well, my name is Shingai, and my attitude is this: You don't have to be from Scotland to have a history. (National Film Board, 1992)

Conclusions

Education is synonymous with being young. Adolescents are properly seen to belong in high schools and those in their twenties belong in colleges and universities. Specifically, the expansion of the post-secondary education system in the second half of the twentieth century signifies the prolongation of the stage of youth. However, despite popular imagery of youth roaming the hallowed halls of colleges and universities, social class, gender, race, and ethnicity continue to determine one's access to, experiences in, and success in the educational system. Patterns of advantage and disadvantage are likely to be perpetuated as young people situate themselves in the labour market.

3 | Work

In terms of supervision, there is none. [The employer] says: "Oh, I'll be around to check on you," but I think it's impossible because he gives each kid such a huge area with buildings with ten or twelve floors. There's no way he can know where you are...Also he sends kids out on their own...He doesn't care where you go, if you wander, go to houses, buildings, as long as you sell flowers. (Female teenager, about selling flowers door-to-door, National Film Board, 1994)

From the Frying Pan into the Fire: Youth Labour Markets

Whether combining education and employment or in transition from education to full-time employment, young people face a range of problems that have less to do with their qualifications and preparedness for the labour market and more to do with the structure of the economy. This chapter will outline the central features of the youth labour market, including patterns of employment and unemployment, with a focus on gender, race, and ethnicity.

Currently, the labour market has few pieces of good news to offer to young people. The 1980s and 1990s were particularly characterized by "global economic restructuring, new technologies, unemployment and underemployment, the growth of low-tier service industries, and an increase in temporary, part-time, and other 'flexible' forms of work" (Lowe and Krahn, 1994–5: 3; also see Blanchflower and Freeman, 1998). Consequently, youth are facing a worsening labour market with fewer opportunities for jobs that match their education. Most offered are in the service sector, which utilizes young people as a pool of poorly paid, temporary, part-time, and flexible workers. Additionally, patterns that emerge in secondary and post-secondary education (Chapter 2) are mirrored in young people's work experiences. Streaming based on social class, gender, race, and ethnicity continues in the labour force. Young people's chances of resisting the deterioration of their work experience by unionization are reduced by the transient nature of their employment. Just as not all youth have access to education, not all are able to participate in the formal economy. Some become victims of the many ills of society and are claimed as casualties of the streets. Thus, the lives of "squeegee youth" will be addressed as a part of informal economic activities.

Youth Employment and Unemployment

Generally, young Canadian people are less likely to be employed and more likely to be unemployed than people over twenty-five. There was a significant drop in the labour force participation of males aged 15–24 from 69.7 percent in 1981 to 65.3 percent in 1999. The declines were even greater for the younger age groups with an increase in the participation gap between those aged 15–19 and those aged 20–24 (Archambault and Grignon, 1999; Jennings, 1998).

The labour force participation rates of female youth are generally lower than for male youth (see Table 3.1). In 1981 the total participation rate for females between the ages of 15–24 was 61.2 percent. It rose to a high of 64.9 percent in

1991, and dropped again in 1999, to 61.7 percent (Statistics Canada, 1999d).

In December 1997, only eight percent of the working age population was composed of youth between fifteen and twenty-four years of age, while this age group formed twenty-nine percent of those who were unemployed (Nakamura and Wong, 1998: 8). The unemployment rate of males aged 15–24 rose from 12.7 percent in 1981 to 18.4 percent in 1996. With the late 1990s economic recovery, the unemployment rate declined to fourteen percent by October 1999. Overall, the trend from the 1980s onward has been upward, with some cyclical fluctuations. The unemployment rate of female youth has always been lower, with a 4.1 percent difference in women's favour in the period 1990–1996 (Statistics Canada, 1999d; Kerr, 1997).

There are also wide differences in the unemployment rate of those in the age group 15–24. As seen in Table 3.1, teenagers typically have higher unemployment rates than those in the age group 20–24. In the time period 1990–1996, the difference between these two groups' average annual unemployment rate was 3.7 percentage points, and there was no change from the 1980s (Kerr, 1997).

A most disturbing trend is the growing proportion of non-student youth dropping out of the labour force (Jennings, 1998). Associated with this are ever longer periods of unemployment among youth since the 1970s. The proportion of youth unemployed for more than a year increased three-fold between 1976 and 1995 (Kerr, 1997).

Cohort Effects and Economic Cycles

A point often made is that there is heightened job competition as the "echo" of the baby-boom offspring entered the labour market (Lowe and Krahn, 1994–5: 3; Kerr, 1999). Although this may be a minor factor in explaining cyclical shifts in youth employment, there is increasing evidence that this proposed "cohort effect" is negligible in face of economic factors (Blanchflower and Freeman, 1998; Beaujot, 2000: 304). For example, Statistics Canada (1999g) reports that: "Roughly 12 percent of the drop in the youth employment rate between 1989

**Table 3.1. Population 15 Years and Over by Sex, Age Groups,
and Labour Force Activity, for Canada, Provinces and
Territories, 1981–1996 Censuses (20% Sample Data)**

Sex, Age Groups, and Labour Force Activity	1981	1986	1991	1996
Canada				
Both sexes				
15–19 years	2,303,580	1,917,245	1,872,230	1,956,115
Participation rate	46.6	47.0	48.3	43.8
Unemployment rate	15.6	20.7	15.3	19.0
20–24 years	2,334,420	2,243,945	1,960,595	1,892,910
Participation rate	84.1	85.5	84.7	79.5
Unemployment rate	11.5	15.2	15.7	17.0

Source: Statistics Canada http://www.statcan.ca/english/census96/
mar17/labour/table6/t6p00b.htm.

and 1998 was due to the change in the composition of the youth
population. The other eighty-eight percent is a reflection of
poorer job conditions or other factors." When the economy is
poor, youth are more likely to suffer disproportionately in
comparison with older age groups (Blanchflower and Freeman,
1998; Kerr, 1999) and youth labour markets are less likely to
recover from economic downswings. While the numbers of jobs
for adults increased by 1 million between 1992 and 1997, youth
were offered 100,000 fewer jobs (Elton and Brearton, 1997). The
economic upswing of the late 1990s brought youth employment
rates up, added 145,000 jobs, and led to a reduction in the youth
unemployment rate (Statistics Canada, 2000c). In other words,
youth are the least employable group when the economy

worsens. This has much to do with the types of jobs generally available to young people.

Where are the Jobs?

There is a distinct pattern to the type of employment youth are able to get. In the past, major employers for graduates (regardless of level) were found in the public sector: health, education, and public service. In contrast, during the 1990s and beyond, youth employment is generally found in the service sector. As indicated in Table 3.2, young people, regardless of education level, are substantially over-represented in traditional service industries, in clerical, sales, and service occupations where wages and benefits are poor, promotions rare, and the work force transient. In contrast, youth are under-represented in non-service job sectors. There is a trend of higher concentration in "bad jobs" since the mid-1970s (Betcherman and Leckie, 1996, in Nakamura and Wong, 1998: 8; Marquardt, 1998: 81–82; Côté and Allahar, 1994). Graduates are also competing for jobs in the private sector with high levels of stress and competition (Marquardt, 1998: 81–82).

Another significant feature of the youth labour market is the dramatic increase in the part-time employment of youth relative to age groups over twenty-five. Approximately forty-five percent of young people worked part time in 1995, compared with around twelve percent of adults. This represents a near doubling of youth part-time work since 1980 (Nakamura and Wong, 1998: 8). In effect, the increase in the overall part-time work participation rate between 1981 and 1991 is accountable by the age group 15–24 alone (Beaujot, 2000: 302; see also Marquardt, 1998: 80–81). As was noted in Chapter 2, part-time employment of young people has gone hand in hand with the rising cost of education, as young people's own financial contributions are needed in addition to parental contributions (Baker, 1989: 43).

One of the growing areas of employment for young people, particularly in high school, is in door-to-door sales. This is a completely unregulated sector of youth employment, often

Table 3.2. A high proportion of post-secondary graduates work
in clerical, sales, service, or blue collar jobs

Type of job held when interviewed

Educational attainment	Felt over-qualified	Management, professional	Clerical, sales, service	Blue collar
	(%)	(% distribution by occupation)		
Post-secondary graduates	22	64	23	13
Community college certificate or diploma	21	46	30	24
Undergraduate diploma or certificate	23	58	32	10
Bachelor's or first professional degree	22	78	17	5
Master's degree, earned doctorate[1]	27	83	12	5

[1] Includes university diplomas or certificates above a bachelor's degree.
Source: Statistics Canada, 1994 General Social Survey (from Kelly, Howatson-Leo and Clark 'I Feel Overqualified For My Job' in Canadian Social Trends 3, 2000, p.183.)

characterized by misrepresentation of the nature of the business, where youth who are sent to sell flowers, chocolates, or other light items. They are instructed to represent themselves as "poor students who are not getting help elsewhere" (National Film Board, 1994), giving the impression that they are a part of a youth service geared toward providing a livelihood to industrious and deserving young people. As quoted in the beginning of this chapter, some of this type of work is both exploitive and dangerous. These young people are promised at least a minimum wage for work but the realities are quite different:

> There are some kids out there earning maybe a dollar for an
> entire night's work and he'd also yell at the kids [that] you've
> been stealing flowers from him so you'd have to pay him
> (National Film Board, 1994).

Lately, more attention has been paid to the dangerous
working conditions that young people face in their workplaces.
In 1998, 61,620 workers aged 15–24 were injured and fifty-
seven were killed (Philp, 2000). Among the cases that made
the news were David Ellis, who died at age eighteen, Jared
Dietrich, aged nineteen, and sixteen-year-old Ivan Golyashov,
all of whom died of separate workplace injuries suffered while
dealing with a dough-making machine (Freeze, 1999;
Hargrove, 2000). Another youth, twenty-year-old Steve
MacDonald, died after being entangled in a metal lathe
(Hargrove, 2000). James MacMillan was crushed at age twenty-
four, pinned to his truck while a ten-tonne agricultural sprayer
lurched from its trailer (Philp, 2000).

Some of the blame for these and other serious workplace
accidents is put on young people themselves, who are described
as seeing "themselves as invincible." However, in not providing
health and safety training to young employees, most of the
blame must fall on employers (Philp, 2000), either in businesses
that are small enough to be left outside workplace safety
training legislation or those who give only lip service to
informing young workers about factors having to do with their
health (Hargrove, 2000).

The Benefits of Education vs. Educational Inflation and Credentialism

According to many reports, including a recent one by
Human Resources Development Canada (1999b: 12), staying
in school longer pays off as education increases one's chances
of employment. This link is demonstrated through statistics
which show that high-school dropouts have a significantly
higher unemployment rate (also see Kerr, 1997) and they work
longer hours and earn less (Nakamura and Wong, 1998: 9). In
1996 the total unemployment rate for youth with some high
school was twenty-eight percent, while the unemployment rate

for high-school graduates was sixteen percent. The unemployment rate of young women without a high-school diploma in 1995 was over thirty percent (Marquardt, 1998: 75–77).

The fates of those with more education are better. A report from Human Resources Development Canada (1999b: 12) states that sixty-seven percent of graduates from vocational or trade schools, seventy percent of graduates from college, and sixty-eight percent of graduates from university had found employment within two years of graduation. Similarly, the unemployment rate reflected levels of education. The unemployment rate of vocational school graduates stands at fifteen percent, compared with ten percent for college graduates, nine percent for university BA graduates, seven percent for masters' graduates, and eight percent for doctorate graduates (also see Marquardt, 1998: 75). The National Graduates Survey (Clark, 1999) interviewed 43,000 young people in 1997 who had graduated in 1995. The study found that ninety-five percent of these graduates had found a job since they graduated.

However encouraging these statistics may seem, there is also a serious discrepency between education and quality of employment. Half of post-secondary graduates experience unemployment in the first two years following graduation (Marquardt, 1998: 75). Of the 43,000 graduates in the National Graduates Survey (Clark, 1999), about a quarter of the college and bachelor's graduates had difficulty finding employment while about one third had difficulty finding work related to their field of study. As shown in Table 3.3, the chances of finding full-time work and high wages have gotten progressively worse for graduating classes between 1982 and 1995.

The terms "educational inflation" and "credentialism" have entered our vocabulary. As more people are getting educated, the value of education is inflated; credentials such as degrees and diplomas are required for even entry level jobs that previously required no such credentials (Côté and Allahar, 1994: 36–37, 124–125; Naiman, 2000: 176–177; Baker, 1989: 41–43; Blanchflower and Freeman, 1998). Despite holding a degree many youth find themselves "under-employed" in

---

Table 3.3. 1995 graduates were least successful finding full-time work and high level jobs

Two years after graduation	Class of 1982	Class of 1986	Class of 1990	Class of 1995
Working full-time		%		
College	77	82	76	70
Bachelor's	71	73	72	66
Working full-time in high level jobs[1]				
College	51	54	56	47
Bachelor's	78	77	77	73

---

[1] Six highest categories of the Pineo-Carroll-Moore socio-economic classification of occupations including self-employed and employed professionals, semi-professionals, technicians, and senior and middle managers.
Source: Statistics Canada, National Graduates Survey, 1997 (from Clark 'Search for Success: Finding Work After Graduation' in Canadian Social Trends 3, 2000, p.174.)

unskilled jobs offering low wages and benefits (see Table 3.4). In 1976, forty percent of university graduates in social sciences were in a job unrelated to their field of study; the graduating class of 1986 found forty-one percent with a B.A. underemployed while sixty-two percent of M.A. and between thirty-five and forty percent of Ph.D. graduates were underemployed (Côté and Allahar, 1994: 38–39).

These trends continue. According to the 1994 General Social Survey, large numbers of well-educated Canadians feel overqualified for their jobs. Of those with a college or university education, twenty-two percent felt overqualified for their job, with women more likely than men to feel this way. College and university graduates in the age group 20–29 were the most likely (thirty-seven percent) to feel overqualified, reflecting the fact that they are most likely (thirty percent) to be employed

---

**Table 3.4. Over one in four graduates reported great difficulty
in finding a well-paying job**

	College	Bachelor's
	%	
Finding a job that paid enough	28	27
Finding a job related to my field of study	25	33
Finding a job where I wanted to live	17	16
Knowing how to find job openings	7	8
Deciding what I wanted to be	7	14
Performing well in job interviews	2	2
Completing job applications, writing résumés or letters of introduction	1	1

Source: Statistics Canada, National Graduates Survey, 1997 (from
Clark 'Search for Success: Finding Work After Graduation' in
Canadian Social Trends 3, 2000, p.177.)

in clerical, sales, service, or blue collar positions (Kelly et al,
2000: 182–183).

Life-Long Learning?

Ironically, a pattern emerging from the mismatch between
education and work is a pressure for more education. One of
the recent buzz words is "life-long learning," a process whereby
young people entering the labour force are pushed toward
obtaining ever increasing amounts of training and education
even as they are already overqualified for the labour market
(Lowe and Krahn, 1994–5; Jennings, 1998). During the 1970s
and right through the 1990s the student labour market grew
while formal education was "prolonged and co-existed with
employment" (Marquardt, 1998, 48). There is a significant
upward trend in full-time educational enrolment in the 1990s,
among those aged 15–24, and particularly marked for the 20–
24 age group (Jennings, 1998).

Lowe and Krahn (1994–5) raise concerns about increasing
labour market polarization, in that most of the job training

programs favour young well-educated male workers, as programs are more likely to take place in larger work organizations and among full-time workers. Other research (Côté and Allahar, 1994: 124–125; Naiman, 2000: 176–177; Baker, 1989: 41–43; Blanchflower and Freeman, 1998) supports the conclusion that the current system favours those who have the means to pursue education and that it discriminates against lower income groups, women, or members of ethno-racial minorities.

An additional concern is that combining education and employment seems to suppress labour force performance. The National Graduates Survey (Clark, 1999) reports that youth who had jobs before graduation, to finance their studies, were more likely to work in clerical, sales, and service occupations, and were more likely to stay in the same job. Those who started work after graduating were more likely to work in professional or technical jobs and were more likely to have changed jobs.

The Canadian Council on Social Development (2000: 5) found that at least half of Canadian-born youth aged 15–19 combine school and full- or part-time employment. Statistics Canada (1999g) also reports that in 1998, thirty-five percent of full-time students had a job, an increase of three percent from the year before. This means that while an adult work week is on average thirty-seven hours, the average working teenager's combined weekly time at school and work amount to between fifty and sixty hours (Waldie, 1993).

Although enrolment in full-time studies has been identified as an important factor behind the decline in youth labour force participation (Jennings, 1998), high proportions of youth combine these experiences. Lowe and Krahn's (1994–5) study of 404 high-school and 357 university graduates from the class of 1985 in Alberta showed that in 1992, high proportions in each group were engaged in a process of combining periods of education with periods of employment. This signifies a prolonged process of transition from school to work. Notably, most education was aimed toward improving personal labour market options rather than improving skills required in one's current job.

Gender and Employment Experiences

Not surprisingly, considering the gender-typing in education (Chapter 2), the type of youth employment varies, based on gender and levels of education. Studies find that most girls aspire to a narrow range of traditionally female occupations (Maxwell and Maxwell, 1994: 153). Patterns from the 1970s and 1980s indicated that young women find it very difficult to enter nontraditional work in a highly gender-segregated labour market. Their primary employment is in the clerical and service industries and other female dominated professions, such as teaching and nursing (Guttman, 1991; Anisef et al., 1980).

These gender-based differences are carried over to the 1990s and beyond. Male youths without a high school diploma are generally found in unskilled blue-collar jobs: deliveries, grocery clerks, kitchen helpers, or general labourers. By the age of twenty-four, one quarter will be in skilled trades as carpenters, welders, heavy-duty mechanics, and auto mechanics. A minority will be in supervisory sales or service positions. Meanwhile, two thirds of female youth without a high school diploma will be in consumer service industries as sales clerks, cashiers, and waitresses, while only fourteen percent will have a blue-collar job like seamstress or food processor. Even with a high-school diploma seventy percent of young women will be in clerical, sales, and service industries with most in consumer services. Only one in ten will be in blue-collar jobs in comparison with half of the males (Marquardt, 1998: 77–78).

Of male graduates from community colleges or other non-university diploma graduates , over one third work in skilled blue-collar jobs while female graduates find employment in "professional, managerial, and technical occupations, particularly nursing, teaching, and skilled administrative and business occupations" (Marquardt, 1998: 78). Almost half of female post-secondary graduates and one third of males are still working in unskilled or semiskilled jobs (Marquardt, 1998: 78–79).

Holding a post-secondary degree spells more success relative to less educated youth. Of youth with a post-secondary degree by the age of twenty-four, half will work in managerial occupations. Reflecting the gender-segregated education system discussed in a previous chapter, females will more likely become elementary or secondary teachers while males will be in "professional jobs in the natural and applied sciences, including engineering, as well as in business, finance, and administration. However, over a third of both male and female university graduates under 24 work in the typical student labour market, consisting of work in the service sector or blue-collar labour market" (Marquardt, 1998: 78).

Studies document the effect of both socio-economic background and gender on education. Thiessen and Looker (1993) studied a sample of 567 males and 639 females, all seventeen years of age, in Hamilton, Ontario, and Halifax, Nova Scotia. Their study suggests that working-class youth distance themselves from the manual work of their fathers, and that middle-class youth expect a pattern of work after their fathers. This finding also supports a study by Weis (1990; in Thiessen and Looker, 1993) suggesting that there is a gender equalization in expectations and that young women take it for granted that their work patterns would be those of middle-class males.

As in the case of education, work settings reflect general patriarchal power patterns. Women may be subjected to sexual harassment in the workplace (Nelson and Robinson, 1999: 264–271, 345, 494). Sexual harassment is typically divided into two varieties. The *quid pro quo* cases are the most obvious, involving threats to employment if the woman does not agree to sexual encounters. The other variety, called "poisoned work environment" is more difficult to recognize and refers to subtle ways in which the work environment is intimidating, uncomfortable, or offensive to the worker (Nelson and Robinson, 1999: 268).

The Canadian Violence Against Women Survey found that eighty-seven percent of Canadian women have experienced sexual harassment of a "memorable" variety and that nearly half of these were work-related. In work-related incidents, co-workers were the most frequent (twenty-five percent) perpetrator, while bosses or supervisors accounted for eighteen percent, and clients, customers, or patients another six percent (Johnson, 1996: 97). Young women are particularly vulnerable to the unwelcome advances in workplaces where their bosses are likely to be male and their male co-workers are socially defined to have power over women (Larkin, 1994: 24–28; Johnson, 1996: 103). According to Johnson (1996: 103–104) young and unmarried women are more likely to be subjected to harassment.

Race, Ethnicity, and Employment Experiences

Visible minority status in Canada typically translates to being under-employed in the labour market. Although they are likely to have more credentials, racist barriers continue to plague job entry (Livingston, 1999: 215). In 1992, unemployment among visible minority males aged 15–25 was fourteen percent (Marquardt, 1998: 76).

Unemployment is a particularly serious problem among Aboriginal populations and is partly linked to the poor educational histories discussed in Chapter 2. Even those with education have a difficult time getting employment. In 1996, the unemployment rate among young Aboriginal adults without a high school diploma was forty percent, compared with twenty percent among the general youth population. Similarly, the figures were twenty-three percent and thirteen percent, respectively, for Aboriginal people with a high school diploma, twenty percent and nine percent for those with a college diploma or degree, and nine percent and five percent for those with a university degree. The corresponding figures for non-Aboriginal people in the same age group showed the same pattern but at significantly higher respective rates: twenty percent, thirteen percent, nine percent, and five percent (Tait, 1999; Tait, 2000: 260; see also Marquardt, 1998: 76).

Another population facing serious problems with employability are black youth. James (1993: 93) reports that black youth believe that "as visible minority individuals they would be labelled, stereotyped, and discriminated against, and that their race would impact on their occupational experiences and opportunities." These fears are well founded. In the late

1980s, the unemployment rate for Caribbean-born black males aged 15–24 was fifty percent higher than for Canadian-born males (Christensen and Weinfeld, 1993: 31). More recently, Ornstein's (2000: 59) analysis of the 1996 Census in relation to Toronto found that there are three groups with "frighteningly high" youth unemployment rates: Africans and blacks, the Jamaicans, and the Trinidadians and Tobagonians. What is significant in relation to these groups is that their high youth unemployment is not due to settlement difficulties. For example, "70 percent of the African and Black group are born in Canada and another 10 percent arrived before 1976." At the same time, justifiably, there is a growing and more public restlessness among these segments of the population. An increase in the size of the black population combined with the increase in the visible minority population in general has been accompanied with a rise in awareness and community activism (Walker, 1985: 19–22).

Immigrant youth are at a particular disadvantage in searching for employment. They lack contacts and networks, may have language difficulties, and may deal with different sets of familial expectations regarding combined responsibility to family, school, or workplaces (Canadian Council on Social Development, 1998). This is reflected in the lower rates at which immigrant youth combine work and education. The Canadian Council on Social Development (2000: 5) reports that while about half of Canadian-born youth aged 15–19 combine school and employment, only one quarter of immigrant youth in this age group who have been in Canada less than ten years are holding a job while in school. In the age group 20–24, seventy-nine percent of Canadian-born students work, while under half of the immigrant youth in Canada for less than ten years work. However, the study also found that eighty percent of immigrant students of this age group who have resided in Canada for longer than ten years did work.

Earnings: Are Youth too Greedy?

One persistent image in the public is that young people are lazy. Not only that, they are too inflexible and demanding in their expectations of starting level jobs. In other words, youth themselves and particularly their "excessive" demands and expectations are to blame for youth unemployment. This argument has no bearing in reality. It has been shown that virtually in all OECD countries workers in young age groups have experienced declines in their earnings relative to older workers in the 1990s (Blanchflower and Freeman, 1998).

The Canadian Economic Observer (Corak, 1999: 3.2) reported that in 1994 young men (aged 17–24) were earning the same as their counterparts in 1969. When inflation was accounted for, there was a nineteen percent decline in the earnings of full-time working males aged 17–24 between 1979 and 1992, while there was a similar drop of ten percent in the age group 25–34 (Picot and Myles, 2000: 131). Meanwhile, those in the age group 45–54 earned over thirty percent more than their counterparts in 1969. It is said (Corak, 1999: 3.2; also see Beaujot, 2000: 302–303) that:

> these changes reflect a pervasive decline in the earnings capacity of the young regardless of industry, occupation, union status, and the prevailing macroeconomic climate. Even if unemployment had been the same, youths in the 1980s would have started their careers with earnings almost twenty percent lower than their counterparts ten years earlier.

The beneficial effect of education is demonstrated in earnings. In 1990, there was a difference of nearly $10,000 a year in income between those who have bachelor's degrees and those youth without one (Kerr, 1997). In 1990, high-school graduates earned approximately $22,600 a year, compared with $46,000 for doctoral graduates (Education Today, 1996: 5). Nevertheless, a decline in earnings for young workers has occurred "regardless of industry, occupations, education level, or union status" (Marquardt, 1998: 93). Moreover, according to Statistics Canada data from 1988 (in Little, 1998):

> Young people, those aged 15–24, accounted for a staggering 58 percent or 316,000 of all those making the minimum wage

or less. They represented 18.4 percent of all young people who had jobs, almost four times the 4.8 percent figure for the whole work force. Of the same 316,000, about sixty percent — 191,000 people — were students who lived with their parents; 155,000 were between fifteen and nineteen, the other 36,000 were 20–24.

These low earnings are reflected in the living conditions of youth. In 1981, just under half of the youth under the age of twenty-five that lived on their own were below the poverty line. By 1996 the figure had risen dramatically to two thirds (Marquardt, 1998: 97). With increasing proportions of the youth population working dead-end service jobs and under minimum wage conditions that do not provide them with a subsistence wage, this is hardly surprising. Provincial governments set minimum wage levels, ranging from a low $4.75 per hour in Newfoundland to a high $7.00 in British Columbia (Kerr, 1999). In Ontario and Alberta there is a sub-minimum wage for students despite the fact that other provinces eliminated it because they believed it was against the Canadian Charter of Rights (Marquardt, 1998: 126–128).

Because of the significant drop in the incomes of young males and the slight increase in young women's wages, some have concluded that "young men and women increasingly have more in common with their age-mates than with older persons of the same sex" (Beaujot, 2000: 304; Allahar and Côté, 1998). The common elements are increasing job ghettoization, a general deterioration of wages, and being trapped in dead-end work areas with no chance of advancement (Allahar and Côté, 1998: 132). Nevertheless, the wages of young women reflect the general male-female wage gap; it is estimated that young women earn fifteen percent less than young men (Elton and Brearton, 1997).

The image of young people as lazy slackers is put in a new light. If young people are lacking in faith in the benefits of hard work, it is because they see no evidence of their efforts being rewarded. Whatever slacking may be taking place (and there is no real evidence for it) would be rooted in knowing that they will have to work twice as hard as their parents or even the cohorts of youth before them to obtain a smaller share of the wealth around them. What is surprising is that so many young people can still bring themselves to keep on trying.

Employment Policy

According to Marquardt (1998: 109–135), prevailing labour market policies reflect a two-pronged approach. On the one hand, there is a goal to create good jobs in the labour market and to ensure that the education system is in keeping with this policy. To this end, there are a number of quality control mechanisms in the education system, including tests of literacy, math, and science, while students are encouraged to stay in school. Various school-to-work transition programs are created, including co-operative education, internships, and youth apprenticeship programs, to allow high-school students to finish their schooling while getting training for skilled trades or to get on-the-job training opportunities.

Thus, the federal government works with the provinces under Youth Internship Canada providing either community-based, sector-based, or school-based programs, which consist of both on-the-job and in-class training. In 1996/97, $124 million was committed to this program. Further, the Summer Jobs Program was allocated $120 million in 1996/97, which covered the wage-subsidies toward 45,000 jobs in the non-profit, private, and public sectors. Youth Services Canada also develops working opportunities for youth in the area of community service. Community-based organizations are given funding to bring together teams of between ten and twenty youth, for a project lasting between six and nine months. Some of the projects are: mentoring teenage parents, setting up after-hours sports programs, or elderly escort programs. Most recently, Human Resources Development Canada is also developing a First Jobs program, which will provide college and university graduates with entry-level internship positions in the private sector. This program has been criticised by student groups for providing subsistence wages at a proposed $1,000/month (Association of Canadian

Community Colleges, 1996; see also Marquardt, 1998: 109–135). Generally, opportunities given to students come at a cost of low wages, while the short-term employment opportunities do not necessarily result in good permanent jobs.

On the other hand, programs that aim at creating good jobs and easing school-to-work transitions are complemented by policies that support the "expansion of low-wage employment to reduce the jobless rate" of those who do not fall into the first scenario. This includes measures such as lowering or eliminating minimum wage and lowering other labour costs by employers, such as unemployment insurance premiums and pension plan contributions. It is expected that as labour costs fall, the number of jobs will increase. On the other side of the coin are measures to create incentives for workers to accept low-paying jobs, such as lowering unemployment insurance benefits and social assistance (Marquardt, 1998: 109–110). A part of this strategy are wage subsidies to employers toward hiring young workers. The ironies are multiplied in that as this trend is taking place, youth wages are deteriorating with a significant drop in the last two decades.

Aside from these general problems that apply to all youth, not enough has been done to assist either female or visible minority youth in their educational or employment experiences. For example, Aboriginal youth need a range of different support programs (Gabor, Thibedeau, and Manychief, 1996; Wood and Griffiths, 1996). Young women also need a range of programs, including employment equity or anti-harassment policies to help them along the way (Varpalotai, 1996). One of the major policy challenges is to help young people establish a healthy connection between wage work and family life in a manner that does not unduly penalize women (Looker, 1996: 160).

Youth and Unions

The working conditions in youth-dominated jobs are often poorer than those in adult workplaces and the rates of work-related injury are higher among young workers. They may be even higher than officially reported because many young people are not aware of their rights or are afraid to report any injuries (Waldie, 1999). Meanwhile, job growth has "concentrated in the largely non-union, private-service sector, where work is likely to be part time and precarious." The shift from full-time union jobs in manufacturing and resources has had a disastrous effect on incomes (Eaton, 1997).

In recent years young workers in the service industry have started to realize that their situation isn't getting any better. In 1994 a McDonald's outlet in Orangeville, Ontario attempted to become the first unionized McDonald's in the world out of 13,000 outlets. Headed by seventeen-year-old Sarah Inglis, the attempted unionization was overwhelmingly defeated by the employees (Klein, 1997). However, the desire for higher wages and better benefits has since then led to other attempts to unionize other franchises in the service sector that offer employees "McJobs." In 1996, Vancouver employees of Starbucks managed to organize and won better wages (Irvine, 1997), and in March 1995, seventy workers in three Ontario Tim Hortons voted to join the Retail Wholesale Union, Local 448, part of the United Steelworkers. The average wage for Tim Hortons employees ranged from $6.85 to $8.00 an hour before unionisation (*The Hamilton Spectator*, 1995).

As young people of both sexes have entered the ghettoized youth labour force, unions are changing in composition. Nearly half of union members in Canada are now women, compared with only one sixth thirty years ago. Women are unionizing at a more rapid rate than men, reflecting both their increased portions in the labour force, and the increasing attempts of unionization in the female-dominated, part-time labour force (*The Kitchener-Waterloo Record*, 1998).

The Informal Work Sector: Toronto's Squeegee Kids

A small but significant number of young people end up making their lives on the streets. The complex reasons for young people leaving homes and ending up on the streets will be discussed in the next chapter. Here, the subject of the informal squeegee work performed by these young people is taken up.

Squeegee youth are young, homeless people who earn their livelihood by offering to clean car windows in busy intersections in large urban centres, such as Edmonton, Calgary, Saskatoon, Montreal, Hamilton, and Toronto. Squeegee workers are the most marginalized of the youth population. They tend to be alienated not only from their families but also from the rest of society and the services geared to helping individuals who are homeless. This phenomenon is not just a product of the twenty-first century. As explained in Chapter 1, early stages of industrialization and urbanization led to the detachment of large numbers of youth. This process was then, as it is now, associated with fears of youth vagrancy and criminal activity, which will be further explored in Chapter 7. As earlier in the twentieth century, street youth in the twenty-first century are also blamed for their precarious situations. Society on the whole has condemned squeegee cleaning activity and culture. O'Grady et al. (1998: 315) argue that the public perception of Toronto's squeegee youth is that they are "tarnishing the image of the city, or more seriously, that these youths are responsible for elevating levels of violence in the urban core."

In response to that claim, many street youth advocates claim just the opposite. They argue that, due to the visibility of squeegee youth, they themselves have become targets of police harassment. During the summer of 1998, a "war" was declared on squeegee youth. The attack was led by the Toronto mayor Mel Lastman, who was quoted as saying, "We're getting rid of the thugs...The city is becoming safer and I like a safe city. And those who don't like it, it's too damn bad" (Spears, 1999).

Lastman created a program to target specific downtown areas with extra police whose purpose is to remove "squeegee kids, panhandlers, and street criminals" (Giese, 1999; Spears, 1999). The irony of his attacking homeless youth at the same time that the well-publicized interim report of the mayor's homelessness Action Task Force was released was overlooked by the media.

Following the initiative of the mayor, Ontario Premier Mike Harris joined the anti-squeegee bandwagon during the election race in the spring of 1999. In a bid to have "a safer Ontario" (Progressive Conservative Party of Ontario,1999: 27), the government of Mike Harris pledged to "stop aggressive panhandling by making threatening and harassing behaviour, such as blocking people on sidewalks, a provincial offence. We'll also give police the power to crack down on 'squeegee kids'" (Progressive Conservative Party of Ontario, 1999: 31). Local bylaws against squeegeeing are in place in Hamilton, Saskatoon, Edmonton, and Calgary. Ontario has the only government to pass a provincial law against this form of informal labour.

Bill 8, the *Safe Streets Act*, which amends the *Highway Traffic Act*, was passed by Ontario Legislature on December 9, 1999, and was implemented on January 31, 2000. Under the new legislation fines will range from $500 for the first offence to $1,000 and/or six months in jail for repeat offenders. It makes it illegal to engage in "aggressive panhandling" as well as stopping or approaching a "motor vehicle with the intent to offer, sell, or provide any product or service." Andrew Bolter (1999), a London lawyer and poverty advocate, argues that "Harris's answer to the problem of poverty is to try to ban its visible manifestation; out of sight, out of mind." A Toronto lawyer, Edward Sapiano, and thirty of his colleagues are ready to represent charged squeegee youth and challenge the Conservative government constitutionally all the way to the Supreme Court. Sapiano argues that "the challenge will turn on whether individuals are allowed to perform this type of job and whether the Constitution protects an individual's choice of employment" (*The Cambridge Reporter*, 2000). On June 14, 2000, the lawyers were in court for the first time launching their constitutional challenge. Defense lawyer Peter Rosenthal argued "the wording is so general it makes the simple act of asking a friend for money illegal" (*The Toronto Star*, 2000a). The trial date is pending as this book is going to print.

Many poverty advocates, members of the opposition, as well as squeegee youth are concerned that this law will force those affected by it into a life of crime. Liberal justice critic, Michael

Bryant argues that exactly that has occurred in Montreal, where "squeegee kids turned to prostitution, the drug trade and other crimes...It's going to throw them into the revolving door of criminal justice" (*The Cambridge Reporter*, 2000).

In fact, rather than being lazy and criminal, most street youth want to be gainfully employed. When involved in squeegeing, this was the next best thing, "the most viable means of generating income that they are currently able to engage in" (Gaetz et al., 1999: 19, 21). Further, O'Grady, Bright, and Cohen (1998: 319) found that rather than this activity leading young people into crime and ruin, squeegee cleaning street youth reported fewer criminal acts than non-squeegee street youth. These acts included: selling marijuana or other drugs (forty-four vs. sixty-six percent); breaking into a car or building (thirty-four vs. sixty-one percent); taking something worth $50 or less (twenty-four vs. seventy-five percent); damage to or destruction of property (thirty vs. sixty percent); use of physical force to get money (thirty-nine vs. fifty-nine percent); and getting into a fight "just for fun" (twenty-four vs. fifty-one percent).

Another significant pattern was that only twelve percent of squeegee cleaning youth, compared with thirty-three percent of non-squeegee cleaning youth, reported depression and/or suicidal thoughts. O'Grady et al (1998: 322) conclude that the non-traditional labour of squeegee cleaning provides not only financial and social support through closely linked groups, but it also reduces depression and criminal activity and provides an indication that these youth are on their way off of the streets.

Conclusions

Education is seen as an important pathway toward gainful employment. However, the kind of jobs and wages young people are getting are no match to the extensive and expensive education they receive. The dramatic economic shifts of the 1980s and 1990s have hit the youth population particularly hard, leaving some segments especially vulnerable. The patterns of youth employment mirror those of educational pathways: those from lower classes, women, and members of race and ethnic minorities are at a disadvantage.

While increasing numbers of young people combine their education with part-time wage work, the longer weeks they spend in these "constructive" pursuits might also be seen as a form of diminishing their "idleness" and chances of getting up to no good. The fates of those youth not fortunate enough to benefit from access to socially valued goods and services signify what happens if this control mechanism does not work. Youth who fall completely out of the official labour force become casualties of the street. Yet, by attempting to engage in an informal economy that provides them with some meager subsistence, they are subjected to draconian legislation, excessive policing, and social ostracism.

4 | Family and Intergenerational Relationships

I left home because my father was abusive, physically, sexually, mentally. I went through it for years, I blamed my mother because she wasn't there to protect me. I kind of blamed everybody even though my mother didn't know. I blamed her at the time, I was only a kid. That's why I started running. I was only twelve. (Maria, aged nineteen, a homeless Toronto youth, in Gaetz et al., 1999: 10)

Power in Families

When we think of families, we tend not to see them in terms of power and control. Yet, families are the most common site for children and youth to be subject to expressions and effects of power relations. As social institutions, families are shaped by power relations prevalent in society, based on social class, gender, race, and ethnicity. There are also direct manifestations of power and control in families, based on differentials in age-based resources and gender of family members.

This chapter will focus on young people's family lives, primarily their relationships with parents. Topics to be explored include parenting and socialization issues, including gender socialization and the manifestations of intergenerational power as well as the notion of "generation gap." There is a prevailing stereotype that adolescence is characterized by intensified and hormone-driven processes that necessarily lead to conflict with parents. Its corollary in immigrant families is the view of heightened intergenerational conflict in which the "old world" values of parents are pitted against those of their "new world" children. Another major area of concern is young people's patterns of leaving and returning to their parental homes.

Families are commonly viewed as places that protect and nurture children and youth. However, large segments of youth are subjected to abuse and neglect by family members. Sometimes seen as a natural part of "character building," abusive behaviours can escalate to create an unbearable family environment. A lot of young people put up with years of violence; some (such as Maria, quoted above) become "castaways," living on hostile streets. Yet others come into contact with youth protection agencies where, despite the best efforts and intentions of hardworking social workers, they may be subjected to further maltreatment and neglect due to poor funding and impossibly large caseloads.

Family Structure

Research into adolescents' relationships with their parents is increasingly complicated by the wide variety of family contexts. We are increasingly hard pressed to find a "typical" family setting. In the 1996 census, most families (fifty-one percent) were composed of a married or cohabiting couple with never-married children at home. One increasingly common form of family is the single-parent family. Currently twelve percent of all family types are of this variety, with most of them (83.1 percent) female-headed (Nelson and Robinson, 1999: 29). Additionally, there are an estimated 444,000 families with gay or lesbian parents (Nelson and Robinson, 1999: 129).

Divorce rates reached a peak in 1987, after two rounds of legislative reforms, and began to decline slightly after that. Currently, it is estimated that between thirty and forty percent of all marriages will end in divorce (Richardson, 1996: 228–239). There is consequently also a significant increase in the proportion of families where one or both partners have been previously married. In 1967, only 12.3 percent of all families were of this variety with an increase to 32.3 percent by 1991 (Baker, 1996: 30a).

The sole-parent situation is more prevalent in some ethno-racial minority groups than others. For example, although black families come in many varieties, in Canada they are 2.5–3 times more likely than families on average to be headed by a sole parent. The consequences of this are risk due to family instability, poverty, racism, and discrimination (Christensen and Weinfeld, 1993: 41; Calliste, 1996: 252–259). Single-parent families are more likely to live in poverty and be stigmatized. Blacks and other visible minorities are likely to be carrying a double burden in both regards due to a higher likelihood of lower-level and poorly paid employment and the additional stigma of racism.

Family Poverty

Most families living in poverty are intact families (Richardson, 1996: 238), demonstrating the deterioration of overall family incomes over the last few decades. The wage gap between the wealthy and middle-income or low-income families has grown from the 1980s to the 1990s. In 1991, the average poor household was over $1,000 further below the poverty line than it was in 1981 (Cameron, 2000), as measured by the Canadian government's official low income cutoffs, adjusted for the cost of living.

Most families who live in poverty have at least one family member employed outside the home. The myth of poverty being associated with not working for pay is exploded by statistics on the working poor. In 1993, fifty-six percent of poor couples with children were among the working poor, as were fifty-one percent of poor couples without children and half of poor, unattached women (Cameron, 2000). This means that the biggest factor behind poverty is insufficient wages to sustain families, particularly those with one breadwinner.

Thus, the significant fact of prevalent poverty means that

children and youth in these families are subject to poverty because their parents do not earn enough to support them. The latest statistics show that more than one in five Canadian children under the age of sixteen live in poverty. This is the second highest rate (after the United States) among industrialised countries (Cameron, 2000).

In contrast to other types of families in poverty, most of whom have at least one wage earner, the majority of the heads of household in single-parent families are not employed (Cameron, 2000). One of the often cited facts is that poverty is associated with lone-parent, female-headed families. Based on the above discussion, we have to note that poverty may prevail prior to divorce and the establishment of a sole-parent household. However, the second important item to note is that economic consequences of divorce are worse for women than men. Upon divorce, women's standard of living goes down and men's improves. It is estimated that about one in ten divorced fathers live under the poverty line, whereas two thirds of divorced women live in poverty (Richardson, 1996: 238). A government study found in 1997 that women experience an average loss of twenty-three percent in after-tax income in the first year after divorce while men register a gain of ten percent in their income (Nelson and Robinson, 1999: 412).

There are several reasons for this, including the lack of social support mechanisms (such as affordable daycare) to assist women in finding and keeping employment, and the generally lower-paying work areas for women rooted in the gender division of labour. "Lone-parent mothers are more likely to be younger, less well educated, have lower earnings and less income, and typically are responsible for younger-aged children than are lone-parent fathers" (Odekirk and Lochhead, 1992, in Nelson and Robinson, 1999: 407). One major reason for the poverty of mother-child families is "deadbeat dads," or fathers who don't pay child support regularly or at all. Research has found that most fathers do not pay the court-ordered child support, while a minority pay partial support. According to one estimate from the 1990s, the default rate is between fifty and seventy-five percent (Richardson, 1996: 232–242; see also Nelson and Robinson, 1999: 413).

This fact is particularly important for youth in two ways. First, poverty in sole-parent households is age-specific in that ninety percent of those families where the female head is under twenty-five years of age live in poverty, while the same can be said of fifty-eight percent of families with female heads aged 25–33. This is all the more difficult for black sole-parent families. The 1991 Census shows that eighty-five percent of the young black female lone parents aged 15–24 in Canada and ninety-one percent in Nova Scotia earned less than $20,000 (Calliste, 1996: 257). Second, as we have seen in previous chapters, it is not the sole-parent environment per se but the poverty of these families that leads to negative child development outcomes and to difficult circumstances for the children and youth.

Remarriage

One of the most significant trends is an increase over time in the numbers of remarriage (also called reconstituted) families. By the mid-1990s, approximately eighty-one percent of divorced people remarried. One important feature of remarriage families is that they are more likely to end in a divorce than first marriages (Richardson, 1996: 243).

About one third of divorces in Canada involve children under sixteen years of age. A major area of concern for adolescents and youth is how they cope with parental divorce and remarriage. Divorce and remarriage mean several adjustments for young people. Generally, it has been noted that most young people, regardless of age, do eventually adjust to shifts in their family situation.

Social scientists have searched for negative effects of divorce on children. Research shows that the gender and the age of children are important. Boys tend to be more negatively affected by divorce than girls. This may have to do with the fact that in the vast majority of the cases, custody goes to the mother (Richardson, 1996: 233; Nelson and Robinson, 1999: 410) so a boy may miss the same-sex parent, whereas girls have their mothers present. Age of the child is also important; teenagers tend to have more problems adapting to parental divorce and remarriage than younger children. Teenagers have lived for a longer time with their two biological parents and tend to make negative comparisons between their biological and step-parents, who are seen as intruders. This has been shown to result in diminished marital satisfaction and increased instability in the remarriage (Baker, 1996: 31–32; Richardson, 1996: 244–245). There are also additional problems for young people as they adjust to the presence of step-siblings and half-siblings (Richardson, 1996: 245).

On the other hand, some research shows positive and stabilizing effects for both children and their parents. Step-families are found to be a better alternative than remaining in an intact but conflict-ridden family or one-parent and poverty-stricken household (Baker, 1996: 31–32). In terms of other outcomes for youth, arising from non-traditional families, it has been found that parents in these types of situations are "less likely to gender stereotype their children than parents living in traditional families" (Nelson and Robinson, 1999: 129).

Parenting and Socialization

Socialization is the process through which we develop a sense of who we are and learn to function in our social group or society (Nelson and Robinson, 1999: 123). This learning process is lifelong and happens in the context of human interaction. It is commonplace to distinguish between *primary* and *secondary* socialization. Primary socialization takes place in the context of significant others, usually family members. Secondary socialization takes place in the wider society, in the context of socializing institutions like schools, workplaces, the media, and peers (Nelson and Robinson, 1999: 122–127). We have addressed in previous chapters how school and workplaces socialize youth into normative behaviour, and we will take up the issue of peers in the chapters to follow. In this chapter, we will focus on primary socialization.

The most prevalent theories in this area are the learning theory and the social learning theory. The former sees socialization as a process directed by socializing agents and individuals, based on rewards for normatively acceptable behaviours and punishment for unacceptable behaviours. Through this process, a child learns and adopts normative limits. The social learning theory arose in response to criticism of learning theory as too mechanical a representation of the complex learning process. This theory put more emphasis on the way young people process information and examined the many different ways in which this takes place, including imitation (Howe and Bukowski, 1996: 183–184).

In practice, social learning theory is characterised by a near obsessive attention to parenting techniques. There is a wide range of socialization literature that is essentially parenting literature in that it concentrates on examining the kinds of "effective" parenting strategies that produce good outcomes in terms of young people's socio-emotional competence and their capability of behaving in a mature and responsible manner (Noller and Fitzpatrick, 1993: 145). This includes research into parents' roles in juvenile delinquency, school and career success, sexual behaviour, and general attitudes and values. One widely cited finding is that parents have an influence on their adolescents' decisions about educational, financial, and vocational choices, whereas peers are more influential about decisions about adolescents' social activities (Noller and Fitzpatrick, 1993: 145). These are seen to be mediated by different types of parenting styles, which is a relatively popular topic in American research but not really addressed in Canadian studies. Parenting styles are usually classified into authoritative, authoritarian, permissive (or indulgent), and indifferent (or neglecting) (Anderson and Sabatelli, 1999: 212–214; Paulson and Sputa, 1996; Howe and Bukowski, 1996: 188).

Parenting styles are usually seen as based on two main dimensions: control and warmth. From the different combinations of these, four categories of parenting are created: authoritative (high control/high warmth); authoritarian (high control/low warmth); indulgent/permissive (low control/high warmth); and indifferent/neglecting (low control/low warmth) (Paulson and Sputa, 1996; Howe and Bukowski, 1996: 188). Authoritative parenting is linked to the most positive outcomes, measured through high levels of adolescent adjustment, psycho-social competence and maturity, high self-esteem, and academic success. Further, in taking apart the dimensions of control and warmth, specific aspects of these dimensions are found to correlate positively with adolescent outcomes. In the control category, it is involvement, not strict controls on behaviour, that results in good outcomes. Involvement refers particularly to parental values, parental expectations aimed at school success, parental interest in the child's grades, helping with homework, and involvement in school functions. The authoritative parenting pattern can be linked to the notion of "sponsored independence," which is specific to adolescence, and involves a gradual relinquishing of parental control over the child, in a supportive and warm atmosphere which allows the adolescent to gain more control over his/her decisions and actions (Nett, 1993: 196).

However, there is far less research into the perceptions of children or adolescents themselves regarding these parental styles. In fact, an extensive search found no Canadian studies and only one American study that asked young peoples' views on their parents' parenting styles (Paulson and Sputa, 1996). This study of mostly white and middle-class families in the American Midwest interviewed children and their parents while the children were in grade nine and later in grade twelve. Their study was aimed at distinguishing between the parenting styles of mothers and fathers, including adolescents' perceptions about parenting styles. Some results are consistent with other research. First, the results showed that, regardless of the age group, both adolescents and parents perceived mothers to be more demanding as well as more responsive than fathers. Further, both mothers and fathers perceived themselves to be more demanding and more responsive than adolescents perceived them to be. Both adolescents and parents perceived mothers to be more involved in homework/schoolwork and school functions than fathers were. However, both parents were seen to be equal in their values toward achievement. The study found that parents reported themselves to be more involved with their adolescents than the adolescents reported. This is consistent with the concept of "generational stake" (Koller, 1974: 224; Nett, 1993:

199–201), which proposes that parents have a higher investment in their children than vice versa. Because of this, for example, parents tend to report being closer to their children than children report being to their parents.

Some age-group specific results arose, but they have to be treated with caution due to the smaller size of the follow-up group. Nevertheless, the study found that both adolescents and parents reported that mothers and fathers were less responsive in grade twelve than in grade nine. Parents also reported that they were less demanding when their children were in grade twelve. This reflects the increasing level of autonomy and independence of adolescents and goes toward the point made earlier about "sponsored independence." Consistent with this, both the older adolescents and their parents reported lower levels of parental involvement in school work and in maternal involvement in school functions, but no changes in parental values toward achievement. The results are consistent with the generally perceived decrease in parents' involvement in adolescents' school work and activities as they get older. An important omission from this study is that the results were not reported based on the gender of the adolescents, even though parental gender was a variable.

Parenting styles and socialization practices seem to vary by social class. It has been found that working-class parents are more likely to use "power-assertive" techniques, including physical punishment, and to demand more conformity from their offspring. In comparison, middle-class parents use less overtly punitive methods. Instead, they use reasoning and withdrawal of privileges, love, and affection to guide their children toward self-control, while encouraging their curiosity and self-expression (Nelson and Robinson, 1999: 130–131; also see Nett, 1993: 196).

Ironically, the social learning theory proves to be at least as mechanical if not more so than the learning theory. Social learning theory can be criticized for its lack of attention to the relationship involved in socializing. There is an emphasis on one-directional socializing in which the active participation of the socializers, or parents, is paramount, while the young people remain targets or objects of socialization, rather than active participants in the process (Ambert, 1992). In fact, socialization involves an active bi-directional relationship. In the interactive process, children are not likely to just go along for the ride but push the limits and mediate them according to their own wishes. Becoming knowledgeable about limits, norms, and expectations does not necessarily translate into following them. The active element in socialization is all the more evident as adolescents become young adults, in prevalent myths about how difficult it is for adolescents and their parents to find common ground, and the general view of adolescents as challenging to their parents. Parents of adolescents often have difficulty dealing with youngsters who are becoming aware of their own individuality and independence and are looking to put their own mark on their environment.

Gender Socialization

Feminist scholars have addressed ways in which gender differences are socially created, affirmed, and changed, instead of emerging naturally. The term "doing gender" has been used to capture the notion that getting a sense of ourselves as gendered beings is an everyday process, a "recurring accomplishment" based on minute details of daily life (Mackie, 1995: 49).

Gender socialization is the process by which individuals develop a gender identity and acquire the normative behaviours associated with masculine and feminine in society (Nelson and Robinson, 1999: 128). From our earliest years onward we learn to understand the place and meaning of our gender in society, and we learn shared ideas and meanings of femininity and masculinity that are culturally specific. These social behaviours, values, and attitudes are passed onto us in various ways throughout our lives. Traditionally, there are clusters of acting, thinking, and feeling associated with female and male socialization. The dominant themes of female socialization are "sociability, popularity, and attractiveness" (Udry, 1971, in Nelson and Robinson, 1999: 128) and "nurturance, sympathy and warmth," and submissiveness (Mackie, 1995: 49). Male socialization centres on "independence, emotional control, and conquest" (Udry, 1971, in Nelson and Robinson, 1999: 128), and aggression (Mackie, 1995: 48).

It has been observed that independence is encouraged more among adolescent boys than girls. Girls are expected to be more passive, and there are more controls on their behaviour. In this way, "sponsored independence" is more of a pattern associated with the socialization of males than females (Nett, 1993: 196).

Generally, there are gender-linked socialization practices in all social classes. However, social class differences in the socialization of boys and girls are exhibited in the degree to which gender-based differences are emphasized. Those in the upper socio-economic classes are most likely to promote relatively egalitarian gender relations. Those in the lower socio-economic groups are more traditional and less egalitarian in their gender expectations (Nelson and Robinson, 1999: 131).

The gender of the parent is also important. Despite hype about "new" and "more involved" fathers, mothers continue to provide most child care. Most men still have limited involvement with their children. The consequence is that by teenage years, young people are more likely to want to communicate with their peers, mothers or other relatives, than with their fathers (Bibby and Posterski, 1992, in Nelson and Robinson, 1999: 417–420). Other studies from the 1980s (discussed in Noller and Fitzpatrick, 1993: 209–210) also show gender differences in communication patterns between parents and adolescents. Daughters communicate more with their parents than sons do, with mothers seen as more communicative than fathers. This is supported by a recent Health Canada study (Fine, 1999) of 2,500 teenagers, which found that fathers have a big communication gap with both male and female children, but particularly with their daughters. In all age groups, representing students in grade six, eight, and ten, both male and female children reported that they found their mothers much more approachable than their fathers. The trend got worse over time, with significantly fewer children in grade ten than in grade six reporting that they could talk to their father about things that really bother them.

Racial Socialization

It is recognized (and discussed in Chapter 2 in relation to education) that living in a racist, sexist, and capitalist society is a particular challenge for members of minority populations. Calliste (1996: 262–264) points to the problems of raising black children to be physically and emotionally healthy in an anti-black racist society. Various strategies are used to accomplish this: teaching black heritage and history, including personal stories of resistance; emphasizing the positive aspects of being black; and stressing education.

There is a process of racialization that children and youth are subjected to as they mature. This process involves an internalization of the messages that one is exposed to in the social environment, including schools, workplaces, peer groups, and all other social institutions. This will be discussed in more detail in the chapter on youth culture and identity.

Impact of Children on Parents

It is still quite rare to see studies that examine the way in which older children, namely adolescents or young adults influence their parents or the manner in which intergenerational relationships evolve (Ambert, 1992: 16–19). This notion is embedded in the criticism of traditional socialization theories and carries the name "bidirectional socialization" (Nett, 1993: 203).

Where the impact of children or adolescents on parents is acknowledged, they are most commonly seen as a drain or a problem for parents. Examples of the wide range of these are: limitations to parental residence and community involvement due to the educational and recreational needs of children; diminished social, intimate, and sexual lives of parents; increased domestic work; disruptions to parental and particularly maternal wage work patterns; and the general financial drain from children and particularly adolescents (Ambert, 1992: 33–43). Not to mention the worry that particularly adolescent children cause their parents with sex, drugs, and their choice of peers and leisure activities (Noller and Fitzpatrick, 1993: 208–209; Ambert, 1996: 102–103). It is rare to see studies that entertain an idea of positive aspects in the presence of children and adolescents in their parents" lives. One such finding is that children provide companionship and support to their parents (Boulding, 1980, and deMause, 1974, as reported in Ambert, 1992: 41–42). A select few studies found that divorced custodial parents are grateful for the structure and stability that having children provided at the time of divorce (Ambert, 1992: 165). Nett (1996: 203) also reports a study from the mid-1980s that showed that university-attending youth influence their parents in a variety of ways, ranging from sports to politics, to personal care habits. The parents reported having become more tolerant and acknowledged that they had gained from the knowledge passed onto their children from their university courses. The influence was more evident for fathers than mothers. Nett (1996: 203) suggests that the closing of the gap might be more evident for fathers who had a longer distance to make up with their children. Mothers may already have been primed to being accepting and learning from their children through years as primary caregivers, while fathers may be coming onto this more recently.

Where parental attitudes are explored, it is usually in terms of the presence of children, not in terms of the interaction between parents or children, or with an acknowledgment of the active role of children. For example, a standard sociology of the family textbook approach is to address how parents adjust their parenting techniques to the child's age, temperament, or gender (see Baker, 1996b: 193–194). A typical example of the latter is from research by Ganong and Coleman (1987) who suggest that the presence of children of different sexes may lead parents to think in more sex-typed ways. The authors found that parents of sons were more sex-typed than parents of daughters. This is explained by the higher value societies put on sons than daughters, which would lead to parents investing more into raising their sons into sex-appropriate roles (reported in Ambert, 1992: 46–47). The possibility is not raised that interactions between adolescents and parents would influence this in any manner. It is hardly surprising that young people themselves are oblivious to the impact they have on their parents; even when asked about relationships with their parents, they are not likely to spontaneously report their impact on their parents, but focus on their parents" impact on them (Ambert, 1992: 133,147). It is even more rare to see studies in which the parents are being socialized into parenthood by their children or where young people are shaping their family environment. There is a huge literature on parental transmission of values to their children but far less on the impact of children on their parents" values and attitudes (Ambert, 1992: 42–46).

Intergenerational Power

The reasons for general neglect of the agency of young people are doubtless many, but an important parallel can be detected with the omission of other less powerful yet numerically large groups as subjects of study.

As stated earlier, young people are at the bottom of the age hierarchy. Adults, particularly those in their middle years, hold economic, political, and social power, and they also control access to information, knowledge, and research. Adults in their full wage-earning years have access to most of the resources and thus have power and control over their children's behaviour, goals, and values. At issue are the power and control of parents over their children (Nett, 1993: 204).

Developmental Stake and Generation Gap

As noted earlier, parents have a greater developmental stake in their children's lives than vice versa. This notion comes from aging and life course research of Vern L. Bengtson and associates (in Koller, 1974: 224; also see Nett, 1993: 199–201). It is suggested that parents have a greater investment in their children because they represent continuity. On the other hand, children need to distance themselves from their parents as they develop a separate identity. This distance is exhibited by, among other things, the more negative attitudes by adolescents than their parents about the communication in the family. Adolescents tend to report less openness and more problems than their parents (Noller and Fitzpatrick, 1993: 267).

Interestingly, it has been reported that parents tend to see more similarity in the values and ideas of themselves and their adolescent children, whereas adolescents tend to point to differences. This is a normal part of the developmental process and relates to the notion of "generational stake," in that older people have more of an investment in the younger generation than vice versa. Parents want to minimize the differences between themselves and their adolescents because they are the ones experiencing the loss of the youngsters as they gradually move away from them. Meanwhile, adolescents are in the process of leaving their family of procreation and moving toward other relationships. In this process, they are more likely to emphasize differences to make the separation more palatable. As pointed out by Baker and Dryden (1993: 209), it is only later that young people once again are able to realize that perhaps they and their parents have more in common than they previously believed.

This imbalance between the generations is particularly exhibited in the line of thinking that flows from it. It is assumed that if parents engage in controlling behaviours, this will naturally cause conflict as young people strive toward independence and start to rebel. The expectation of a generation gap and resultant intergenerational conflict is reinforced by psychoanalytic and developmental stage theorists, who see adolescence as a period of identity confusion that needs to be resolved by the adolescent becoming autonomous (Koller, 1974, esp. 208–209; Seltzer, 1989: 227; Beaumont, 1996). This phenomenon is rooted in the 1960s and 1970s with the associated student and youth rebellions (see Duncan, 2000). However, the concept has been less clearly demonstrated empirically in the post-1970s era (Nett, 1993: 175).

Generally, we do expect some type of intergenerational conflict to emerge between parents and adolescents. The two or three decades separating young people from their parents' age group are likely to lead to a generation gap. There is so much social change taking place that it would be quite abnormal if there weren't any areas of disagreement about values and expectations between parents and adolescent children. Also, those parents who were adolescents in a different era often go through a developmental process themselves and have a very selective memory about the kinds of things they did when they were adolescents. For example, it was noted in a survey of young women in Canada (Holmes and Silverman, 1992: 31–32) that young people's satisfaction with their family life decreases with age. Even though most adolescents, male and female, are satisfied with their family relationships, there is a decrease between ages thirteen and sixteen, from eighty-seven percent to eighty percent for girls, and from ninety-two percent to eighty-five percent for boys.

It seems that this sequence of parental control leading to rebellion is generally culturally accepted in North America. For example, in one rare study, Canadian sociologist Anne-Marie Ambert (1992) explored the perceptions of 109 university students of their effect on their parents as teenagers. Notably, all but seven reported having had a negative or more negative effect on their parents as teenagers than in any other age group. They linked this factor to having been more "rebellious/ difficult," or to parental styles which they experienced as challenging (Ambert, 1992: 131–149). Interestingly, Ambert (1992: 133–137, 148) also found that the students went on to explain that as their parents adjusted to their new behaviours and needs, life became more harmonious, indicating a socializing effect by the children of their parents. The general trend was that, excepting the rare few who engaged in truly delinquent acts, "not a single student ever questioned their *own* mentality or the need to change it." The sense was that parents need to adjust and peer culture supported this view (Ambert, 1992: 133–137; 148).

In a recent study (Beaumont, 1996) of twenty-eight girls in grades eleven to twelve and the same number in grades five to six in southwestern Ontario, it was found that girls perceive their conversations with their friends to be more positive than those with their mothers. It is suggested, based on research of others, that as adolescents begin to engage in intimate communications with their friends, they learn that all relationships can be based on a more reciprocal model. This influences them to shift the basis of their interactions with their parents from a unilateral authority model toward a more adult model of interaction.

Some researchers now question the applicability of the control/rebellion model, or the generation gap, in present times (Nett, 1993: 201). Vivian Center Seltzer (1989: 228–229) suggests that this may be both a self-fulfilling prophecy and a matter of interpreting regularly occurring parent-child conflicts in a new light once the child gets into adolescence. In the words of Marvin R. Koller (1974: 224), it seems that "generational dissension is far easier to contemplate than consensus."

Adolescent-Parent Relations in Immigrant Families

When discussing socialization and parenting in terms of ethno-racial variation, there is an ongoing debate over the significance of race and ethnicity over social class. Some argue that social class differences override race and ethnic influences, whereas others argue the opposite (Nelson and Robinson, 1999: 132).

Where parenting and socialization of adolescents in immigrant communities is concerned, there is a tendency to focus on intergenerational conflict. Much is made of the generation gap in terms of expectations of "old world" parents and their "new world" children, including issues related to peer relations and social behaviour (Wong, 1999; Wade and Brannigan, 1998), dating and spouse selection patterns (Chimbos, 1980: 34–35; Dhruvarajan, 1996; Arruda, 1993; Isajiw, 1999: 103); educational and career choices (Li, 1988: 74–83; Fuligni, 1997; Dhruvarajan, 1996; Arruda, 1993: 16–18; Christensen and Weinfeld, 1993: 32–35), and retention of culture/ethnicity (James, 1999: 95; Pizanias, 1996: 350; Ambert, 1992: 236, 241–245).

Research into specific immigrant communities suggests that gender differences may be heightened in some immigrant communities with adolescent girls having much less freedom of movement and decision-making power than their brothers. For example, Arruda's (1993) research on the Vancouver Portuguese community confirms the traditional pattern of expectations of girls and boys in the 1970s. While boys were given some freedoms in adolescence, girls were subjected to strict parental controls. They were "*kept* at home" (Arruda, 1993: 11 - emphasis in the original). They were not allowed to date or go out after school. Both girls and boys were subjected to parental, and particularly paternal, authority and discipline, including corporal punishment.

In these studies, there is a real need to guard against generalizations based on studies of selected immigrant communities. There are significant differences not only between different immigrant groups but also within immigrant communities. These generalizations are known to lead to an overemphasis of the generation gap in immigrant families. They stereotype all immigrant parents as conservative throwbacks to old world values and behaviours. In contrast, adolescent immigrants are seen in a particularly problematic light, as potentially more rebellious and troubled and prone to delinquency (as exemplified in the media stereotyping of "oriental youth gangs") as they supposedly work out their confusions between their ethnic heritage and North American values.

Anne-Marie Ambert's (1992: 131–149) previously mentioned study of university students' perceptions of their impact on their parents is one of the rare studies on this topic in Canada. In this study, children of immigrants reported a wider variety of perceptions of their impact on their parents than children of non-immigrants. However, differences arise in relation to the specific immigrant groups. Contrary to the general immigrant family stereotype, children of immigrants from the Caribbean, British Isles, or Israel did not generally link any impact they had on their parents, to their parents' immigrant status (Ambert, 1992: 133, 134, 139–140). In comparison, responses by children of Italian, Greek, and Portuguese immigrants were in line with the Old World/New World intergenerational gap, which was particularly acute for girls whose parents were Southern European. Their parents were seen to be more restrictive and protective and even coercive than they would be toward sons. Girls described a significant impact they had on their parents, including their rebellion against parental control.

These youth also mentioned their contributions to their parents because of their better ability to speak English. Other research also suggests that because immigrant children often learn the new language quicker than their parents, there is a tendency of parents to rely on their children, reversing the normative patterns of dependency. It is suggested by some that this may initially be good for parent-child cooperation but that it may result in producing more gaps. For example, children may feel embarrassed or ashamed of their parents or develop feelings of inferiority because of them (Isajiw, 1999: 103). Arruda's (1993) research among Portuguese immigrant families confirms that parents rely on their children in dealing with social institutions, schools, hospitals, etc. in the host society. Adolescents may also contribute in tangible ways to family finances. All of these elements may both enhance and create difficulties in families, depending on the ethnic group in question and other background variables, including social class or urban/rural differences.

Intergenerational Cultural Retention

In previous chapters, I addressed the integration of ethnic and racial minorities into mainstream institutions. An interesting question related to the sociology of family is how ethnicity is retained intergenerationally. How much of ethnic identity changes over time and under what circumstances? What tensions may arise within families, over different conceptions of acceptable behaviour, due to intergenerational change in ethnic identification? The most common approach to these questions is the "acculturation thesis," which sees a natural progression in which each successive generation adopts more of the "behaviours, rules, values, and norms of the host society" (Boyd, 2000: 138).

A study by Isajiw and associates (1990, in Isajiw, 1999: 189–191) of 2,338 Torontonians belonging in nine ethnic groups, including a more detailed examination of four groups (German, Italian, Jewish, and Ukrainian) suggests that identity retention varies across ethnic groups. The researchers used an index of internal and external aspects of ethnicity. Internal aspects refer to images, ideas, attitudes, and feelings about one's ethnic group, whereas external aspects refer to observable behaviour, both cultural and social. He found that internal ethnic identity measures dropped in each of the generations following the first generation who immigrated to Canada. The only exception were the Jews, where there was little loss. The greatest loss was among Germans, then Italians and Ukrainians. The general pattern was one in which external ethnic traditions (food, cultural articles) were retained across generations more than the internal aspects. The use of the parental language declined, but people in the following generations retained some knowledge of it, although they did not use it.

In the most recent studies and theorizing, assimilation and acculturation are seen to be linked in that a continued emphasis on ethnic identity often means that a particular group is not integrated into mainstream institutions. This also tends to go along with the process of "racialization" in which a (most often visible) minority group becomes an underclass with associated low status. Most likely candidates for this process are Arabs, Blacks/Caribbeans, Latin/Central/South Americans, Spanish, Vietnamese, or West Asians (Boyd, 2000: 140–141).

Leaving Home

Leaving home is a normative expectation when people reach adulthood. However, young people leave home for a variety of reasons and at different ages, some voluntarily and others compelled by difficult situations, including family violence. Some become castaway youth on the streets, while others return temporarily and leave once again more permanently.

The Empty Nest

The event of a young adult leaving the parental home and establishing independent living quarters is commonly seen to mark an important transition, a passage to adulthood. There is ample evidence to show that there is a sense of normative timing for this to take place (Mitchell, 1998: 22–24), usually associated with significant life course events, such as higher education, employment, or marriage (Zhao et al., 1995: 32).

There has been a steady decline in the median age of home-leavers in Canada for cohorts born in 1910 to 1960, and an increase for cohorts born after the 1960s. There is general agreement that the prolongation of time spent living at home has to do with the worsening of the economy and various recessions (Zhao et al., 1995: 32, 47).

The age at which children gain residential independence from their families was estimated to be sixteen in 1911, seventeen in 1921, and nineteen in 1931; it went into a decline, with another reversal taking place since 1981. It was the 1960s and 1970s affluence that permitted single young people to set themselves up in independent households. As education has lengthened, the age of independence has risen (Nett, 1993: 216–217).

Women typically leave earlier than men, but for both, marriage has declined as a reason for leaving home. Instead, the reasons for leaving home have more to do with a desire for independence and getting post-secondary education. For men, employment was always more important as a reason for leaving home, but the general importance of getting employment has declined (Ravanera et al., 1992, 1993, in Zhao et al., 1995: 32). Gender differences in home-leaving patterns were confirmed by Zhao et al. (1995: 47), who also cite four reasons (from Ravanera et al., 1992) to explain it: earlier physiological and psychological maturation of girls than boys; earlier age of marriage for women than men; a longer period of preparation for males as breadwinners; and more household tasks for girls than boys that may act as an incentive to leave.

Zhao et al. (1995) examined the results of the 1990 General Social Survey on home-leaving in Canada. They found that there were important family and parental characteristics that explained the timing of leaving home. First, stepchildren and adopted children leave home earlier than other children. Second, except for widowed families, children in all different types of non-intact families (divorced, step, single-parent) leave earlier than children of intact families. Third, children in immigrant families, especially non-European, leave home later, perhaps due to a greater emphasis on familial values that hold them together for a longer period of time. Fourth, lone children tend to leave home later than children with siblings, except if the lone child is a girl who is more likely to be a target of parental protectionism. Further, female children whose parents have post-secondary education are more likely to leave later than females whose parents are less educated. This may be explained by more parental emphasis on their daughter getting an education and a career than on getting married and leaving home.

The Crowded Nest

Since the 1990s, the "empty nest" stage has proven to be less permanent, as more youth return to live with their parents, as "boomerang kids," or "velcro kids" (Kingsmill and Schlesinger, 1998: 13–34) resulting in a "crowded" or "cluttered nest" (see Table 4.1). In fact, Canadian statistics show a significant increase in this phenomenon as of 1991, compared with previous decades. As of 1991 in the age group 20–24, 70.5 percent of unmarried men and 63.4 percent of unmarried women were living with their parents. These percentages reflect both extended residence by children who have not left and those who returned after having left (Mitchell, 1998: 22–24).

As of 1996, twenty-three percent of young women aged 20–34 were living at home, an increase from sixteen percent in 1981. Among young men, the increase was from twenty-six to thirty-three percent in the same time period. Thus, the notable trends are the increasing age of children living at home, the majority being men (Boyd and Norris, 2000).

As in the case of delayed departure from home, the return to the parental home is reflective of the economic conditions. Although intergenerational co-residence patterns and reasons

Table 4.1. The proportion of young adults living at home has been rising over the past 15 years

Percent living with parents

		Unmarried				Married*		
	Total	20-24	25-29	30-34	Total	20-24	25-29	30-34
Women								
1981	44	60	27	18	1	3	1	1
1986	46	64	32	18	2	3	2	1
1991	44	63	33	19	2	5	2	1
1996	47	67	36	19	3	7	4	2
Men								
1981	55	69	40	28	2	3	2	1
1986	57	72	45	30	2	4	2	1
1991	53	71	44	29	3	6	3	1
1996	56	74	48	32	4	9	5	3

* Married includes legal marriages and common-law relationships.
Source: Statistics Canada, Censuses of Population (from Boyd and Norris 'The Crowded Nest: Young Adults at Home' in Canadian Social Trends 3, 2000, p.158)

behind them have shifted over the last century, Côté and Allahar (1998: 137) argue that "not until now...has it been a result of the inability of the young to support themselves." This argument is reinforced by the previous chapter presenting the poor financial situation of young people. Similarly, Boyd and Norris (2000: 159–160) link extended co-residence with economic factors and the lengthening of education of young people, both of which serve to keep them dependent for a longer time.

There is a tendency to depict adult child/parent co-residence in a negative light, as typical of children who have "failed" at marriage or in their careers and are returning to further burden their parents (Kingsmill and Schlesinger, 1998: 13–34; Allahar and Côté, 1998: 136–138). It is often a very difficult situation for both the parents and the returning children, as appears in the following segment entitled "How do your children feel about returning home?":

> ...Returning home is not easy. Many boomerang children feel they have failed, and envy their friends who have made it. It was exciting and stimulating living away from home, and it is often discouraging to move back. They have become used to living on their own and to doing things their own way; now, suddenly, they have to swallow their independence. They may be wondering if they will ever be able to leave home and make a life for themselves. They may be depressed and unsure of themselves.
>
> Moving home can be a real blow to any adult's pride, self-esteem and self-confidence, and the worries of what the future holds can seem overwhelming. Most do not return home by choice, no matter what the precipitating event, and the return is usually temporary. Unfortunately, many people see young adults who return home as moochers and cop-outs scurrying home at the first sign of trouble. This is unfair: in any age group there are some deadbeats, but most boomerang children are home to regroup before leaving again. (Kingsmill and Schlesinger, 1998: 20)

Meanwhile, other studies report positive effects from generational co-residence, including sharing of household tasks and positive family interactions (Mitchell, 1998: 22–24; also see Kingsmill and Schlesinger, 1998: 13–34). For example, Mitchell's (1998) study of 420 families in the Greater Vancouver area found that co-residence can be both a positive and a negative experience for the parents. Most parents reported that the co-residence was working very well, and fewer than ten percent reported that it was working out either somewhat well or poorly. This goes contrary to the current negative views of co-residence as characterized by "intergenerational tension, conflict, and dissatisfaction" (Mitchell, 1998: 40). The most positive aspects were related to companionship and the child's helping at home. Further, if the child had a full-time job or if s/he had initially left to go to school, parental attitudes were more positive. Fathers were somewhat less positive than mothers, possibly because they are not likely to have as close a relationship with their children as mothers do. Single parents also reacted more negatively toward co-residence with their children, because of possible privacy issues. Further, the return of sons was more welcome than daughters, possibly because of different expectations regarding marriage and participation in household tasks. Those who returned twice were welcomed more readily, probably because issues related to co-residence had been worked out previously.

Research has not looked at the effect of ethnicity on home-leaving patterns. Some immigrant and ethnic groups have an expectation of continued closeness between parents and children even as children approach adulthood. Indeed, some aging parents expect their older children to look after them. These familial values no doubt encourage young people to either prolong their co-residence with parents or to freely return to their parental home if the need arises.

Family Violence and Castaway Kids

Not all families are safe havens for a secure transition from childhood into adulthood. Some young people's lives are marked by abuse and violence by other family members. We have quite a lot of information about the different types of child abuse, including physical, emotional, and sexual abuse, and neglect (see Raychaba, 1993). Data have been collected primarily for younger age groups. For example, the data collected by the Canadian Centre for Justice Statistics stop at seventeen years of age. However, some trends can be summarized from a Statistics Canada (2000b: 31–38) report of assaults told to police in 1999 (see Table 4.2). The main findings show that "children and youth under eighteen years of age made up twenty-three percent of the Canadian population and were the victims of twenty-four percent of assaults reported to the police." They are dramatically overrepresented among sexual assault victims (sixty percent). Physical assaults, however, are more common in general, and children and youth form one fifth of victims of physical assault. Young victims are more likely to be assaulted by acquaintances (fifty-two percent) than family members (twenty-four percent) or strangers (nineteen percent). Family members were the perpetrators in nearly one-third of sexual assaults and over one-fifth of physical assaults. A similar proportion of girls (thirty-one percent) and boys (twenty-nine percent) were sexually assaulted by family members. However, girls were much more likely (thirty-six percent) than boys (sixteen percent) to be physically assaulted by family members, whereas they were less likely (fourteen percent) than boys (twenty-four percent) to be assaulted by strangers. This is consistent with the pattern of physical assaults among adults.

The report also states that parents are the most likely family members to engage in violent behaviour toward the young, whether physical (sixty percent) or sexual (forty-two percent) assault. Significantly, fathers are more likely to be abusive regardless of the type. The study found that fathers were the perpetrators in ninety-eight percent of sexual assault cases and seventy-one percent of physical assault incidents. Of all family assault, girls are more likely than boys to be victimized; they form eighty percent of sexual assault and fifty-three percent of physical assault victims. There are differences based on age. Girls are more likely to be victimized sexually between ages twelve and fourteen, while the peak sexual assault years for boys are three to six. Generally, up to age thirteen, boys outnumber girls as victims of physical assault, at which point girls start to outnumber boys. Physical violation of both boys and girls increases with age, peaking at seventeen for girls and fourteen for boys. The higher rate among older girls is also reflective of spousal assaults, which formed forty-one percent of assaults by family members against girls aged seventeen. This issue of relationship violence will be taken up in more detail in Chapter 5. These trends show the particular victimization of young people and the continuing and escalating violation of adolescent girls by family members. Whereas the sexual abuse of boys tends to end as they reach

Table 4.2. Child and youth victims of assault reported to police by accused-victim relationship, 1999[1,2]

Relationship of accused to victim	Total Assault		Victim Sex				
		Sexual Assault[3]			Physical Assault		
	No.	Total	Female	Male	Total	Female	Male
Total	25,231	6,461	5,141	1,320	18,770	7,092	11,678
	%	%	%	%	%	%	%
	100	100	100	100	100	100	100
Family	24	30	31	29	22	30	16
Acquaintance[4]	52	49	48	54	53	51	54
Stranger	19	15	16	12	20	14	24
Unknown	5	5	5	5	5	5	6

Percentages may not total 100% due to rounding.
[1] Data are not nationally representative. Data are based on a sample of 164 police departments, representing 46% of the national volume of crime in 1999.
[2] Includes victims under the age of 18 years.
[3] Sexual assault includes the "other sexual crimes" category which includes sexual interference, sexual touching sexual exploitation and incest, etc.
[4] Acquaintance includes any relationship in which the accused and the victim are familiar with each other, but not related, or in a legal guardianship relationship.
Source: Statistics Canada, Canadian Centre for Justice Statistics, Incident-based Uniform Crime Reporting (UCR2) Survey (from Family Violence in Canada: A Statistical Profile 2000, Catalogue no. 85-224, p.32)

adolescence, the sexual abuse of girls tends to continue. This finding is consistent with other patterns of female victimization and abuse in families (Duffy and Momirov, 1997: 67–72).

However, this is just the tip of the iceberg. There tends to be underreporting of incidents of abuse by children and young people in general, and of sexual abuse in particular (especially of male children — see Mathews, 1996) and emotional abuse. The underreporting is due to several factors, including children not understanding what is being done to them; children's fear of and dependence on their abusers; and lack of training of professionals to recognize signs of abuse (Statistics Canada, 2000b: 31).

There are no general Canadian statistics on the prevalence of abuse of adolescents and young adults by family members, past the age of eighteen. This is partly due to the problem of defining the dimensions of abuse of children in general. The lack of attention to the abuse of adolescents and youth has been explained (Duffy and Momirov, 1997: 86) by the general stigmatization of adolescents. This time is seen to be generally confusing in that young people are in-between childhood and adulthood and subject to more stresses. Because of this, there is the expectation of heightened family conflict on the one hand while, on the other hand, there is a perception that anything that teens and youth have coming to them may somehow be deserved, due to their being "difficult," or "rebellious," or "obnoxious." There is also a perception that youth are better able to defend themselves, being larger and more capable of handling themselves.

The discussion of child and adolescent abuse is complicated by the Canadian Criminal Code, which allows the corporal punishment of children by their parents. Those who have fought to strike down this section argue that "corporal punishment is part of a continuum with spanking at one end and physical abuse and homicide at the other. It can sometimes be very difficult to assess when a parent or caregiver has crossed the line" (Mathews, 1996). Ultimately, corporal punishment is a show of power by the parent, an imposition on the child that, were it directed at anyone in "adult" categories, would be a criminally punishable offence.

Abuse of young people by their adult family members is at least an acknowledged aspect of family relations. On the other hand, sibling violence is mostly ignored. This kind of behaviour tends to be dismissed as sibling rivalry, and parents tend to downplay its severity and long-term consequences. A study by DeKeseredy and Ellis (1994; also see Baker, 1996a; Duffy and Momirov, 1997: 84) found that 47.8 percent of 215 undergraduate students reported having experienced harm inflicted on them by their siblings. Statistics Canada (2000: 31) found in their 1999 study of reported violence that siblings formed nineteen percent of perpetrators of physical and twenty-nine percent of sexual violence. Once again, it is difficult to compare results, because of the different definitions and measures used to capture dimensions of violence (Duffy and Momirov, 1997: 80–86).

Family violence is found in all income groups and social categories. However, some minority groups have been found to be particularly vulnerable. The 500-year colonial legacy of large-scale pauperization and alienation experienced by Native communities is shown in the prevalence of family violence, estimated to be several times higher than in the general Canadian population. In the 1960s and 1970s, this resulted in the removal of large numbers of Native children from their families who were cared for in white foster homes. The outcome was the removal of almost an entire generation of children and a disruption of intergenerational continuity. The system was gradually changed, and Native communities have gained more control over what to do with their children and youth. However, this does not solve the larger problems of unemployment and poverty at the root of the problem (Duffy and Momirov, 1997: 73, 184–185). Further, as discussed below, there is a widespread concern over the physical and emotional well-being of young Native people, because of their alarmingly high suicide rate.

Family conflict can also be exhibited in the violence of young people against their parents. Even though parents have the power in the family, including control over resources, some of them become victimized by their own children. There are no Canadian studies in this area that involve children or adolescents; most focus on abuse of elderly parents by their adult, mostly middle-aged children. However, American estimates of abuse of parents by their younger children put the incidence somewhere between five and thirteen percent. Only a small minority, around three percent, involve severe instances like the use of a weapon or severe kicking or beating. Parent abuse is often associated with the presence of other violence in the family, such as spousal abuse or child abuse, or with generally distant or "disengaged" family relations. Some authors also argue that abuse of parents is a way for young people to assert some order and control over a chaotic family setting. Abusive adolescents are most commonly detached from the school environment and have experienced trouble with the law, or they have dealt with social services or have been abused in their homes. They are more likely to have developed delinquent values and peer groups, and substance abuse is more prevalent than among other adolescents (Duffy and Momirov, 1997: 91–95).

Youth in Care and Street Youth

Two significant measures of long-term abuse of adolescents and young people by their parents are the numbers of youth in the care of child protection services and youth on the streets (also see discussion in Chapter 3 on Squeegee Kids). There are an estimated 45,000 children and youth who live in state-sponsored alternative care settings, including approximately 30,000 in foster care homes, 10,000 in residential care settings, and 5,000 in institutions such as psychiatric wards, treatment facilities, and young offender centres. They are put in these facilities due to neglect or sexual, emotional, or physical abuse, or living in a setting where they are exposed to spousal abuse. In some studies, youth behaviour problems in the school setting, ongoing conflict with and running away from families, or delinquent behaviour are identified as the reason for alternative care arrangements. However, these instances frequently cover up the true causes of youths' disruptive acts: violence and neglect by their families and other social institutions (Raychaba, 1993: 4).

Raychaba (1993) documented the lives of abuse young people have experienced, giving a rare glimpse of youth perspectives on both their families and the child welfare system. By the time some of these young people reach adolescence, they have been repeatedly abused by their parents or other adults whom they trusted. This is one such story (Raychaba, 1993: 19), reflecting how normal this young person thought it was to be seriously physically abused:

> There wasn't very much. It's just that I came into care because my dad was kind of being an asshole. He would knock me around and throw me down the stairs and lock me in my room and stuff. That's really it, I guess. I left home one night when my dad went to pick up my mom at work. I went over to my friend's mother's house and she called family services and told them that I would be staying there and that I needed a foster place. So, I stayed there and then I went to my group home. It wasn't really that serious. It's just that I wouldn't put up with his shit no more. If he had just given me a slap on the face I wouldn't have minded. It's just when he started throwing me down the stairs I started thinking about my back. Then he'd lock me in my room.

Another one described sexual abuse (Raychaba, 1993: 16):

> I was more sexually abused and emotionally abused than physically abused...To this day I remember certain things, as clear as if they happened yesterday. If you would ask my father the first time he sexually abused me, he'd lie to you and tell you that it was two years after it actually happened...He used to make me sit and read stories out of Playboy magazines. These were stories with explicit swear words and explicit sexual things going on and he'd make me read them out loud to him and all that type of stuff which I thought was being weird. If I didn't do it, you know, it was "Do it, or else?" Yes. He'd do things like that or he'd do things like wake me up in the middle of the night when some porno movie was on and tell me to come and watch with him, that type of stuff. I mean, he did any and everything basically, you know. And it was just like, "if you

tell anybody, I'll kill you." I mean, I've been threatened, I've been threatened with everything from being stabbed to being strangled and all that type of stuff...I think my stepmother knew. I think she knew. I think she's a real bitch because she didn't do anything about it...

Yet another youth described extensive emotional violence (Raychaba, 1993: 19):

> My mother never physically abused me. But she was really mentally cruel. I guess I sort of consider that violent too because it was really, really destructive. It was much more subtle than physical abuse and it was hard to explain to anybody. When I was in the [psychiatric] hospital everybody kept asking me, "What made you do this? What made you want to kill yourself?" I couldn't tell them because, as far as I knew, I wasn't being "abused." I hadn't been sexually abused and it wasn't like someone had beaten me. It was this whole conglomeration of all the things my mother ever did to me, like these mental things. It was so hard to explain to anyone what she was like and how she treated me on a daily basis. It was so subtle that I didn't understand what was happening or why I was feeling the way I was feeling. I either just thought I was crazy or I felt sorry for myself...

The impact of violence on young people is serious. Youth are traumatized to the extent that their behaviours become destructive and self-destructive, and they have difficulties trusting anyone or forming lasting relationships. A common reaction is suicide (Raychaba, 1993: 25):

> You know like with me, I've just about always slit my wrists. When I slit my wrists I used to always do it in an active way. It was fun. It was a way of taking things out on myself. In one foster home I always took everything out on myself. It's scared me because I was very abusive toward myself, like my wrists and everything. In the foster home that I was at, where I'm at now, they felt "Well, if you believe in God then he should take your problems away." It's like, that

was bullshit! How can you take away problems that have been there for ten years. And then they turn around and yell at you, "Well, you don't have problems. Your past is past. Just leave it. Go on." But you can't do that, man.

One of the big problems has to do with the lack of facilities and programs to deal with young people in need of help. It is estimated that between five and ten percent of all young people under the age of sixteen suffer from "some significant social adjustment problem," but only one in ten of them receive any form of treatment. Not only is there a problem with adults not believing or not wanting to hear what young people are telling them, but existing child welfare services are so stretched that young people often experience this as an unwillingness or inability to help. Young people often also feel that they have no control, are being pushed around, coerced, and harassed by child welfare professionals (Raychaba, 1993: 27–42).

In the most extreme cases, the family violence and dysfunction that young people are removed from gets replicated in the child welfare system itself. It is estimated that between five and seven percent of substitute care providers abuse their wards (Raychaba, 1993: 68–69). Not all foster families are the safe havens of healing and support they are supposed to be. The problems of traumatized youth are extensive and foster parents are not always given adequate training to deal with the demands they pose. The stresses of caregiving by poorly trained foster parents in an inadequately funded and supported system make the situation ripe for abuse (Raychaba, 1993: 68–96). In the words of one young ward of the state (Raychaba, 1993: 69–70):

> I was being constantly told that I was worthless and a piece of shit and everything and stuff, being told how stupid I was. We had a foster parent who would physically beat all of us. He'd physically beat all of us kids, saying "You guys deserve it! You're all shits!" and saying that all of us deserved to die and everything else. I mean to me that was verbal attacking and stuff on me. I think he was crazy. I mean it wouldn't take anything really. He'd come home. He'd

be upset. Somebody would do something or could drop
something, could trip or whatever, and he would just fly.
She [foster mother] was like that too. To cope I stayed in
my room a lot, started bashing my head against the wall a
lot, and then I finally just took off. It's really important to
check more into the people who are being foster parents.
The second most important thing is that somebody working
in the system, whether it's a social worker or a children's
advocate or whatever, has to be letting these young people
know that if any of this stuff happens they can phone and
that they're there for them.

Another way of measuring the abuse of adult power and
exploitation of youth in families is through the phenomenon
of "street kids," who are also seen to be either "castaways,"
"throwaways," or "runaways" (Duffy and Momirov, 1997: Webber,
1991; Fitzgerald, 1995). According to estimates from the early
1990s, there were between 10,000 and 20,000 homeless youth
in Toronto alone (Fitzgerald, 1995). As seen in the quote that
starts this chapter, young homeless people are not youth in
search of thrills. They are there because their family
circumstances have become unbearable and leave them no
alternative but to depart. They come from families
characterized by persistent family conflict, sustained sexual
and/or physical abuse, and parental substance abuse problems
(Baron, 1999: 3; Fitzgerald, 1995; Duffy and Momirov, 1997:
89–91; Webber, 1991).

A recent study done in Toronto (Gaetz et al. 1999), of 360
Toronto youth in shelters, reports a profile of homeless youth
consistent with other studies. A significant number of these
youth are gay or lesbian (generally estimated between twenty
and forty percent of the street youth population), who left home
due to conflict with parents or peers over their sexual
orientation. They also found a higher proportion of females
than males; and the young women left home at a younger age
than the males. The youth are not clearly representative of
any one type of background, based on social class as measured
by parental employment or education. On the other hand, Gaetz
et al. (1999) found a very high percentage (sixty-five percent)

from families where the parents do not live together, or with one or both parents deceased (seventeen percent). These features of family structure indicate that street youth typify a situation where, for one reason or another, their "attachment to a nurturing adult has broken down" (Gaetz et al., 1999: 9).

When these young people escape their families, they are faced with a precarious life on the streets or in shelters, a life of unemployment or underemployment, poverty, hunger, poor health, and conditions of extreme deprivation. They are also more likely to be substance abusers than other youth and more likely to commit crimes to make a living and to finance their addictions (Baron, 1999). Baron's (1999) research also shows that homeless youth have backgrounds, including parental substance addiction and child abuse, which are linked to youth's substance abuse, particularly alcohol abuse and use of soft drugs, such as marijuana. However, street life itself also contributes to the drug and alcohol problems and criminal acts to finance substance abuse. These factors, and long-term stay on the streets, are likely to encourage the use of hard drugs.

Gaetz et al. (1999) found in Toronto that the major way (thirty-six percent) street youth made money was through panhandling or the unsolicited cleaning of car windows, squeegee cleaning. Other ways of making ends meet on the streets involve criminal behaviours such as breaking and entering or selling drugs (nineteen percent); social assistance (eighteen percent); or sex work like prostitution, escort services or stripping, or phone sex (ten percent). A surprisingly high percentage (twenty-one percent) reported being employed at the time of the study, but seventeen percent reported that this was their primary economic activity in the last three months. Similarly, although one-tenth reported sex trade as their main economic activity, a much higher thirty-one percent of both men and women reported that they had engaged in one form of these activities at least once. In terms of criminal activity, seventy-six percent of the males and fifty-two percent of the females reported that they had been arrested at least on one occasion in the past, and another sixty-three percent and thirty-six percent, respectively, have served time in jail or a detention facility. The connection between poverty and crime will be discussed in more detail in Chapter 7.

Youth and Mental Health

Even if not driven out onto the streets by their family circumstances alone, large numbers of young people experience mental health problems, including depression and suicide. The many pressures of young people's lives, including school and work, sometimes create a situation in which a young person will find it difficult to function. If, in addition, youth have problems in their family lives, they are left without support from the source held socially to be most responsible for looking after them. The instability of family life and absence of support combined with economic and social isolation can lead toward increased vulnerability of youth to mental illness. A general lack of social networks is similarly detrimental. Further, institutionally rooted discrimination based on race, gender, sexual orientation, religion, or other characteristics is a contributing factor, as are cultural or political patterns which are not supportive of family life (Cochrane, 1988). The difficulties in the lives of non-heterosexual youth will be addressed in Chapter 5.

Canadian studies from the early- to mid-1990s show that between ten and fifteen percent of youth in public schools experience moderate to severe symptoms of depression. Statistics from a recent Ontario Child Health Study stated that 1.8 percent of adolescents aged twelve to sixteen years had experienced a major depressive syndrome within the last six months (Sears and Armstrong, 1998). According to Statistics Canada (1995) depression is more prevalent among women than men. In the younger age groups (12–17) 41,000 males compared, with 93,000 females, reported depression, while the respective numbers in the age group 18–24 were 79,000 (6.1 percent of the age group) and 128,000 (10.3 percent of the age group). For example, the 1992 Adolescent Health Survey (The McCreary Centre Society, 1998) in British Columbia found that five percent of males and eleven percent of females reported having been emotionally distressed in the month prior to the survey. In fact, the young women's emotional distress rose steadily from grades seven to eleven and twelve, while the rate increased between grades seven and eight, and levelled off in grades nine to eleven.

According to the Ontario Secondary School Study of 45,000 adolescent students (King et al., 1988: S46), those enrolled in basic level courses in high school were the most well adjusted while students in the advanced stream exhibited the most mental health problems. This was attributed to "unrealistic expectations from parents and from society as a whole." What made the biggest difference was their relationships with their parents, including parental support and expectations. In this study, girls were found willing to pursue further education, and they were generally more hard working and got better grades in school.

Adolescent suicide has increased four-fold since the 1960s. Canada now has one of the highest rates of youth suicide in the industrialized world (Links, 1998). According to the 1992 Adolescent Health Survey, sixteen percent of youth in B.C. had considered suicide at least once in the past year fourteen percent had actually planned a suicide, and seven percent attempted suicide. Suicide experiences were reported more by male B.C. youth than by female B.C. youth. A longitudinal study of 131 adolescents from Nova Scotia (Sears and Armstrong, 1998) found that adolescents' depression can be predicted by observing their risk behaviours, behaviours that challenge familial and social standards and pose some risk to their own or others' well-being. These include alcohol and drug use, school misconduct, and antisocial acts. Depression in youth rarely occurs on its own. It is usually experienced at the same time as anxiety, conduct disorder, substance abuse, and eating disorders. The Ontario Child Health Study determined that all but four percent of those who were depressed also suffered from other afflictions. Studies also show that there are some gender differences in the causes of depression. Girls' depression, for example, is often linked to anxiety, whereas boys' depression can be more frequently associated with substance abuse and anti-social behaviours (Sears and Armstrong, 1998).

Of particular concern are the alarmingly high suicide rates in Quebec and among Native youth. In Quebec, the discussion was spurred after five high-school students from the same school in Coaticook took their lives in separate incidents. There is increasing pressure on the Quebec government to deal with the issue, linked to the rapid social changes that have taken place since the 1960s, including secularization, increased divorce, and unemployment (Daly, 1999).

The fates of Canada's Aboriginal children and youth are likewise under closer scrutiny. The suicide rates of Native youth on reserves are many times the national average. The blame for these is put squarely on the legacy of colonialism, which has left these communities to struggle with no resources, no spirit, and at the mercy of financial mismanagement by misguided or unscrupulous leaders (Cheney, 1999; Barber, 1999). Young people commit suicide because they are left without any hope for improvements in the future, are often caught in a cycle of family violence, and engage in a range of self-destructive behaviours, including abuse of drugs, particularly sniffing of gasoline and solvents (Cox, 2000).

Conclusions

Families are seen in popular culture as safe havens from the ills and temptations of the world. At a closer look, they both replicate the power relations of society and have power relations of their own. When young people get exposed to the multiple direct and indirect effects of inequities, their lives can take a turn for a worse. Although large segments of youth live in perfectly well-functioning families, significant numbers end up as casualties of family life, subject to poverty, discrimination, abuse of parental authority, neglect, and violence, with detrimental effects on their chances of optimum development, or making it in the world.

In some ways, the discussion in this chapter gives the impression that problems related to family are somehow more universal. Whereas previous chapters pointed to specific time periods and the multitude of issues facing young people in education and work toward the turn of the twenty-first century, the information on families shows a slightly different pattern. On the one hand, the many problems that young people face in their families seem to have become worse. On the other hand, our heightened awareness has resulted in more attention to the problems of poverty, abuse, and the establishment of one's own home.

In the end, a large number of family-related issues have not received the attention they deserve. Most importantly, there is a need for research that examines young people's perspectives to changes in their families due to divorce, death, or remarriage of their parents. While some recent research (Church, 1996) explores step-families, this is done mostly from an adult perspective. Another area in need of more research are parent-adolescent relations, particularly with sensitivity to race, ethnicity, and gender. Also of note is the lack of Canadian research into sibling relationships, another sign of adult-oriented family research. Generally, we need to pay more attention to the lives and perspectives of youth in the Canadian family literature.

5 | Intimate and Sexual Relationships

Well, if you are labeled a fruit or a fag or so on socially, you might as well forget about it, because you won't get a girlfriend, you won't get invited to any parties, you won't play any sports, and you won't get invited to come over and jam on the drums. You have to sit at home or work at Towers. Being a heterosexual is definitely at the top. But at the same time, 'you're not allowed to hang out with girls or be nice to them. That's a real no-no. (Derrick, homosexual, in Frank, 1994: 51–52)

Relationship Patterns

Forming sexual and intimate relationships is a large part of the adolescent and young adult experience. Relationship formation reflects the society around us and is subject to the same kinds of power issues that characterize other social relationships, particularly patriarchal power, including heterosexism. These are manifested in the variety of both subtle and overt pressures put on single young people to form lasting intimate and sexual relationships as they get into their twenties. Youth receive these signals from their parents and other adults, their peers, and a wide range of media influences, including popular magazines and television sitcoms with societal preferences favouring heterosexual relations. Thus, young people who are gay, lesbian, or bisexual are frequently subjected to bigotry and rejection by their families and friends.

In all sexually based partner relationships, there are issues of power and control; old double standards still prevail in dating practices. As young people form cohabiting and marital relationships, they are faced with multiple pressures as this tends to be the time for building one's career, and there is pressure toward having children. Combined with social structures and norms that support male power over women, these pressures can result in relationship violence.

Living Single

The term single refers to people who were never married. About ten percent of all Canadians are likely to remain single throughout their lives. There are more men than women in this category. In the 1991 Census, about 3.6 million men and three million women were single, and single men outnumber single women in all age categories. A trend since 1973 has been an increase in the general numbers and proportions of single people. We see corresponding changes in the average age of marriage, as outlined below.

Traditionally, there used to be a strong stigma attached to being a bachelor or a spinster, particularly for women whose unmarried status was associated with a host of negative associations. Men's singleness was more readily accepted as a chosen stage of "sowing wild oats" while single women were pitied because "nobody asked them yet." Today singleness as a choice is more socially accepted, but the pressure toward relationships is still there, and single people are still faced with having to explain why they haven't found "the right one" yet. Well-meaning friends and relatives will go to any length to try to set single people up with potential partners. The recent growth in the acceptability of singleness has to do with the lengthening of education and the increased acceptance of casual relationships due to contraception and the women's movement (Nett, 1993: 223; Baker and Dryden, 1993: 64–67).

Research finds that never-married people are less happy than married people but are happier than those who have been divorced, separated, or widowed. The reasons for being less happy than married people have to do with a lack of a readily available sexual partner, costs incurred from living on one's own rather than sharing a household, more effort needed to find company, and the general pressure toward a "couples culture" (Nett, 1993: 224).

Interesting gender differences appear. Never-married women at all ages are healthier and better satisfied with their singleness than never-married men. This is quite the opposite of the stereotype. The exception are women in their thirties, due to increased pressures from family and friends, and the wish to have children — the "biological clock." Being single is associated with higher educational levels, higher median income, and higher occupational status. Women who delay marriage and live independently, compared with those who continue to live with their parents, are more likely to plan for employment, lower their expected family size, be more accepting of employment of mothers, and be non-traditional in their sex role expectations. Women who never marry also retain stronger ties to their family of procreation and extended kin (Nett, 1993: 224).

But, the simple fact is that only a small portion of people remain single throughout their lives. Ninety percent of Canadians select mates and form long-lasting relationships and family units at some point of their lives. The expected time for this to take place is in one's youth.

Courtship and Dating

Mate selection is traditionally associated with courtship, defined formally as "the institutional way that men and women become acquainted before marriage" (McCormick and Jesser, 1991). This was historically prevalent and still continues today in some societies, where young women and men are kept apart as much as possible during puberty and early adult years. In these kinds of societies and cultures, courtship is a way of introducing young men and women to their prospective mates. Traditional courting behaviour includes formal visits between the young woman and man in the presence of an adult chaperone. There are strict limitations on the ways time together is spent. Sexual self-control is valued, but there is often a double standard whereby the sexual indiscretions of unmarried men are tolerated more readily than those of women (Hobart, 1996: 144).

Essentially, courtship and arranged marriages are about the use of parental power. Parents play the primary role in mate selection, with some degree of input by the young people themselves, and courtship usually does end in marriage (Hobart, 1996: 144). The practice is still implemented in southern Europe where Catholicism is the dominant religion. Arranged marriages are also normative in large parts of Asia and the Middle East, as well as Southern Africa.

Because Canada receives large numbers of immigrants, these practices still exist among some ethnic and racial minorities in this country. However, through the processes of urbanization and the global migration of populations, children are more likely to be exposed to alternative patterns and gain more control over their mate selection. For example, some parents from India and Pakistan arrange marriages for their children, even if they are university graduates (Hobart, 1996: 144). However, even where marriages may be arranged, there is more intergenerational consultation involved than may be the case traditionally. For example, Dhruravarajan's (1996) study of Hindu Indo-Canadian families in Winnipeg indicates that parents first screen potential matches based on considerations of caste, class, and linguistic background. After that, the young people have the final say about their choice for a partner. Further, it is becoming more acceptable for young people to date and seek their own partners.

The prevalence of courtship and arranged marriages declined in Europe from the middle of the eighteenth century onward, and love became the basis for marriage. With this transition, in modern industrial societies, free choice of mate became the standard and dating gained in popularity (Hobart, 1996: 144–145; Nett, 1993: 205–207). Dating refers to an institutionalized pattern of association among adolescents and young unmarried adults that provides a series of companions for purposes of recreation and socialization (modified from Nett, 1993: 206). It is more casual than courtship, based on mutual fun, on a short-term basis, without any immediate expectations about the future of the relationship. In Western countries this practice dates back to the 1920s, and it gained popularity in the 1950s, when freer social association of young women and men was formalized, particularly in North America. With the 1960s, the dating setting changed, and formal dates began to be described in more casual terms, as "going out," "seeing" someone, or "getting together with" someone. Some researchers suggest a three-step process involved in contemporary dating. Albas, Albas and Rennie (1994) propose that the process begins with dating as a less serious step in which you want to find out about someone. This progresses to "going out" which is more serious and exploratory, and then to "seeing someone" which implies a more permanent situation, likened to courtship.

There is a power relationship involved in dating, evidenced in the different expectations from young males and females. It has been argued that adolescent socialization gives poor preparation for young men to be responsible and nurturing in relationships, or young women to strive for independence. Both, and particularly young men, are ill prepared for sexuality and reproduction (Orton, 1999: 133).

It is customary to view young people's dating relationships and first relationships as puppy love or infatuation, in contrast with adults' deeper and more committed relationships. However, at least one study (Connolly et al., 1999) involving 1,755 Canadian adolescents aged 11–14 found that adolescents' views of romantic relationships and friendships "show parallels" with those of adults. Specifically, they found that adolescents, just like adults, identify passion and commitment as the distinguishing features of romantic relationships, with strong affection as a hallmark of friendship. Passion was linked with infatuation and sexual contact, while intimacy was seen to be part of both romantic relationships and friendships. Among differences between parents' and adolescents' views was that adults put more emphasis on emotional intimacy in both relationships and had a stronger sense of commitment in terms of romantic relationships. The authors found that generally, the views of older adolescents got closer to those of adults. The study found no significant differences between boys and girls. The authors suggest that age may change this as gender patterns in behaviour get more established.

This conclusion gains support from a study (Kolaric and Galambos, 1995), which examined the verbal and non-verbal behaviours of fifteen-year-olds engaged in conversations in female-male dyads. Although literature on adult male-female interactions generally confirms that men dominate conversations, interrupt and gesture more, and challenge their conversation partners more, this study found no such differences between adolescent males and females, other than a gender-typed choice of topics. The only finding consistent was that women smiled more than men did, and there were gender-specific gestures, such as more chin-stroking by males and more hair-flipping by females.

Sexual Orientation

In a recent book on post-war Canadian youth and the "making of heterosexuality," Mary Louise Adams (1997) maps out the ways in which teen sexuality was geared toward heterosexuality in the 1950s, through the demonizing of homosexuality and its association with abnormality and delinquency (see also Maynard, 1997). There has been increased acceptance of homosexuality over time, resulting from the battles of gay rights activists (Baker and Dryden, 1993: 66–67). Yet we still live in a heterosexist, homophobic, lesbophobic, and biphobic society. One study (King et al, 1988, in McKay and Holowaty, 1997: 34) reported that only about a third of youth asked believed that homosexuality is acceptable. The attitudes of females were more positive than those of males, a trend supported by the McKay and Holowaty (1997: 34–36) results.

In this kind of a setting, discovering that you are gay or lesbian or bisexual can be a frightening experience.

Homophobia and hostility are exhibited in schools, workplaces, and families. Some young people feel particularly rejected by the older generation, who represent power and authority in these social institutions. This is combined with the general ideology in heterosexual and queer communities alike that being young means that a person cannot possibly know his or her sexual orientation. Seventeen-year-old Anna-Louise Crago (1996: 15) has this to say:

> When I began coming out, somewhere between 14 and 15, I started playing around with the word bi. No one believed me. They swore I'd change when I matured. (I'm seventeen and still here). I worked tirelessly on gay and lesbian issues hoping I might gain credibility. I didn't, nor did I gain shelter from the queer-bashing in high school as the only one out. Biphobia fed into ageism and vice versa. Established lesbian and gay groups were there for people in their thirties. They did/do not have the resources or necessarily the understanding of the gamble of being out *in* and *dependent on* one's home.

As the above quote shows, some young people face rejection by their families, due to their sexual orientation (Crago, 1996; Lenskyj, 1990). The stigma of "sickness" is still associated with homosexuality, and it was not too long ago that young people were encouraged to be "cured" from their same-sex sexual attraction by forming heterosexual relationships, including getting married (Lenskyj, 1990), or having children (O'Brien and Weir, 1995: 119).

Being openly gay or lesbian can result in many problems for youth. It has been said that "families are a hazard for gay and lesbian youth" rather than a support (O'Brien and Weir, 1995: 121). Coming out to family and friends is a difficult process. Because of the fear of rejection, taunts, and hostility, they may be forced "into the closet" for longer than they would like and cover up their true sexual identities. Economic dependence on parents and fear of loss of family affection are likely to delay the coming-out process (O'Brien and Weir, 1995: 118–119). Typical family reactions to coming out include lack of support, anger, harassment, and parental attempts at restricting the young people's activities. Parents may also be misinformed, engage in denial, or think the child too young to decide. Parental and sibling abuse as an outcome of coming out is well documented (O'Brien and Weir, 1995: 119–120).

In schools, gay and lesbian youth are subject to ill treatment, including physical and psychological abuse by students and teachers. Frank's study of fourteen white young men, aged 16–20, in a Canadian high school in 1987–1988 is a rare examination of the ways in which youth's views of sexual orientation, and particularly masculinity and sexuality, are shaped. The study shows that heterosexual privilege is taken for granted and that it is important to be perceived as a heterosexual male. The young men in this study are clear about "what it takes to be a man": sports, building your body, acting tough, and getting girls. Among the least acceptable were behaviours by peers: "acting like a girl," homosexuality, not doing sports, and being friends with girls. Negative reactions were to follow, including verbal, physical, and psychological abuse. In the words of Sean (Frank, 1994: 54):

> The teachers hear the name calling all the time. There's no way they don't hear "faggot" and stuff everyday, even in their classes. Sometimes they do it themselves.

Another participant, Jim, tells the following (Frank, 1994: 55):

> A friend of mine took about thirty stitches on various places of his body. Five guys kicked him repeatedly with steel toe boots. These guys didn't know who my friend was, they were just down looking for fights with anyone who doesn't fit their stereotypes. When I'm chased, I think it's because of my appearance.

Frank (1994: 57) concludes that the hegemony of heterosexual masculinity is very difficult to work against because it permeates every aspect of social life.

As a consequence of family and peer rejection, the risk of suicide among gay and lesbian youth is significantly high.

Further, it is estimated (as was also pointed out in the previous chapter) that the homeless street youth population has extremely high proportions of gay, lesbian, and bisexual youth (O'Brien and Weir, 1995: 120–121).

Sexual Behaviour

Until the 1950s, pre-marital sexual abstinence and virginity in heterosexual relationships were normative for women, while the double-standard allowed men to engage in pre-marital sex. This meant that women would be of two types: potential wives or "easy" sexual partners (Hobart, 1996: 148).

Following the 1960s, sexual encounters in dating patterns became more common for both young men and women. According to Hobart's research, there was, between 1968 and 1988, a general increase in the proportions of all young Canadian men and women who thought that pre-marital intercourse was acceptable if you loved someone, or if you had sex "for fun" (Hobart, 1996: 148–149). More recent studies confirm this trend toward more acceptability of sexual relations among young people (Belyea and Dubinsky, 1994: 20).

Pre-marital sexual abstinence among Canadian youth declined from 45.3 percent among Anglophone women and 27.5 percent among Anglophone men in 1968, to 21 percent and 12.8 percent in 1988, respectively. The pattern for French-Canadian women and men in 1968 was similar, with slightly higher percentage of women and slightly lower percentage of men reporting abstinence. However, a significantly lower proportion of French-Canadian males (4.4 percent) and females (1.9 percent) reported abstinence in 1988. Hobart (1998: 148–149) suggests that this dramatic difference is explained by the decline in influence of the Roman Catholic Church during the Quiet Revolution in Quebec.

Canadian studies show that between the late 1960s and the late 1980s, there was more than a doubling of the proportions of high school and university students who were sexually experienced. While in the late 1960s only approximately one third of university-aged males and one fifth of females had sexual intercourse, by the 1970s and the 1980s, the majority of males (sixty to seventy percent) and females (fifty to sixty percent) had sexual experience (Hobart, 1996: 149–151). By 1988, the gap reduced to seventy-seven and seventy-three percent of Canadian college and university male and female students, respectively (Netting, 1992; Hobart, 1996: 149–151).

Netting's study from 1990 (reported in 1992) of a sample of college students shows that there are distinct types of sexual culture among youth. About one third of men and women reported that they practice celibacy or sexual abstinence. About one third of men and almost half of the women reported being monogamous, having had only one lover in the past year, whereas thirty percent of men and twenty percent of women had more than one partner. Most men (sixty percent) and women (fifty-three percent) had had more than one partner since they began dating. More men (thirty-three percent) than women (fourteen percent) reported at least one one-night stand, and more men (twenty-eight percent) than women (six percent) reported that they currently have multiple sexual partners.

In fact, studies from the mid-1980s show that sex is important for adolescents in dating relationships. There is a great deal of acceptance and even expectation of sexual intercourse in dating relationships. About one half of teens approve of sex after a few dates, if the partners really like each other. This does not mean that teenagers are promiscuous, with many partners and frequent intercourse. It means that they are sexually experienced, having had sex a few times with one partner or consecutive partners. They may not be having frequent sexual intercourse. Although young people may endorse more relaxed sexual standards, this does not necessarily translate to actual sexual experience (Hobart, 1996: 150–151).

Nevertheless, sex has now become a natural part of being a teenager. Canadian health studies have found that approximately sixteen percent of male and twelve percent of females have had sexual intercourse before age fifteen. By the time they are seventeen years of age, forty-seven percent of males and forty-five percent of females have had sex, and thirty-six percent of the males and seventeen percent of females have had more than one sexual partner. These rates are much higher among high-school dropouts aged 16–19, eighty-nine percent and eighty-four percent, respectively, and were ninety-five percent and ninety-three percent among street youth aged 15–19. Among college and university students aged 18–21, seventy percent of males and sixty-six percent of females had experienced sex (Orton, 1999: 131–132).

A national study of high school students in 1992 found that the vast majority, or ninety percent of both males and females, approved of pre-marital sex for a couple in love. The percentage declined to fifty-one percent for women and seventy-seven percent for men in cases where the couple liked each other (Hobart, 1996: 151). Similar patterns were found in another national study of adolescents in the early 1990s (Orton, 1999: 132). This is usually taken as a sign of women's greater emphasis on emotional aspects of the relationship while men value physical elements more (Hobart, 1996: 151).

Some gender differences still prevail in terms of how young people value their dating or sexual partners as compared with their families or other significant areas of their lives. For example, a survey of Canadian adolescents by the Canadian Advisory Council on the Status of Women (CACSW) (Holmes and Silverman, 1992: 37–39) found girls much more concerned with their families and friends, rather than boyfriends. Young women paid more attention to the emotional aspects of their relationships with boyfriends, while young men expressed more concern over "getting sex."

Sex is not as high on the list of priorities for young high-school-aged women as are friends and getting good grades and "it is still not considered appropriate for young women to take control over their sexual lives." Thus, young women's sexuality is along the lines of social expectations, namely that they remain passive (Holmes and Silverman, 1992: 39–40).

Since the late 1960s, there has been a gradual decline in the double standard among university and high school students (Hobart, 1996: 150-151). However, it remains prevalent. Witness the continued assumption of "availability" of single women who date many men (Baker, 1996: 304). Studies continue to show that girls can lose their reputation if they engage in sexual activities such as being flirtatious or having more than one boyfriend (Belyea and Dubinsky, 1994: 32–34). However, there has been some shift toward a liberalization of sexual norms and more attention to female sexuality. There has been an erosion of the double standard, as shown in the reduction of the male-female sexual experience gap (Otis et al., 1997: 17).

These new patterns of relaxed sexual norms are due to wider availability of contraceptives and the general loosening of sexual standards among adults, including the portrayal of sex in media. There is less morality associated with sex, and Hobart (1990, in Hobart, 1996: 151) found that only eight percent of young people believe that pre-marital sex is morally wrong. That sexuality is a part of youth culture is borne out by the fact that most adolescents find out about sexual matters from their peers, not their parents, and about birth control in school, not at home (Nett, 1993: 210). Adults tend to view adolescent sexuality, and particularly that of their daughters, with a great deal of alarm, convinced that young people are obsessed with sex (Belyea and Dubinsky, 1994: 22–23). One issue for young women's sexuality is the glamourization and sexualization of youthful female bodies as displayed in advertising, pornography, and popular culture. This objectification of a specific type of ideal female body can lead young women to feel inadequate. The social ideal is a thin body, which has been linked with high levels of dieting among young women. It is also reflected in the increased incidence of eating disorders, such as anorexia (Belyea and Dubinsky, 1994: 29–30).

This exemplifies the fact that sexuality essentially involves power relations. Among other things, this is seen in the idealization and objectification of a specific female body. While young women strive to attain this ideal, they may also have difficulties with accepting their bodies even as they are engaging in sex (Belyea and Dubinsky, 1994: 29–30; Otis et al., 1997). A further asymmetry, based on the privileging of male sexual needs over women's, is the association of male sexuality with aggression and pleasure and female sexuality with passivity in the context of wanting love and romance.

Thus, women who express their sexuality more aggressively and freely are more likely to be labelled as deviant or promiscuous (Otis et al., 1997: 18). Male power in sexual relations is exhibited in three major indictors: the ability to choose the place and time and progression of sexual activity; the ability to communicate one's sexual demands explicitly; and sexual pressure or strategies used to obtain sexual favours (Otis et al., 1997).

These patterns and expectations in dating raise questions about some of their consequences, including sexually transmitted diseases (STDs) and specifically AIDS, teenage pregnancies, and dating violence.

Safe Sex and Sexually Transmitted Diseases

Chlamydia trachomatis infection is the most common STD in Canada, with over 36,000 cases reported annually. Young people in the age group 15–29 account for approximately eighty-five percent of the reported cases. Infection rates vary by province; the highest infection rate was among youth aged 15–19 living outside of Whitehorse in remote areas of the Yukon (Wackett, 1998). Additionally, seasonal tourism offers an opportunity for youth to engage in high-risk sexual behaviour. For example, the STD rates in Jasper, Alberta, are among the highest in the province and the country (Burrows and Olsen, 1998).

There has been a gradual increased in the diagnosed AIDS cases, to an estimated 16,000 by 1994. Alarmingly, the median age for people with human immonudeficiency virus (HIV) has declined, from thirty-two prior to 1982, to twenty-seven in the early peak years of 1983 and 1984, and to twenty-three years during 1985–1990 (Frank, 2000: 61, 64). There has been a gradual decrease in the number of new reported cases, from 1,206 in 1993, to 443 in 1997. Most of the cases (eighty-four percent in 1997) are among males (Statistics Canada, 1999e).

The prevention of sexually transmitted diseases, and specifically AIDS, raises questions about safe sexual practices. There is general concern over the failure of young people to practice safe sex (Nett, 1993: 212–213; Belyea and Dubinsky, 1994). In 1988, Hobart found that only thirty-two percent of young men and fifty-nine percent of young women strongly agreed that it is risky to have sex with someone you have known only for a week. A further alarming finding was that those who rated this type of sex as the least risky tended to know more AIDS victims and rated the threat of AIDS as very high. This group also tended to be the least inclined to use a condom during sex with less well-known partners. This pattern was more prevalent among French-Canadian respondents and among those with multiple (more than nine) sexual partners (Hobart, 1996: 151).

Although young people are aware of the dangers of unsafe sex, they still also subscribe to the view that condoms interfere with sexual pleasure (Belyea and Dubinsky, 1994: 31). Netting (1992) notes that before the late 1980s, condoms were not widely used by Canadian youth. About one fifth of the forty percent of sexually active teenagers used condoms, compared with only about eight percent of all sexually active persons of any age. National studies from the mid-1990s indicate that only sixty-six percent of male and forty-seven percent of female adolescents who had more than one sexual partner in the previous two years, reported having used a condom each and every time. Earlier studies found that only twenty-four percent of sexually active teens aged 15–18 used the double protection (contraceptive pill and condom), and twenty-six percent did not use any protection (Orton, 1999: 132). According to the National Population Health Survey of 1994/95, more young women (fifty-one percent) aged 15–19, than men (twenty-nine percent) in the same age group reported having had sex without a condom. The corresponding percentages for the age group 20–24 were fifty-three percent and forty-four percent, respectively (Statistics Canada, 1998b). Significantly, condom use is linked to the extent to which sexual topics are discussed at home, while some studies find that most young people find out about sexuality from sources other than family or parents (Nett, 1993: 209–210). This shows that sex education is a required element not only from schools but from parents.

By the end of the 1980s, reports of increased condom use appeared in North America in response to AIDS, but Canadian researchers still found in the early 1990s that only a minority of sexually active people were using condoms. These results relate to ignorance about AIDS as a disease that could effect the whole population, rather than being only a "gay disease." It also reflects the fact that when questions are asked about people's sexual practices and number of partners, only about ten percent are engaging in sex with multiple partners. In other words, they are aware that one sexual partner whose history they know is the best protection against AIDS (Netting, 1992).

Teenage Pregnancies

Physiologically, many eleven to thirteen year olds are ready for intercourse and young girls can potentially bear children as young as age eleven. One of the significant phenomena of the twentieth century has been the reported rise in babies born outside of wedlock. In 1921, only two percent of babies were reported born outside of marriage, a figure which rose to twenty-seven percent by 1991. The lower rates for the earlier decades of the twentieth century no doubt reflect the unacceptability of births outside of wedlock, and there were likely many more births than we know of. The most rapid increase in non-marital birth rates took place in the 1980s. The increase reflects the increased acceptability of sex before marriage and the prevalence of common-law relationships, a trend particularly significant in Quebec (Belle and McQuilan, 2000: 115; see also Baker, 1996a: 29; Nett ,1993: 214–215). The rate of babies born to unwed mothers is higher in Quebec, where more couples live common-law. Still, only one fifth of these births are to women under twenty years of age, while two thirds are to women aged 20–30. Contrary to popular imagery, there has been a significant decline in teenage birth rates since the 1950s (see Table 5.1), partly due to better contraception and legal abortions (Baker, 1996a: 29; Nett, 1993: 214–215).

The majority of these pregnancies are unplanned (Orton, 1999: 125). Also, the majority (eighty-one percent) of teenagers who gave birth in 1994 were single, compared with only one quarter in 1974. This reflects the increased social acceptability of single motherhood, as opposed to the compulsion to marry when pregnant. Pregnancy rates of older teenagers (aged 18–

**Table 5.1. Estimated number of pregnancies
and pregnancy rates, women aged 15 to 19
at the end of pregnancy, Canada, 1974 to 1994**

	Pregnancies	Total 15-19	15-18	18-19	Female population aged 15-19
		Pregnancy rate			
	Number	Pregnancies per 1,000			'000
1974	61,242	53.7	33.8	83.7	1,141
1975	61,964	53.6	34.3	82.9	1,156
1976	61,267	52.2	33.1	81.4	1,175
1977	59,923	50.6	32.2	78.5	1,184
1978	59,210	49.6	31.4	76.8	1,194
1979	57,423	48.0	30.6	73.4	1,196
1980	56,784	47.7	30.5	72.6	1,189
1981	53,782	46.2	29.4	69.6	1,163
1982	52,163	46.4	29.6	68.5	1,123
1983	46,190	43.1	27.2	63.1	1,073
1984	43,233	42.2	27.0	61.8	1,024
1985	40,892	41.5	26.3	62.3	986
1986	40,000	41.2	25.8	63.7	970
1987	39,340	41.1	25.3	64.3	958
1988	39,636	41.6	25.7	64.4	952
1989	42,133	44.4	26.9	68.3	949
1990	44,750	47.3	29.6	72.1	947
1991	44,745	47.6	29.8	73.8	941
1992	45,323	48.1	30.2	74.9	943
1993	45,412	47.8	29.9	74.4	950
1994	46,753	48.8	30.2	76.2	957

Data sources: Statistics Canada (reference 7), Health Statistics
Division, and Canadian Vital Statistics Data Base (from Health
Reports, Winter 1997 Vol. 9, No. 3, p. 11.)

19) were twice that of the younger group (15–17). The total of
those aged 18–19 who gave birth in 1994 was around 16,000.
Nearly 8,000 women in the younger age group gave birth in

1994, approximately 700 of them for at least the second time (Wadhera and Millar, 1997: 12–14).

In 1994, there were close to 24,700 babies born to mothers aged 15–19, while another 21,000 pregnancies in this age range were terminated, and there were 2,000 stillbirths or miscarriages (Wadhera and Millar, 1997: 9). However, the age of unmarried mothers is rising, and today, most mothers are twenty-five years or over (Belle and McQuillan, 2000: 116).

Overall, what is significant about teen pregnancy is not the increase in the actual rate but the greater numbers of young women who want to keep their babies rather than abort them or give them up for adoption. Indeed, as shown in Table 5.1, Canadian statistics indicate a drop in the birth rate to teens to under half the rate between 1960s and the 1980s (Wong and Checkland, 1999: xv). By 1989, only 3.6 percent of unwed mothers under twenty-five opted for adoption (Orton, 1999: 125).

Teenage pregnancies tend to be viewed in a way that can be described as alarmist. Having a baby as a teenager is associated with medical risks for both the baby and the mother, including a greater chance of premature births and identifiable congenital abnormalities, or having a low-birth-weight infant (Wadhera and Millar, 1997: 9). A child also causes multiple economic and social problems for teenage mothers, especially if they remain single and without support from either the father or their own parents. The kinds of items that cause concern are high school dropout rates, which lead to lower level wage work involvement, or dropping out of the system to be reliant on social assistance. This means that young women can create and perpetuate a cycle of poverty for their children. Generally, single parent mother-headed households are at high risk for poverty, as are young families in general, because of their lower earning power. Concerns are also raised about the emotional maturity of young parents, whether on their own or with a partner, to raise children (Baker, 1996a: 29–30; see also Wong and Checkland, 1999; Orton, 1999: 127).

A typical story is that of Debbie from Newfoundland (National Film Board, 1990) who got pregnant after having been with her boyfriend for one month, because they did not use birth control. The boyfriend became abusive toward her while she was pregnant. She reported it to the police, and he got a jail sentence. She tells of the "struggle to get by" on a welfare cheque of $823, $550 of which goes to rent. She gets most of her stuff from garbage, is constantly hungry, and has no money. She sometimes eats in restaurants and slips out without paying, just to have a meal. She did not finish her education, nor is she gainfully employed.

In contrast to the alarmist approach to teenage motherhood, there are recent critical voices pointing to general shifts in societal attitudes over time. Wong and Checkland (1999: xv) point out that "The age at which it is "normal" to begin raising children has varied across cultures and times." They also question why the issue is raised now, and why it is framed. Among other things, Wong and Checkland (1999: xviii) conclude:

> The issue of teen parenting...should bring to the forefront the needs and status of adolescents and "youths," a group towards which political, ethical, and social theory have generally been ambivalent. Adolescents are poised between the legally full autonomy of adulthood and the dependent, non-autonomous status of childhood. Psychologically, adolescents — perhaps especially female adolescents, given the changing conceptions of women's rights and roles — are also in a "no-man's land" that has been neglected in public discussion. Developmental paradigms and common sense...locate the adolescent as capable of much that "adults" are capable of, but at the same time suspect as a decision maker because of attributed immaturity. Clarifying the appropriate weight to give to developmental considerations unavoidably complicates issues of responsibility, blame, opportunity, entitlement, rationality, and choice.

In fact, others (e.g. Orton, 1999: 127-128) question the stigmatization as illiterate, dependent, or immature of teenaged women who choose to keep and raise their children. She raises important issues rooted in the prevailing social inequalities, including unequal or inadequate access to pregnancy prevention. Teenage pregnancy is far more prevalent in lower socio-economic classes. The Ontario Health Survey found in 1990 that eighteen percent of teenage women in households with incomes below $30,000 reported a pregnancy in the past five years, compared with only four percent in households with incomes over $30,000. Meanwhile, pregnancy prevention and educational programs concentrate in more affluent areas.

Teenage pregnancy has social class, gender, and racial components. Kaufman (1999: 30) also points to the vilification of teenage mothers while the role of young fathers is taken less to task. Teen mothers are seen as irresponsible unwed mothers, contrasted with good girls whose life path involves an orderly planned sequence where sex and children follow marriage (Addelson, 1999: 85–87). Also teen pregnancy among blacks is seen as a sign of widespread social dysfunction, whereas white girls are subjected to an interpretation of psychopathology while their offspring is at least seen to contribute to good quality stock (Caragata, 1999: 103–104). Further, because of the correlation with poverty, teen mothers are more likely to be seen as evidence of "those poor who breed like rabbits." In fact, Susan Clark (1999) questions whether the condition of poverty by teenaged mothers is an effect of early parenting or whether it was the condition which led to the young woman making a rational choice given her circumstances. Motherhood may be a pathway toward independence and maturity, and a way out of a bad family situation (Davies et al., 1999: 46–47).

A critical approach to teenage pregnancy does not see births by young women as unproblematic, but it frames them in a different way with attention to the power relations involved and the interpretations of the young people going through the experience. Particularly important consideration is given to the way young single mothers are seen to be a drain on the public purse (Caragata, 1999: 106; Kelly, 1999). North American studies show that neither do welfare payments entice young women to become pregnant, nor are teen mothers any more likely than older mothers to be welfare recipients (Kelly, 1999: 56–59). The conclusion from this is that the negative attitudes toward teenage pregnancy have more to do with ageism grounded on the generally upheld view that young people are incapable of looking after themselves much less their children, the conservative discourse on dependency, and moralistic middle-class values about proper families, than with the actual circumstances among teenage mothers.

There is a direct link between the weak youth job market and the dependency of teen mothers on welfare. As more jobs are becoming part-time, short-term, and temporary, wages are declining. As teen mothers try to support themselves and their children, they often have tough choices to make between welfare and a poorly paid job that would not allow them to cover the cost of child care and other expenses. Davies et al. (1999: 48) interviewed sixteen teen mothers having to make tough choices between going on welfare or having to spend large portions of their wages toward new costs that come from living with a child. Pam, who had supported herself as a factory worker and cashier, observed:

> The way I see it, I could go to work right now, but I wouldn't really make it, because I would be making about $600 a month and that's not even enough — already with the money that you get from welfare, you don't get enough for the month. And imagine: if I go to work, I'm going to have to pay the babysitter, the bus pass, this and that, so it wouldn't really work...Some people might imagine that it's fun for us to get pregnant because we get out of working, and we get out of going to school or whatever, but it's not. It's pretty hard, you know.

Marriage and Common-Law Relationships

We tend to see modern mate selection as a free situation where people can date or marry whomever they please, but there are several factors that contribute to the selection of dating partners. First, prospective dating partner's proximity in one's neighbourhood, community, workplace, or school tends to prevail. Second, there is still homogamy: people tend to select mates who are similar to themselves in terms of social class, education, religion, and race or ethnic group. Third, there is also hypergamy for men: they tend to "marry down" in terms of education, income, social class, or even height (Hobart, 1996: 145).

There has been a gradual increase in positive attitudes toward religious, ethnic, and racial intermarriage, as well as an increase in the actual rate. For example, public opinion polls from 1968 and 1983 show that (Goldstein and Segall, 1991: 165, 173) tolerance of intermarriage between Jews and non-Jews rose from fifty-two percent to seventy-seven percent, and acceptance of black-white marriages rose from thirty-six percent to seventy percent. Younger people between eighteen and forty-nine are more tolerant than those over fifty. Chimbos' (1980: 34–35) research of Greek-Canadian immigrant families in the 1970s shows a stronger preference for endogamy than among some other immigrant families. There is a strong resistance to inter-ethnic marriages, and parents are particularly disturbed if their children start to date outside the ethnic group. A similar pattern was found in the Hindu Indo-Canadian families in Winnipeg (Dhruvarajan, 1996: 314–318).

Statistical analyses show that ethnic intermarriage increased between 1871 and 1991. Studies also show that the least likely group to intermarry are the Jews. Northern, Western, and Eastern Europeans have the highest rates of ethnic intermarriage, followed by recent immigrant groups, namely Greeks, Italians, and the Portuguese. Blacks/Caribbeans and Latin/Central/South Americans and Arabs are about at the same level with the recent European immigrant groups. Among the most recent non-European immigrant groups, East Indian and Chinese people have the lowest rates of ethnic intermarriage (Kalbach, 2000; see also Baker and Dryden, 1993: 73–76).

There has been a general trend toward increased age at first marriage for both women and men. In 1992, the average age at marriage was twenty-seven for women and twenty-nine for men (Nett, 1993). By 1997, the average age rose to 30.9 years for brides and 33.5 years for grooms. Approximately fifty-six percent of brides were aged 20–29, and fifty-two percent of grooms were 25–34 years of age (Statistics Canada, 1999c). The rising age of marriage should generally be good news because the younger the age at marriage the more likely the couple is to divorce. Divorce rates for those who marry between the ages of fifteen and nineteen are significantly higher than for people who marry at an older age (Oderkirk, 2000: 97).

However, there has been a decrease in marriage rates. When in 1981, eighty-three percent of all families were married couples, this decreased to seventy-seven percent by 1991 (Baker, 1996b: 306; Figure 13.2). There has been a corresponding "cohabitation explosion" in Canada since the 1980s (Hobart, 1996: 155; Oderkirk, 2000: 97–98).

Since common-law marriages were officially counted by the Canadian Census in 1981, there has been an observation that this is one of the fastest growing family types. In the 1991 Census, approximately 1.5 million Canadians lived in 726,000 common-law families, forming ten percent of all family types (Hobart, 1996: 155). In 1990, thirty-seven percent of married people in their twenties had cohabited before getting married (Baker, 1996b: 305). While six percent of couples lived common-law in 1981, this rose to twelve percent by 1990, and to 13.5 percent in 1996 (Baker, 1996a: 16; The Vanier Institute of the Family, 2000: 36). There is inter-provincial variation, with the most common-law relationships in Quebec (24.1 percent) and with the fewest (8.9 percent) in Ontario and Prince Edward Island, as of 1996 (The Vanier Institute of the Family, 2000: 36).

Living common-law is correlated with age. Young people are more likely than older people to live common-law. For example, in 1990, twenty-one percent of women and ten percent of men aged 20–24, who had married at age twenty, had lived common-law. This compares with eighteen percent of women and nine percent of men in the age group 25–29, and fourteen percent of women and six percent of men aged 30–34. The corresponding figure for those in the age group 45–54 was 0.3 percent for men and 0.2 percent for women (Baker, 1996a: 16-

17; Oderkirk, 2000: 98). By 1996, seventy-seven percent of those aged 15–19 and fifty-six percent of those in the 20–24 age group were living common-law. In the somewhat older age groups, the percentages were: 25–29 (thirty-two percent), 30–34 (twenty percent), 35–39 (fifteen percent), and 40–44 (twelve percent) (The Vanier Institute of the Family, 2000: 38).

This increase in the prevalence of living together among younger generations has been linked to caution on the part of young people about getting into a potentially financially precarious situation. In fact, common-law relationships are more widespread among younger people. In 1991, three quarters of all marriages in the 15–19 age group were common-law, forty-three percent of marriages in the age group 20–24 were common law, and twenty-two percent of those 25–29 were in common-law marriages (Conway, 1993: 27–29).

Although more young people live common-law, it is also likely that they will end up getting legally married. In 1984, sixty-three percent of common-law unions ended in marriage, thirty-five percent ended in separation, and two percent ended with the death of one of the partners. Because of this trend, living together is often referred to as trial marriage, with the anticipation that if all works out well, legal marriage will ensue. On the other hand, there are people for whom living common-law is an alternative, particularly if they are separated, but not divorced. Other people object to legal marriage as state interference in their lives, or they try to avoid the rigid traditional gender-based expectations that go along with legal marriage (Baker, 1996a: 16; Hobart, 1996: 155). The tendency to view cohabitation as an alternative to marriage has risen overall, but it is particularly high among French Canadians. In a study from the early 1990s (Hobart and Griegel, 1992, in Hobart, 1996) about one quarter of French Canadians but only five percent of other Canadians agreed that "Since living together is becoming so common, I doubt that I will ever get married." In 1995, one quarter of Quebec couples lived common-law, compared with eleven percent in other provinces (Turcotte and Belanger, 2000: 107). Common-law relationships are less acceptable in some ethnic communities than others. For example, Italians and Greeks have traditionally frowned upon cohabitation (Ishwaran, 1980, in Baker and Dryden, 1993: 76).

Common-law unions differ from legal marriages in that they tend to last for a shorter time and produce fewer children. Further, if marriage follows, it is more likely to end in divorce, possibly because cohabiting people hold less traditional views and see that divorce is a legitimate way out of an unhappy marriage. However, as cohabiting becomes more prevalent, these distinctions seem to be diminishing (Baker, 1996a: 17–18; Hobart, 1996: 155–156). One of the important factors in the equalization of marriage and cohabiting couples are legal changes that have given equal status to these relationships (Hobart, 1996: 156).

Finally, the last hurdle to cross in terms of equalizing relationships is the question of the rights of gay and lesbian couples to marriage. Some movement took place on this in the 1990s, with federal legislation granting some rights to homosexual couples, but the legalization of marriage between same-sex partners has not yet taken place.

Domestic Division of Labour

As seen in Chapter 3, young men and women are almost equally likely to be found in the wage labour force. This raises important questions regarding possible changes in the gendered division of labour in the family/household. We would like to think that younger generations are more likely to share all tasks. On the other hand, we know that the gender divisions are pervasive, leaving women in charge of most of domestic chores, including childcare, and men responsible for "helping" and doing more of the outdoor chores and household repairs.

As young couples form cohabiting marital relationships, are they entering increasingly into egalitarian relationships? Some evidence comes from non-Canadian studies indicating that cohabitation increases the likelihood of more egalitarian relationships. This would mean that the popularity of cohabitation might translate to more equality in the distribution of domestic work. However, as we see, patterns of marriages and common-law relationships are becoming similar. As time goes on, cohabitation is less of a conscious alternative to traditional divisions involved in marriage, and more of a generally accepted choice to legal marriage (Baker, 1996b: 304–305).

Nevertheless, some studies conclude that younger husbands who are married to full-time working wives are most likely to share childcare and housework (Marshall, 1993, in Baker, 1996b: 307–308). Although there is more pressure on men to share household labour, it is still the case that the shift is more ideological than actual. Studies from the early and mid-1990s indicate, that although young couples claim to favour equality in marriage, traditional roles and task divisions prevail in most households (Baker, 1996b: 308).

Relationship Violence

Under Canadian law, date or acquaintance rape is classified as a form of sexual assault. Sexual assault involves the forcing of any form of sexual activity such as kissing, fondling, touching, or sexual intercourse by one person on another. The main issue is one of consent. Legislation sets specific parameters for understanding whether the sexual behaviour taking place is consensual or not.

Alarmingly, in relation to the growing trend toward cohabitation, violence against women is more common in cohabiting than married or dating relationships (Hobart, 1996: 152; Nelson and Robinson, 1999: 360). Marital violence is also much more likely if there has been violence during courtship (Nelson and Robinson, 1999: 360).

Violence in dating relationships can be either ongoing between a dating couple or so-called date rape or acquaintance rape by a casual date. A study by Rhynard and Krebs (1997) shows that acquaintance or date rape occurs most frequently among females ages 16–24 and that about half of all rapes are perpetrated by someone known by the victim. Further, the better known the perpetrator, the less likely it is that the rape will be reported.

Acquaintance rape is also often associated with alcohol use (Hobart, 1996: 153). For example, Rhynard and Krebs (1997) report that approximately one quarter of the rapists in their study were intoxicated at the time. This is a point of contention because, in the past, alcohol consumption by men has been used as a defence in that these men claim they misread the woman's signals because of intoxication. Some studies find that alcohol use by the victim is also associated with rape. If a woman is using alcohol, she is less able to defend herself and be more likely to be subjected to claims that she gave conflicting signals.

In dating relationships, both men and women engage in violent behaviour, but more men are repeat offenders and abuse many different partners. Women are more likely to have hit one partner a single time (Hobart, 1996: 152). Women are also more likely to use violence in self-defense rather than be the instigators of violence (DeKeseredy, 1996: 257).

How prevalent is dating and relationship violence among youth? Depending on the type of sexual coercion, from kissing to coitus, studies estimate that anywhere between one in five and four in five of young women have been sexually coerced, with an increase in the last thirty years (Otis et al., 1997: 18). Mercer's (1988, in Price, 1989: 22–24) survey of 304 young women and men in Toronto high schools found that one in five young women had experienced at least one form of abuse (physical, verbal, sexual) in a dating relationship. Further, thirteen percent of the young men admitted that they had inflicted at least one such form of abuse on a female date.

Studies from the 1980s show that coercion or violence are present in 20–47 percent of all dates. In 1991, a study of university men found that forty-three percent admitted to having inflicted some form of physical force on a female date, and one quarter said it had taken place more than once. Another study of 1,835 students in forty-four Canadian colleges and universities in the early 1990s found that twenty-nine percent of women had been abused on a date, including pushing, grabbing, or shoving (twenty percent), slapping (five percent), choking (two percent), or threats at gun- or knifepoint, or beatings. The same study also found that nineteen percent of women had been subjected to unwanted sexual touching, and twelve percent of them had engaged in unwanted sexual intercourse, some of them under threats or use of physical force. Most of the abusers were men known to the women in casual relationships (Hum, 1993, in Hobart, 1996: 152; also see Nelson and Robinson, 1999: 360). DeKeseredy (1992, in Lynn and O'Neill, 1995: 277) also report that of women in colleges and universities, seventy-nine percent report psychological abuse, twenty-two percent report physical abuse, and twenty-nine percent report sexual abuse by the men they date.

Further, the Canadian Violence Against Women Survey found that, in 1993, one in four high school girls had been physically or sexually assaulted by a boyfriend or a male date (Johnson, 1996: 115). This figure was confirmed in a study of high schools in Scarborough, Ontario, which found that one in four women were forced into having sex by their dates, either verbally or physically, and one in seven young men said they had forced their dates to have sex. The majority of the students indicated they did not agree with the use of force, but young men were more likely to excuse it than women (Head, 1988, in Holmes and Silverman, 1992: 48). Other studies confirm this tendency among both young girls and boys to tolerate abusive behaviour and to attribute it to misguided love (Belyea and Dubinsky, 1994: 37–38). Abuse by boyfriends tends not to be reported (Belyea and Dubinsky, 1994: 38; Mercer, 1988, in Price, 1989). Since women are held responsible for regulating their intimate relations, they are not likely to report date rapes (Nelson and Robinson, 1999: 362).

Larkin's (1994: 95–96) study of high school girls in Toronto also addresses the difficulty young women have in reporting rapes, having to do with being able to acknowledge or even name what has happened. According to one of Larkin's participants, a teenage female:

> During the March Break, my ex-boyfriend gave me a call and wanted to talk to me about "things" in our relationship... When I arrived everything went smooth, but then there came a point when he was being aggressive. At that point, I was struggling for him to let go of me. When this occurred, he lifted me up and carried me up and carried me to the basement and I guess you can say he sexually harassed

me...When I told my best friend she said it was a date rape...I said "no" to him and he still forced his way inside of me.

In the early 1990s, the Canadian Violence Against Women Survey (CVAWS) found that, although abuse is not confined to specific categories of males, young men under the age of twenty-five are the most likely abusers. In fact, over ten percent of men in the age group 18–24 were reported to be violent toward their partners in the previous year, while only one in 100 males over the age of forty-five had assaulted their female partners. This pattern is often explained by the difficulties for youth in modern society and the lack of "resources or experience to make appropriate decisions." In fact, the CVAWS found that typically, the abusers would be in common-law relationships, with low levels of family income and education, or they would be unemployed. Further, because of the association of low socio-economic status with some race and ethnic categories, abuse is particularly prevalent in Aboriginal communities (Duffy and Momirov, 1997: 37–39).

Other researchers also point to the reported insecurities of young males that lead them to violate a young female (Larkin, 1994: 96–98). Among male theorists, Horowitz and Kaufman (1987) argue that behind men's aggressive behaviour are fragile emotions and a need for reassurance. In a society based on male power, a woman's vulnerability ensures that she is there to stay and will not abandon him. Any sign from a woman that she is not dependent anymore, or that she will not cater to male needs, is seen as a threat. This threat is countered by the use of violence, to ensure that she will not leave him. This line of reasoning relies on relatively tenuous psychological links, comes very close to excusing the behaviour, and is a part and parcel of how both males and females may justify violent behaviour of males. As Larkin (1994: 97) notes, using a sociological analysis, we can be sympathetic to the kinds of trying times that adolescence imposes on both females and males, while questioning "why young women are considered to be the legitimate recipient of the belligerence caused by males' frustrations."

Feminist theorists (e.g. Larkin, 1994; Duffy and Momirov, 1997; Lynn and O'Neill, 1995; Johnson, 1996: 121–131) have advanced our understanding of violence against women. Generally, they argue that male violence is a part of patriarchal power structures based on male power over women. When social institutions are based on the practice and ideology of male superiority, violence by males is to be expected and women and men alike are put in a position where they are subject to the most extreme and unquestioning internalization of this message. Media perpetuate images of romantic relationships and traditional dating that put women in situations where they are controlled by men, including the mode of transportation, choice of location, etc.

One of the continuously debated issues is over the relative degrees of violence of males and females in dating or couple relationships. Some studies have found that males and females are similar in their frequency of reporting of violence by their partners. These findings are criticized for neglecting the context of violence, noting that women tend to behave violently in self-defense and that women also tend to report and accept responsibility over violence more than men. Further, the consequences of violence by women are different than by men; male violence is more likely to result in serious injuries (Sharpe and Taylor, 1999: 165–175; Duffy and Momirov, 1997: 35–37; Johnson, 1996: 116–118).

Conclusions

Moving from being single to forming intimate and sexual relationships can be a minefield of challenges. Today's young people face age-old problems with a new twist. As dating has replaced traditional courtship, young people are faced with expectations of sexual involvement as a regular part of a relationship. With increasing alarm over sexually transmitted diseases and, specifically, AIDS, more attention is paid to safe sexual practices. Due to multiple economic and social pressures, young people are finding cohabitation a more palatable choice, compared with traditional marriage. Intimate and sexual relationships are also gradually shedding the heterosexual bias. However, issues facing gay and lesbian youth still include concern over physical and emotional safety in a heterosexist environment. In heterosexual relationships, concerns continue over male power and control over women, manifested in relationship violence and the continuation of a gender-based division of domestic labour.

Decisions about child births seem to also manifest biases based on gender and age. Lacking an economic foothold or social supports, often including that of the fathers of their babies, young mothers find themselves stigmatized and forced to choose between different kinds of hardship. In the end, this issue also demonstrates the prevalence of an ideology that sees young people as individually incapable of looking after themselves, while societies set up and run by adults make life difficult for young people.

6 | *Peers, Identity, Culture, and Politics*

Young people like to think we're original, but we also like to fit in with the right crowd. Advertisers take advantage of that every chance they get...You gotta keep on buying more and more stuff just to keep in the game. (Teenage consumer, in *All the Right Stuff*, National Film Board, 1997)

Youth Among Themselves

Although the influence of families (see Chapter 4) in the development of youth identity cannot be underestimated, adolescence is generally a time of forming friendships and getting more involved with one's own peers than one's family. For young people, youth groups and the culture that evolves around them, form a basis for creating something that establishes and validates their own identity in contrast to the adult-dominated world with its own norms, rules, and regulations.

This chapter will focus on peer relationships, youth culture, and political activity. Home-based and street-based youth culture will be examined, paying attention to the invasion of media and commercialization into youth culture. The newest youth phenomenon, raves, will be discussed as will the use of licit and illicit drugs as part of peer culture.

Youth cultures are expressed in groups and activities of varying sizes, premised on commonalities of background (social class, gender, race, and ethnicity), interests, and activities. Some of the main elements of youth culture have been discussed in previous chapters. For example, in Chapter 5, dating was identified as a major part of youth culture. Further, part-time work is a major part of youth culture, as discussed in Chapter 3, and education (Chapter 2) is likewise a major site for youth culture.

Mainstream youth culture refers to anything created by adults and their institutions as acceptable ways of youthful self-expression. Institutional settings include schools, local neighbourhoods, and communities that promote a range of organized leisure and social activities, such as sports. Among major interests and activities among youth are music, television programs, and partying.

As illustrated in the above quote, consumerism is brought to these areas by business and media through a range of goods. However, youth may integrate these mass-produced items in ways unique to them, while also engaging in activities that can be interpreted as protest or resistance, such as political activism and social movements. Friends and peer groups provide a comfortable setting for testing one's individual limits. This includes both positive and negative aspects. Among the negative ones is the link between peers and the abuse of tobacco, alcohol, and drugs.

Friendships, Peer Groups, and Youth Culture

Young people tend to value their relationships with both their families and friends. While relationships with family members are still important in adolescence, peer relations and friendships become central (Sippola, 1999). Moreover, youth tend to be more satisfied with their friendships than with their family relationships (Holmes and Silverman, 1992: 38).

Peers are an important pathway toward identity formation of young people. Close friendships and the idea of a best friend "provide support and feedback during identity formation" (Akers et al., 1998: 1). Peer groups and friendships provide freedom from parents and other authority figures, alternative norms and information about expected behaviours, and a setting for conforming to these expectations about "a given group's *own* norms, attitudes, speech patterns, and dress codes" (Kendal et al., 1997: 145 — emphasis in the original). At the same time, youth are a part of something that is emotionally satisfying and a means toward an identity and a sense of community (Doherty, 1988, in Danesi, 1994: 56). On the other hand, Côté and Allahar (1994: 20) suggest that insofar as youth culture is created from within, it is also a reaction to an exclusion from adult culture and a way of creating something of their own besides the roles granted by adults. In the words of Elkin and Handel, 1989, (in Kendal et al., 1997, 145), the "peer group is both a product of culture and one of its major transmitters."

Diversity and Youth Culture

Peer groups do not arise in a random manner. Similarities between friends are found to be great in terms of sociodemographic factors including "grade level, age, gender, religion, and ethnicity" (Akers et. al, 1998: 1).

As was discussed earlier, the educational and work context for youth differs by race and ethnic background. As well, educational institutions are a context in which youth culture diversifies along race and ethnic lines. Anyone who has either attended or observed the cafeteria and recess groupings in schools can attest to the power of race and ethnicity in the formation of peer groups. For example, Kelly (1998: 82) found that black high school youths in Alberta involved in her study "chose their close friends mainly, though not exclusively, from the Black student population." This, she argues, is due to the fact that for many of these students "high school offered the first opportunity to mix with Blacks who were not members of their church or from their immediate neighbourhood" (Kelly, 1998: 78). Kelly (1998: 78) quotes a student:

> There was not that many Black people in my elementary school so I had to get along with other people. In junior

high there was still a little bit more [Black students] but
not that many. But it was in high school in grade 10 that
you associate more [with Blacks].

Some of the bonding among Black students was due to
stereotypes (also discussed in Chapter 2 on education). The
students in Kelly's (1998: 67–72)) study were aware of the ways
in which their identities and group formation were influenced
by how others viewed them.

Kelly's (1998: 82) study indicated that where friendships
develop between black and non-black youth, they were
generally based on the students' common experiences and
support for each other through difficult times. One respondent
explains:

> Little kids hanging out together, having snowball fights, doing
> little kids things, being there for me when I was getting
> busted for doing this and that. I was there for him. We went
> skateboarding together. We just did things as little kids
> and as you grow up you begin to have respect for those things.
> It's easier to be friends with somebody at that age than it is
> now. At our age everything is about money and it's a different
> aspect.

The construction of gender identity was discussed in
previous chapters, in the context of gender socialization in
families and in other social institutions, including education
and work. Peer groups are also powerful sources of gender
identity. Choice of peer groups seems to mirror young women's
social, economic, religious, and educational backgrounds
(Holmes and Silverman, 1992: 38). This is manifested in clique
formation. Danesi (1994: 59–60) writes:

> When a clique is formed it normally consists of young teens.
> Moreover, at its inception it tends to be mainly unisexual
> and isolated from other cliques. A little later on the cliques
> typically start to interact with other cliques. During
> subsequent stages, the clique opens itself up more and more
> to members of the opposite sex. Finally, heterosexual
> bonding occurs within the clique signaling its disintegration.

Some gender patterns emerge in studies of young male and female culture. One survey of young Canadians in the early 1990s (Holmes and Silverman, 1992: 38) found that young women are more concerned about their relationships with families, friends, and the opposite sex than are young men. Additionally, more young women express satisfaction with their friendships than with their family relationships, and twice as many young women are dissatisfied with their family relationships than with their friendships. Young women consider friendships very important, despite possible conflicts. They also worry about peer pressure, but younger teens (aged thirteen) seem to worry more than older teens (aged sixteen). There is also research to suggest that young women are not generally as willing to engage in anti-social activities due to peer pressure as are young men. Holmes and Silverman (1992) conclude that as young women get older, they seem to be less concerned with conformity and are more secure in what they do.

There are also distinctions based on activities. Sports is a major area for the formation of male peer culture (Frank, 1992). Van Roosmalen and Krahn (1996) found that a lot of teenage males reported music, model plane building, computer games, and working on their cars as their major hobbies. When girls reported involvement with cars, such as washing them, the car was not generally theirs but belonged to their father, brother, or boyfriend. The overwhelming choice of hobby for girls were clothing and fashions.

These same-sex, activity-based peer groups result in some differentiation between activities of young males and females. Overall, however, female youth culture tends to be studied less than male youth culture. Where attention to both exists, male culture tends to be identified with the public sphere (streets and public spaces) and the female culture with the private sphere (home and family). Canadian researchers Van Roosmalen and Krahn (1996) question this distinction because it trivializes the youth culture of females and tends to associate young males' culture with deviance and delinquency found on the streets and public spaces. Van Roosmalen and Krahn (1996) suggest that young men's and women's culture is not strictly divided along the public/private dimension. As part of a wider Youth Employment Study, they interviewed 2,074 (fifty-six percent male/forty-four percent female) high school students in three Canadian cities: Edmonton, Sudbury, and Toronto. The sample included youth from both working-class and middle-class neighbourhoods and covered a variety of academic and vocational programs. The authors examined elements of "normative youth culture," the way young people spend their weekends, both at home and on the streets. They conclude that although youth culture is gendered, it is not completely dichotomous.

Van Roosmalen and Krahn (1996) divide normative youth culture into five distinct areas: home-based youth culture, social youth culture, the culture of work, participatory youth culture, and street youth culture.

Work-based youth culture was extensively discussed in Chapter 3. Van Roosmalen and Krahn (1996) confirm the culture of work that permeates young people's lives, including the domination of part-time work. Boys were found to work more hours per week than girls, generally in restaurants and the service industry. This combined with a gender division in types of work and resulted in a wage gap. A larger proportion of females spent time doing unpaid work and the traditional indoor/outdoor distinction prevailed between young women's and men's activities.

Social youth culture, which relates to dating, was discussed in Chapter 5. Van Roosmalen and Krahn (1996) found that both boys (forty-one percent) and girls (forty-seven percent) reported relatively high levels of dating, going out at least once a week. Dating involved more time spent on preparation for dates and indicated more commitment to the dating partner on the part of the girls than the boys. This is in agreement with other research reported in Chapter 5. On the other hand, more males than females reported higher rates of cruising the streets in a car or a motorbike.

In this chapter, the remaining three categories of Van Roosmalen and Krahn's (1996) framework (home-based youth culture, participatory youth culture, and street youth culture) will be expanded and embedded in a general discussion of the diverse aspects of youth culture, including other relevant Canadian literature on patterns based on race, ethnicity, and gender. In the area of participatory youth culture, the focus here will be on institutional participation patterns. Whereas Van Roosmalen and Krahn's (1996) framework explored school-based activities like sports, I will also discuss youth in relation to political institutions. Further, because of rampant commercialization and the targeting of youth as consumers, the lines between home-based youth culture and street-based youth culture are becoming blurred. Business and advertising practices permeate youth activities to a degree unprecedented in history. At the same time, street-based youth culture is being criticized based on concerns over youth's use of illicit drugs.

Youth and Institutions: Participatory Youth Culture

Peer groups emerge based on connections made in one's communities and schools. In an American study, Stewart (1998: 26) calls high schools and their environments "mini cities," and teenagers are likened to citizens with their own language and value system. Because of school curricular and extra-curricular activities, large numbers of youth are involved in sports. Hudon et al (1991: 27–33) found in their survey of 1,003 grade eleven and grade twelve students that participation in sports groups is highest among all organized activities. 41.6 percent of the young men and 22.8 percent of women indicated participation in sports organizations.

According to the 1992 General Social Survey (Corbeil, 2000: 214–215), over three quarters of young people aged 15–18 participated regularly in sports, compared with just over half of those in the age group 25–34 and one quarter of those aged fifty-five and over. The favourite sports of youth are basketball, volleyball, hockey, baseball/softball, and some downhill skiing. There is a gender gap in that sports tend to be mostly male; eighty-nine percent of males and sixty-four percent of females aged 15–18 were active in sport. Men tend to dominate numerically in sports like hockey, rugby, football, soccer, squash, racquetball, baseball/softball, golf, and weightlifting. Women's presence exceeds that of men's in figure skating, equestrianism, swimming, bowling, and cross-country skiing.

Likewise, Van Roosmalen and Krahn found gender-based differences in the types of sports that youth engage in (see Table 6.1). They also found that most youth participated in sports (seventy-three percent) or clubs (sixty-one percent), with higher participation among boys than girls, who were also more likely to engage in either arts or outdoors-oriented clubs. Interestingly, in outside team sports, and in areas such as working out or running, girls had a higher level of participation. Whereas eighty-two percent of girls participated in unorganized or individual type sports, about fifty-nine percent of the boys participated in these areas and another forty-one percent participated in team sports. Males also engaged in a wider variety of individual and team sports. These results confirm the gender divide in that young women's culture is generally found to be geared toward neatness and looking good whereas young males' culture is more competitive. It also signifies fewer opportunities and supports for sports for younger women.

In addition to being gendered, sports provides an arena for racialization. This is an area in which black students can be subjected to stereotyping. Some of this is not necessarily negative but no less unfair than the blatantly negative ones because of the persistence of an either/or approach. While the stereotype of black youth being academically poor prevails, the stereotype of black male youth excelling in sports completes the picture. In the words of one teacher: "They get positives for being athletic but not for being good students" (Kelly, 1998: 67–72).

Youth in Politics and Social Movements

Political and socially aware groups and organizations are a part of young people's lives. In Chapter 3, we already discussed the issue of youth unionization. In Chapter 2, we addressed the ways in which some black high school youth have organized to inform themselves and others about their own history and

**Table 6.1.   Self Reported Sport Participation
on Referenced Saturday By Sex**

Sporting Activity	Female	Male
Individual activity		
Running/jogging	7.5	3.3
Skating	5.4	1.9
Working out	37.7	15.5
Biking	7.5	11.8
Racquet Sports	4.3	9.0
Swimming	7.5	3.3
Hunting/fishing	4.3	6.6
Golf	—	2.8
Organized/Team Sports		
Hockey	—	5.2
Curling/bowling	6.5	2.4
Basketball	1.1	6.6
Football/Rugby	—	7.6
Baseball	8.6	11.4
Volleyball	—	1.4
Soccer	2.2	6.2

Source: Van Roosmalen and Krahn, 1996, Table 5, p.22-23.

living conditions. These are just a few examples of the wide range of politically oriented activities young people participate in.

Studies of young people's political values and attitudes indicate that those aged 15–29 have a gap between their political perceptions and daily practices. Their ideals are more practical than utopian, and they prefer participation in humanitarian associations to joining established political parties. This apparent contradiction has led to a dualized perception of youth. On the one hand, they are seen as apolitical and passive, and much attention was paid to, for example, the decline of large youth demonstrations in the 1980s compared with previous decades. On the other hand, some see youth to be searching a "new politics," involving militancy and participation on their own terms. They approach traditional politics with suspicion and form their own associations (Hudon et al., 1991: 3–8). This image is perpetuated with media reports of "disaffected" youth who "see no point in casting ballot," which was part of a headline of a major national newspaper (MacKinnon, 2000a) during the latest federal election campaign. The article goes on to quote the views of a group of six people in their late teens and early twenties, exemplified by one twenty-one-year-old woman's views (McKinnon, 2000a): "There is a certain sense of hopelessness...You feel like a million young people could vote for the same party and they'd still never get in."

Although this captures a very real sense of disillusionment among youth, a part of the problem in interpreting young people's behaviours is that studies tend to deal with a very large age segment, which may distort the differences between the younger and older age groups and also present a false picture of averages (Hudon et al., 1991: 3–7). Hudon et al. (1991) went on to remedy this problem by reporting on the results of two studies of young people's political interests, one based on seventy-five interviews with students from Laval University in Quebec, and another one of 1,008 secondary school students in seven schools in Quebec City and Drummondville.

Generally, young people's organizational participation is relatively high, even though their interest in political organizations is comparatively low. Youth tend to be more interested (in order of importance) in sports or cultural (theatre, music, dance) organizations, or organizations with social objectives (cadets, Scouts, religious movements), than in organizations with political objectives or political organizations per se (Hudon et al., 1991: 28–29).

Based on the Laval interviews, Hudon et al. (1991: 8–14) show that youth's interest in politics is low, particularly among young women. Their disinterest reflects their view that traditional politics has little of substance to offer and that it may be based on deceit and trickery. A large segment of these students saw politics as necessary but disagreed with current practices. However, they could not be seen to be in search of a new politics, as proposed above.

The high school questionnaires add to this picture. The vast majority of those aged 16–18 indicated either low levels or no interest in politics. However, nearly forty-one percent claimed that they were either "very or fairly interested in politics," a somewhat higher level than in a previous Canadian Youth Foundation survey. Levels of interest in politics and confidence in political parties were somewhat higher among boys than girls. Private school girls, but not boys, were also more interested in politics than public school girls. This is explained by social class; levels of interest in politics were higher among those whose fathers were from an upper middle-class background (Hudon et al., 1991: 14–17).

Hudon et al (1991: 17) conclude that, first of all, "the phenomenon of indifference to politics is not confined to young people." International studies show that the general level of interest between the young and older age groups tends to be similar. Further, questions about political interests tend to be ambiguous at best, subject to multiple interpretations by respondents. Therefore, it is important to use carefully phrased questions. The authors went on to ask more specifically in their high school student surveys, whether "they felt personally concerned about the decisions made by government." There was a correlation between concern in this regard and being fairly or very interested in politics. However, more notably, more students reported having personal concerns than actually indicated an interest in politics. This result is interpreted as a sign that students distinguish between an image of the word politics, compared with political actions or decisions. This is supported by other studies showing a general level of cynicism and lack of trust in politicians, political parties, and institutions.

Political party affiliation among high school students is low. In the study, one quarter of high-school students claim to be affiliated with a political party. Those who are not report lack of information for their non-affiliation. However, one quarter are disinterested, while the rest indicate that no party captures their ideals (Hudon et al., 1991: 18–24). Further, only one tenth of the students surveyed refused to indicate any political party preference (Hudon et al., 1991: 42). Overall, Hudon et al (1991: 24) conclude that:

> only 38.5 percent of the young people surveyed claimed at the same time to have no interest in politics, to have no concern about political decisions and to feel no affinity to a party...Of this group, sixty percent are young women.

One question related to politics is the right to vote. Currently, Canadian youth can vote once they turn eighteen. There has been an ongoing debate over the lowering of the legal voting age to sixteen. However, Hudon et al (1991: 34–36) found that the majority (close to fifty-seven percent) of students in grade eleven and twelve opposed the lowering of the voting age, with more young women opposing than young men. Meanwhile, two thirds of these same students agreed that voting would be one the best ways to get your views reflected in politics. Age was significant here; "the younger the respondents, the more they were in favour of lowering the voting age to 16."

Political parties are only one aspect of the wide spectrum of political interests and involvements. Hudon et al (1991: 24–27) also examined some of these other aspects. For example, a large majority of the high school students would sign a petition if they believed in a cause. Another third would write to newspapers or politicians or belong in a group or association. A further quarter would stand for election. Overall, if those who would "perhaps" engage in these activities are included, at least half of these young people would engage in these activities. There were also fewer gender differences in willingness to get involved through these means.

Although at least one third of those who indicated little or no interest in politics were willing to lobby for an idea they believed in, this general willingness may not result in actual participation. In comparison with the much higher levels of willingness found by Hudon et al., the Canadian Youth Foundation survey (in Hudon et al., 1991: 26) found that:

Forty percent of those surveyed have signed a petition while only 18 percent have participated in a demonstration, thirteen percent have written to an "official" and eight percent have boycotted products in stores.

However, overall only approximately one third in the Hudon et al (1991: 26) study indicated that they were never willing to take some form of political action.

One of the major youth-driven social movements is the environmental movement. An example of this is the Environmental Youth Alliance (EYA) of British Columbia, with membership consisting of young people aged 14–24. Its membership went up to 20,000 in the first few months since its founding, in early 1990. Another youth environmental group is the Canadian Student Environment Network, also founded early in 1990, and aimed at college students nationwide (Lowe, 1990). Van der Veen (1994) interviewed a group of thirty young people aged 15–25 in British Columbia. The grass roots young environmentalists felt that "adults do not respect them or accord them equal status," and they see themselves as a marginalized population group. They do not have much respect for decision-makers and question traditional institutions.

However, this does not mean that all youth are alike. Young environmentalists may have different values and motives for participating. Van der Veen (1994) found seven different categories of participants. First, there are the "peaceful revolutionaries," who want to overthrow the whole system through non-violent means and endorse environmental activism as only one aspect of their general humanist stance. Second, those who are "socially responsible" feel personally culpable for the environment. It is their duty to help others and hold onto Christian ethics or beliefs. Third, those who are "pursuers of a simple life" want to live in harmony with the environment, while pursuing creative activities. Fourth, "spiritualists" have devoted themselves to protect the environment in all aspects of their lives. They see the earth as a spiritual mother, interconnected with everything around. Fifth, "the self-seeking operators" don't have environment as the primary focus of their lives and are more concerned with possible benefits to themselves first, and then to the environment. The sixth category is "the sacrificialists" who value non-humans over humans, willing to discard humans if other species can be protected. Last, the "conscientious explorers" who want to learn about everything possible, whether it be the environment or anything else. They are into making their "own small contribution" toward a specifically defined environmental cause.

Parental Influence

It is generally held that parents influence young people's political attitudes because they provide the setting for primary socialization, our earliest highly personal and continuous experiences, which have more credibility to the child. A notable influence is, as supported above by Hudon et al (1991), the family's social and economic background. School, peer groups, and television also play a role in forming young people's political attitudes (Mintz, 1993).

Mintz (1993) explored the correspondence between the political attitudes of 251 grade twelve (aged 17–18) students and their parents in Corner Brook, Newfoundland. The study found that young people were much less interested in politics than their parents. The young generation, and particularly young women, were more supportive of feminism than their parents and slightly more pro-civil liberties and pro-peace. However, the majorities of both parents and youth supported environmentalism, and the generations were equally likely to uphold "post-materialist" values (meaning that they value self-expression, participation, and aestheticism, as opposed to material goods). There was also a slight difference in terms of youth favouring welfare measures, compared with the more pro-competition approach of their parents. This is explained through the practical problems of neo-conservatism in a region dependent on government assistance and employment. However, this may also reflect youth's higher support for feminist issues, in light of significant generational gaps in questions related to welfare support to single mothers and public child care provision. The author concludes that parental influence on the political attitudes of their offspring is relatively modest, as are generational changes in political attitudes.

Home-Based Youth Culture: The Media Invasion

Van Roosmalen and Krahn (1996) found that there were no gender differences in the degree to which youth spend time "just hanging around." Only one third reported spending most of their time this way and it was also usually combined with other activities, such as doing homework and chores. Television viewing was a major activity combined with hanging out. Other activities include computers, music, and magazines.

All of these media leave youth prone to rampant consumerism. Special attention has been paid to the role of mass media, including television, magazines, and music, in the relentless marketing and consumerism associated with these areas.

Hooked onto the Screen

In Canada, young people aged 12–17 spend on average 17.9 hours a week watching television, while those in the younger and older age brackets watch more (Statistics Canada, 2000a). In agreement with this, most youth in the Van Roosmalen and Krahn (1996) study reported spending a lot of time watching television, and young men tend to watch more TV per week. Males were also more likely to report the content of viewing like cartoons and sports, where females tended to report the context for viewing, namely with family, with friends. In fact, more females than males spent time with friends, both through visits, on the phone, or in the mall, reflecting a traditional focus by women on relationships.

These results are echoed by McKinley (1996: 118) who interviewed "dedicated viewers" of *Beverly Hills 90210*, *Friends*, and *Melrose Place* and came to the understanding that the talk these young women engaged in during and after the shows was important because it "established a community among the viewers, a community with shared experience and expectations — a shared expertise, if you will, in terms of how females look." She suggests that this is indicative of an ongoing process of identity formation, linked to everyday interaction.

The young people McKinley talked to denied being influenced by the media and argued that there must be something intrinsically wrong with a person (a mental disability) to imitate a person from television. Despite the denial, McKinley (1996: 128) observed:

> instance after instance of the shows not only influencing *what* the viewers talked about, but *how* they talked about it — in short, construction of female identity. One woman commented on the fact that what she was forced to think about was her studies [she was studying to go to medical school], but what she wanted to do was focus on her personal life, like the characters in *90210*.

These gender distinctions also have to be seen in the context of the viewing content of television, which tends to marginalize women. For example, Gerbner (1995: 3) found that:

> women comprise one-third or less of characters in all samples except daytime serials where they are fifty-five percent. The smallest percentage of women is in the news (twenty-eight percent) and in children's programs (twenty-three percent). Even that shrinks to eighteen percent as the importance of the role rises to "major characters."

In addition to stereotypes, there are several other sources for identity formation for black youth, including films, television, and music. Kelly (1998: 61) found that a part of black youth's positive sense of identity came from films and shows that depicted black people in a positive way. Still, with the American domination of the air waves, Gerbner (1995: 5) found that African-Americans are largely invisible in program content while their numbers are larger at peak viewing times. Kelly (1998: 60) also found that, even though films can provide a powerful sense of identity and togetherness, black youth are also aware that films present blacks in a particular way. One informant by the name of Eldridge said:

> The [films] always show that the Black man is always saved by White people. We can never save ourselves, I can't understand that. We do stuff for ourselves, but they always show the White man trying to save the Black person.

For a lot of youths, TV and films are becoming boring because they are not interactive or amusing enough (Ferguson, 2000: 3). A recent survey among youth found that "eighty-five percent of Canada's teenagers were wired [to the Internet], three-quarters of them at home." The study also found that boys are on-line for up to ten hours a week while girls for eight (Ferguson, 2000: 1). Although technology connects one via chat rooms and e-mail, it is basically an individualistic activity and also provides a method of youthful resistance. Recently, two Montreal boys, in separate incidences, were arrested and charged with cyber-vandalism. The first was responsible for Mafiaboy and the second, a seventeen-year old, was charged with interfering with data systems at NASA, Harvard, and the Massachusetts Institute on Technology (Ferguson, 2000: 1). The generally high level of comfort among young people in relation to new communications technologies and the Net are also providing more means for businesses and advertisers to reach youth (Ferguson, 2000: 1–2).

Magazines
Durham (1999: 193) writes:

> Much attention has been paid over the last decade to the role of the mass media in this cultural socialization of girls; clearly, the media are crucial symbolic vehicles for the construction of meaning in girls' everyday lives. The existing data paint a disturbing portrait of adolescent girls as well as of the mass media: on the whole, girls appear to be vulnerable targets of detrimental media images of femininity.

Baker's (1985) study of Canadian adolescents and magazines found that girls were more likely than boys to read magazines (Currie, 1999, 43). This is not surprising, considering that reading in general is more popular among young women than men. According to a survey by Canadian Advisory Council on the Status of Women (Holmes and Silverman, 1992: 43) reading for pleasure and personal interest is more common among adolescent women than men. While seventy percent of females reported reading three or more hours per week, only forty-three percent of the men did. The portion of young men who do not read at all is also higher, at fourteen percent, compared with six percent of young women.

Magazines aimed at the young female audience send a specific range of messages to their readers. For example, Currie (1999: 247) found in her research looking at female youth and magazines that, despite being discriminating readers wanting magazines that focus on the realities of their lives, girls are overwhelmed by the difficulties in pursuing the "cultural mandate to 'look good.' " She (1999: 247–248) states:

> Because physical attractiveness is based on the assumption of others, comments from peers can be both reassuring and devastating when self-esteem is linked to physical appearance. As a consequence, learning how to look good is important for girls growing up in a patriarchal culture.

Graydon (1997: 2, Appendix A) identifies some of the most pervasive trends in media, particularly in advertising that have a negative effect on young women. Young women are presented as objects; their bodies are subjected to unnecessary sexualization; they are presented as infants, needing guidance or rescuing; defined in terms of their domestic relationships with men or children; or portrayed as natural victims of male brutality. Currie (1999: 52) concurs:

> If we look at the content of women's magazines, the evidence seems incontrovertible: the representation of women within women's magazines associates femininity with the sphere of domesticity and heterosexual romance; it emphasizes

youth and the physical beauty of whiteness; and it under-represents the diverse identities and concerns of women as a social category.

Music

Music is a major part of leisure activities of youth (Van Roosmalen and Krahn, 1996; Kelly, 1998: 62). The emergence of music television, MTV in the US and MuchMusic in Canada in the early 1980s, has transformed music into a "comprehensive source of youth culture," and some argue that it is no longer authentic (Hampson, 1996: 77) or that it has led to a simplification of ideas, expressed as "cool attitudes" (Danesi, 1994: 85). Côté and Allahar (1994: 92) also add that MTV and rock videos have a disturbing influence on young people's attitudes toward sex:

> Research has shown that heavy viewers of MTV more readily accept sexual violence. Huston and Alvarez found that the more females watch MTV, the more likely they are to believe that men are violent toward women, that violence is part of love and sex, and that women cannot or should not defend themselves from male aggression.

Music is particularly important to the students in Kelly's (1998) study of black youth. Since rock 'n' roll took hold in the 1950s, music has been marketed for the adolescent audience. Elvis Presley, The Beatles, Punk, Rap, and Hip-Hop all have been empowered by the powerless youth movements of the day. Up until the 1990s, rock 'n' roll has been a part of white youth culture, while black youths have their own music that has "acted as a catalyst for their social lives. It provided meanings and themes with which the students could identify and indicated adherence to their raced origins" (Kelly, 1998: 62). In the 1990s and the rise of Rap and Hip-Hop, white youths are relishing in black culture through its music. Rock 'n' roll has freely borrowed from black music since its beginnings.

However important for black youth culture, Kelly (1998) also points to the violence, hate, and negative portrayals of women in Rap. Some students (Kelly, 1998: 64–65) said:

Snoop [Doggy Dogg] is disrespectful to women by calling them bitches. I don't think they should be disrespectful to their own people when your people are being brought down by outside forces [mainstream white society].

Sometimes it's as if he [Snoop Doggy Dogg] has nothing to say. There is nothing to say other than he is going to shoot someone in the head.

They [rappers] always talk about making a difference, kill the White people on and on and on...They say White people is always prejuiced, but I notice it's us too that's prejuiced. It's not just us, like every other race is prejuiced against one race...If we portray our music like that, it's just going to cause trouble. Especially saying kill all the White people, "cause some of my family are White.

Côté and Allahar (1994: 148–150) conclude that the music industry as well as MuchMusic and MTV are there to sell an image to youth, through a series of fleeting and illusory fads. They exert social control over youth and "stifle dissent among a potentially powerful and disruptive segment of the population." For example, MuchMusic's teen audience has grown eighty percent since 1996 (Clark, 1999: 42).

Marketing and Consumerism

There is no denying that marketing to youth is a major business. As young people have been excluded from full participation in the economy and the political process, they are also targets to be exploited. They are both producers and major consumers. Echoing the sentiment expressed in the youthful quote in the beginning of the chapter, Anton Allahar says: "we are taking more from them than we are giving to them" (National Film Board, 1997).

However, membership to cliques involves acquiring certain specific behavioural characteristics similar to other members. For example, Danesi (1994: 59) points out:

A teeny-bopper who sees himself or herself as a hard rocker, for instance, will eventually develop a "hard" personality. The hard rocker will typically manifest aggressive behaviour, utter obscenities regularly, wear ripped jeans, boots, and long hair, and listen to heavy metal music.

Thus, media and advertising feed into the establishment of a range of goods associated with specific trends. It is easy to make the argument that there is a process of indoctrination of youth in the ideology of individualism and self-fulfillment, through media and advertising, leading to a primary identification with consumerism. These become a major basis for identity formation of youth (Côté and Allahar, 1994: 109–111). In the words of Gerbner (1998: 75):

> Most of what we know or think we know, we have never personally experienced. We know the world, and in a way, we know ourselves, by the stories we're told by others; the stories that we can see, read, and write. We live in a world that is directed by these stories, and a major change in the way in which they are told is represented by the shift from the time stories came from parents, schools, churches, communities, and even nations, to our time when stories are being told not by anyone who really has anything to tell, but essentially by big major global conglomerates that have something to sell.

Teenagers have disposable incomes, evidenced by a wide range of goods and bands and clothing and labels in stores. "It's all about pop culture," says Grainger, an eleventh-grader from Toronto, "and pop culture is all about buying" (Andrew Clark, 1999: 42).

Ad campaigns are geared to teens, and ages 14–18 are the most valuable target group (Stewart, 1998: 26). By the year 2004, there will be an estimated 4.4 million Canadian teens between the ages 10–19; in 1998 that age group spent $13.5 billion in Canada alone (Andrew Clark, 1999: 42). Whether referred to as Gen Y, echo generation, or screenagers, teens are a force with a lot of spending to do.

While it is a dream come true for those with something to sell, Dupont (2000: 2) argues that the teen market is a difficult one to stereotype, and that youth today have grown up with advertising and have been able to evaluate it better. One teenager by the name of Brendan (National Film Board, 1997) had this to say as he went to a mall to spend $200 in birthday money:

> Music is a huge part of youth culture. So naturally the first place I wanna go is the record store...There are so many bands out there and they're all trying to sell me the goods. Everyone likes to have what's cool, and it's important to keep up with the trends. But it's not like I'd buy everything they're trying to sell me, even if I could. I'm not as gullible as people seem to think I am.

However, Andrew Clark (1999: 42) states:

> Annie Grainger, sixteen, says she is wary of commercials and marketing, yet spends $50 a pop for body piercing. Eighteen-year-old Mike Landon proudly wears hip-hop clothes with the Phat Farm label and says: "Show me a commercial that says fifty percent off — that's a good commercial to me."

Street-Based Youth Culture: Partying

Danesi (1994: 66) writes about the signs and meanings of adolescent youth:

> There are many ways in which teens can socialize with their peers. But the desire to be involved in a party scene stands out in all surveys of teen social activities...The main reason the party scene has become such a common locus for socialization is that it involves the enactment of three affective states — sexuality, peer bonding, and identity construction in the peer context...

A recent article published in *Maclean's* (2000: 43) outlines the forms of marginalized activity that captivated kids — and, in most cases, scandalized parents — over the past 80 years:

Flappers 1920s:
Music: Dixieland
Look: short, bobbed hair and slim-cut dresses for women, fedoras for men
Drug of choice: alcohol and roll-your-own cigarettes
Ritual: dance hall parties and the Charleston

Swing Kids 1940s:
Look: sleekly coiffed hairdos, fitted blouses and skirts for women, pleated trousers, sports jackets or the clean-cut GI JOE look for men
Drug of choice: alcohol and cigarettes
Ritual: music hall parties and "cutting the rug" with the jive and the jitterbug

Rock 'N' Rollers 1950s:
Music: Elvis Presley and other early rockers, Paul Anka
Look: bouffant hairdos and bobby socks for women, greasy ducktails and white T-shirts for men
Drug of choice: alcohol and cigarettes
Ritual: parties in darkened rec rooms, group excursions to drive-ins and pool halls, high-school dances

Hippies 1960s:
Music: folk and acid rock, the Beatles
Look: tie-dyed garments, ethnic wear, jeans, bell-bottoms, miniskirts
Drug of choice: just about every legal and illegal mind-altering drug going, especially cannabis, LSD and alcohol
Ritual: love-ins, happenings, rock concerts, and festivals

Disco Diehards 1970s:
Music: mindless dance music
Look: platform shoes, loud shirts, big collars, halter tops, and hot pants
Drug of choice: cannabis, cocaine, heroin, alcohol
Ritual: dancing til you dropped at discotheques

Punkers Late-1970s to mid-1980s:
Music: the Sex Pistols and other punk rock
Look: safety pins, Mohawks, studded leather
Drug of choice: cannabis, heroin, speed, alcohol
Ritual: concerts and mosh pits

Hip-Hop Kids 1980s to the Present:
Music: rap music
Look: extremely baggy sportswear, sometimes worn
  backwards
Drug of choice: cannabis, crack
Ritual: parties, concerts.

Raves

We can now add raves as a new youth party phenomenon
for the new millennium. A rave is a party where the primarily
youth population dance to electronic music created by DJs
orchestrating synthesizers and turntables. One observer (Oh,
2000: 38) writes:

> The sea of grinning faces and flailing arms bobs in sync
> with the jackhammer beats. Door-sized speakers pump out
> music so loud that it registers more through the soles of
> the feet than the numbed eardrums.

A recent Angus Reid survey found that five percent of 3,500
youth aged 16–29 had attended one or more raves in the past
year. Only one percent went to them on a regular basis. This
would amount to approximately 50,000 ravers among the
general population (Oh, 2000: 39).

As with other forms of peer group formulation, different
behavioural characteristics are found within the rave culture
and serve to reinforce presence, identity, and solidarity:

> So called candy ravers cultivate a childlike look, dressing in
> bright colours and big hats and decking themselves with
> toys and candy. "Liquid Kids" wear white gloves and move in
> a fluid, mime-like fashion. Dancing at raves is less
> regimented than at clubs; people tend not to pair off as they

move in quirky, even comical, ways. The clothes tend to be fun and comfortable rather than sexually provocative. (Oh, 2000: 42)

Raves have been described as resembling the rock festivals of the 1960s and 1970s. And like those "celebrations of youthful exuberance, gatherings of the idealistic tribe" raves have caused outrage and concern from greater society, despite the fact that on a larger scale ravers "frown on alcohol" (Oh, 2000: 39). Many in and out of the rave scene see raves as a positive celebration, and as 26-year-old Will Chang, founding member of the Toronto Dance Safety Committee, observed:

You can develop a sense of community...[the raves] have made me more open-minded and accepting of others–no one cares about colour, sex, or age. (Oh, 2000: 39)

'I found a family at raves," says Becky, a nineteen-year-old Toronto student who attended her first one in 1994. Taken into foster care at age twelve, she says she "kept going because of the accepting environment" (Oh, 2000: 41). One mother, who chose to accompany her two older teens and one twenty-year-old child to raves explains that: "At least I know where my kids are...The kids are wonderful. There's never any fights or bullying. Everyone's friendly and respectful of one another" (Oh, 2000: 42).

Imported from Britain, the rave scene was originally a drug-free environment where youths would go to dance and have a good time (Silcott, 2000; Oh, 2000). Some ravers, however, believe the scene is losing its joy and innocence. Profiteering owners distributing and encouraging the use of the drug ecstasy, combined with gang infiltration and control over the drugs, has changed the rave scene (Silcott, 2000; Oh, 2000). An ongoing study looking at drug use in middle- and high-school students from the Centre for Addiction and Mental Health in Toronto found that:

57 percent of students who had attended a rave in the past year had used cannabis but no other illegal substances.

But two-thirds of those who had been to a rave are heavier
drug users than non-ravers. (Oh, 2000: 40)

The highly addictive ecstasy, known as methylenedi-
oxymethamphetamine, or MDMA, sells for $30 a pill and
provides a four- to six-hour period described as "love-your-
neighbour euphoria" (Talaga, 2000: 2). However, a recent study
on the effects of ecstasy found that the drug in combination
with high-energy dancing, high temperatures, and dehydration
found within the rave environment, can cause depression the
next day, as well as long-term problems such as brain damage
and Parkinson's disease. Since 1998, there have been
fourteen ecstasy-related deaths in Canada, ten in Ontario,
including Allen Ho, a twenty-year-old Ryerson student and the
most recent, a twenty-one-year-old mother, Elizabeth
Robertson, who died of kidney and liver failure (Kingstone,
2000: 1). With the exception of Elizabeth, all of the other
fatalities were healthy males between nineteen and twenty-
eight years of age (Bethune, 2000: 1).

Outrage and shock over the deaths prompted Toronto City
Council to issue a ban on raves on municipal property. Despite
the fact that no one had died at a city-supervised rave, the
Mayor of Toronto, Mel Lastman, argued to the council that
raves were:

> dangerous, drug-infested gatherings of out-of-control young
> people. This is not the Toronto I want to be part of and
> these are not things I want to see happen...When people
> take ecstasy they go nuts! (*Toronto Star*, 2000b)

However, as advocates in favour of raves pointed out, the real
danger is underground raves located in deserted warehouses
or parking garages (*Toronto Star*, 2000b).

Approximately 10,000 ravers demonstrated at City Hall to
protest the ban (Stanleigh, 2000: 2). In June 2000, an inquest
jury into the death of Allen Ho recognized that banning raves
was not a solution. They suggested that raves should be
"licensed and organizers required to follow a protocol ensuring

the dancers' safety...[and] restricting entry to 16 and over" (*Toronto Star*, 2000b). The City Council voted 50:4 to allow raves in city-owned buildings, providing the organizers meet a strict police protocol before staging the event. Among the rules are police inspections and background checks on organizers, and the provision of police, ambulance, and security workers by the organizers who will have to pay a $2,500 emergency medical services deposit (*Toronto Star*, 2000c).

The movement to lift the ban on raves mobilized a group of youth who were not closely connected before (Stanleigh, 2000: 2). Brake (1985) argues that resistance in Canadian youth is traditionally found at the individualistic level rather than a collective. Raves offer an experience for collectiveness, which as Brake argued, youths traditionally would not experience. Raves threaten the status quo and have created a backlash of "concern" and criticism from politicians to parents. They also offer unusual exposure to diversity and acceptance including, as Charity (2000: 5–6) argues, the absence of male domination.

But as with other forms of youth celebrations spanning the past few decades, acceptance by greater society leads to exploitation of the cultural form. Marketers have sat up and noticed the rave scene and the commercialization of this cultural celebration has begun. From chewing gum commercials to a new feature film, *Groove*, by director Greg Harrison and complete with soundtrack, the rave scene is a marketer's dream. Along with the music, DJs and dancers, ravers can indulge in various rave merchandise, including jewellery, toys, clothing, and glow sticks. Glow sticks are plastic tubes containing chemical lights that ravers wave about or dress themselves up in. They sell for approximately $3 each (Gordon, 2000: 1).

> With tickets running from $25 to $50, rave organizers stand to net or lose as much as $40,000 from one event alone. Raves have also spawned numerous spin-off enterprises, including shops specializing in rave music and garb. (Oh, 2000: 3)

The Use of Legal and Illegal Drugs

When Van Roosmalen and Krahn (1996) examined street-based youth culture, they focused on patterns of alcohol and drug use and delinquent behaviours. The issue of youth crime and delinquency will be taken up in the next chapter. Here focus will be on the link between youth recreational activities and the use of licit drugs (alcohol and tobacco) and illicit drugs. As is seen in the example of raves, smoking, drinking, and doing drugs are associated with youth and particularly with spending time with peers.

There are different patterns based on social class, gender, race, and ethnicity. Males tend to be more likely users of drugs and alcohol, particularly in younger age groups (Single et al., 1994; Van Roosmalen and Krahn, 1996). Overall, men are also more likely to be smokers, except in age groups under twenty, where young women are more likely to smoke than young men (Statistics Canada, 1996–97).

Among the minority populations, particular concerns have been raised over the abuse of drugs, tobacco, and alcohol among Aboriginal youth (Single et al., 1994; Government of Canada, 1998), and over tobacco use of French-Canadian youth (Government of Canada, 1998). Low socio-economic status has been linked with the more prevalent use of all types of drugs, with unemployed people and street youth being particularly vulnerable (Single et al., 1994).

The pattern that arises from the studies and statistics, presented in more detail below, is that, although youth indulge in various drugs as a part of peer culture, the proportions of heavy users of these drugs are low. Heavy use tends to be linked with lower socio-economic or marginalized status. Among these groups, use of drugs is higher than average overall, not only among young people. Further, young people's use of a variety of drugs is often reflective of family circumstances (also discussed in Chapter 4), including abuse (Vertinsky, 1989).

Illegal Drugs

It is difficult to get reliable data on illegal drug use. Generally, it is estimated that illegal drug use has decreased in the last two decades, but that there are signs that cocaine is becoming more common. About 0.3 percent of Canadians reported using either cocaine, heroin, speed, or LSD in 1993, with higher rates of use among men than women. More men than women use illicit drugs, with 5.7 percent of men and 2.4 percent of women reporting use of marijuana (Single et al., 1994).

Notably, while among adults, abuse of prescription drugs (tranquilizers, sleeping pills, codeine, anti-depressants, and the like) is relatively common, it is much more rare among youth (Single et al., 1994). Similarly, illegal drug use among youth is generally low and declining (Health and Welfare Canada, 1992). The majority of youth, sixty-three percent of males and sixty-nine percent of females, do not use any drugs. In the age group 15–16, eighty-seven percent of males and eighty-four percent of females indicate no use. The figures are seventy-one percent and seventy-three percent for males and females in the age group 17–19, and fifty percent and sixty-three percent in the age group 19–24, respectively (Hewitt et al., 1995).

Where drugs are used by youth, marijuana is the most common, used by nineteen percent of males and twelve percent of females in the age group 15–24 (Hewitt et al., 1995). One study (McCreary Centre, 1998) found that twenty-seven percent of males and twenty percent of females had used marijuana ten or more times in their lives. However, use is not regular and increases substantially with grade levels, peaking at grades eleven and twelve. The use of hard drugs such as LSD, crack, cocaine, speed, or heroin is rare among youth 15–24 years of age, with use levels at one to two percent of all youth. The only exception is a higher use rate (four percent) among males in the age group 20–24 (Hewitt et al., 1995). Health and Welfare Canada (1992) generally reports that illegal drug use peaks among older youth (aged 20–24) and gradually declines with age.

As in the case of alcohol use, drug use is more common among marginalized groups, such as street youth and runaways, and school dropouts (Health and Welfare Canada, 1992; Canadian Centre on Substance Abuse, 1999). One study found that while approximately thirty percent of university students used cannabis, ninety-two percent of street youth did. Likewise, the corresponding percentages for cocaine use among university students and street youth were, respectively, 4.5 percent and sixty-four percent; for crack under 0.5 percent and thirty-nine percent, and LSD use was at 2.6 percent and seventy percent (Single et al., 1994). Also parallel to the alcohol pattern (see below), drug use is more common among Native Canadians, with solvents (paint thinners, glue, and gasoline) being among major drugs used (Single et al., 1994).

Legal Drugs: Alcohol and Tobacco

Alcohol consumption in Canada is declining. However, young people are more likely to drink than older people. Approximately eighty-five percent in the age group 20–24 drink alcohol, whereas forty-three percent of people 65 years of age and older drink alcohol. Males are more likely in all age groups to drink than women, and single young males are particularly likely to engage in high volume drinking (Single et al., 1994: 17–18).

In measuring drinking patterns, Hewitt et al. (1995) defined a drinker as someone who has had at least one drink in the last year. They found that among males, sixty-one percent of those aged 15–16, eighty-five percent of those aged 17–19, and ninety-three percent of those aged 20–24 reported being current drinkers. Among females, the figures were 66, 76, and 83 percent, respectively. According to Vertinsky (1989: 9), twelve percent of Canadian youth begin drinking regularly at age fifteen.

These patterns only tell us about someone having had alcohol, but they are less informative about quantities of alcohol consumed. Hewitt et al. (1995) found that among those aged 15 to 19, forty-two percent describe themselves as light/infrequent drinkers, and another twelve percent are light/frequent drinkers. In the same age group, ten percent are heavy/infrequent drinkers, and another eleven percent are heavy/frequent drinkers. In the age group 20–24, the figures are 34, 29, 8, and 17 percent, respectively. In this study, a heavy and frequent drinker was someone who had five or more drinks per occasion and four or more times a month. This means that the majority of youth are either light drinkers or engage in occasional binge drinking. Along these lines, Health and Welfare Canada (1992) reported that about one fifth of young Canadians consumed five or more drinks per occasion fifteen or more times in the past year. The conclusion is that problem drinking is infrequent among young Canadians and of the high volume (binge) variety. More frequent and heavier drinking is more common among those in their early twenties rather than among teenagers. This may be partly explained by the higher numbers of people in their twenties who attend university and live away from parental controls on their behaviour.

Single et al. (1994) report that there are various reasons for drinking alcohol. Among New Brunswick youth, the overwhelmingly most often cited reason is curiosity ("to see what it is like"), followed by peer influence ("because friends drink"), for fun, to escape worries, because there was nothing else to do, and to feel good. Studies in Newfoundland and Labrador found that the most common reason was "to be sociable," followed by "to relax," "to feel good," "to forget worries," "to feel less shy," and "to add to the enjoyment of meals." These studies indicate a strong peer influence, also confirmed in other studies (Vertinsky, 1989; Hewitt et al., 1995).

One of the major areas of concern related to drug use among youth is tobacco. Approximately one fifth of the population under twenty are regular smokers (Hewitt et al., 1995). Statistics Canada (1996–1997) reports that 21.3 percent of males and 22.8 percent of females age 15–19 smoke, and thirty-five percent of men and thirty-seven percent of women in the age group 20–24 are smokers. As well, there is concern over the rising proportions of smokers in the 15–19 age group (Single et al., 1994). In the older age groups, men are more commonly smokers than women (Government of Canada, 1998). Presently, women and men are generally equally likely to smoke due to an increase in the numbers of young females smoking since about 1990, particularly in the age group 15–19 (Statistics Canada, 1996–1997). Overall, young males are more likely to be non-smokers than young females (Hewitt et al., 1995).

The use of tobacco products is higher among Aboriginal youth. By the time they are nineteen years old, seventy-one percent of Inuit and sixty-three percent of Dene and Metis in the Northwest Territories are smokers, with higher rates for females than males. The highest rate for smokers is among Inuit females aged 15–19, seventy-seven percent of whom smoke (Single et al., 1994). These patterns may once again be related to smoking being more common among marginalized populations with low levels of income and education (Health Canada, 1995).

There are numerous public education campaigns to alert young people to the hazards of smoking. In recent years, however, there has also been an increased realization of the ruthlessness of tobacco companies in targeting youth as a market for cigarettes and tobacco products. Even well-known "tobacco industry whistle-blower" Jeffrey Wigand expressed surprise at the marketing strategies of Canadian tobacco companies, found by Health Canada to have "aimed marketing campaigns at children as young as 12" (MacKinnon, 2000b: A7). This argument gets support from secret documents from Canadian tobacco manufacturers, made public by the Canadian government in 2000. According to a marketing plan (marked "confidential') from 1971 for the Matinée brand (MacKinnon, 2000c: A1):

> Young smokers represent the major opportunity group for the cigarette industry; we should therefore determine their attitudes to smoking and health and how this might change over time.

Aggressive marketing is combined with poor regulation of cigarette sales to minors. According to a recent Health Canada study (McIlroy, 1999), about forty percent of retailers are illegally selling cigarettes to young people.

There is also a demonstrated link between youthful smoking, peer pressure, and parental smoking habits (Health and Welfare Canada, 1995). As in the case of alcohol and drugs, peer pressure is identified as a major reason for smoking (Government of Canada, 1998). In fact, a cigarette-smoking friend is the best predictor of smoking, while children of smokers are twice as likely to smoke than children of non-smokers (Health and Welfare Canada, 1995). The combination of these pressures has resulted in more smoking among Canadians in general and among youth in particular in the late 1990s, after a decline in the early 1990s (Health Canada, 2000).

Conclusions

Youth culture is diverse both in content and composition. The one unified theme of youth culture is that it offers an alternative to the adult-dominated world. Young people band together in order to create something for themselves, a space and identity uniquely theirs. Patterns of cultural expression tend to be clustered along the lines of social class, gender, race, and ethnicity.

Youth culture takes place in the mainstream and against it. Despite concerns about youth apathy, many young people are engaged in politics and social movements, but they want to do it on their own terms. As in other aspects of youth culture, these activities may not necessarily involve any rebellion or demonstration, but separation and isolation, a claiming of territory to explore.

However, a large portion of youth activities are dominated by the adult world. Social institutions, such as education, politics, and business, are adult-dominated and exert their influence in areas where young people are creating something of their own. These institutions also take an active role in organizing cultural endeavours to direct youthful energies and wills. Some of this provides a welcome outlet for youth, such as sports and other recreational activities in schools. Other elements are more exploitive. Even genuinely youth-originated activities, such as raves, which originally begin as youth's own expressions, can be usurped by commercialization, with mainstreaming of youth culture, including music, television and computers, and clothing. Each fad is accompanied by relentless marketing and advertising campaigns. Young people, one of the major groups of cheap labourers (see Chapter 3), are among one of the major consumers targeted by businesses. These businesses include more sinister elements in the form of drug pushers, and tobacco and alcohol producers and sellers. Although the majority of youth do not fall prey to these, a significant minority are vulnerable, particularly those who are already marginalized. The same media that carry advertisements for tobacco and alcohol, tend to emphasize these negative aspects of youth culture over the many positive aspects of it and create unnecessary concern over the state of the youth. This theme will be taken up in more detail in the next chapter on youth crime and delinquency.

7 | Crime and Delinquency

Teenagers like intimidating people. They like the power, it makes them feel good. (Peter Howard, convicted at age fourteen to eleven months in custody for hitting another teenager with a lead pipe, in Pearson, 1993: 75)

Troublemakers?

There is a disturbingly persistent image among Canadian public: young people pose a danger to public safety by engaging in delinquent and violent behaviour. This seems to be both a historical (see Chapter 1) and contemporary (see Chapter 3) phenomenon. As outlined earlier, the prolongation of youth and their tenuous connections to the labour market raise fears that idle hands are a devil's workshop. Youth, who occupy public spaces in increasing numbers, are seen to be a potential threat. The following imagery from *Toronto Life* shows that the late 1900s seem eerily like the late 1800s:

What's with kids today? Take the squeegee punks. We've beaten them up, had them arrested, tried to legislate them out of existence, and even shot at them, and they still won't go away. But these sponge-wielding street urchins aren't the first ne'er-do-wells to raise the ire of local citizenry. Here, a brief history of our wayward youth. - *Steve Brearton.*

1891 Police move to regulate the 500 or so newsboys — you know, the little chaps in tweeds and knickers yelling "Extra! Extra!" — who work the city's street corners. Authorities cite the need "on the one hand...to protect and encourage boys in an honest and industrious course, and on the other, to prevent dishonest boys from making newspaper selling a cloak for idleness and thieving." As a result of the crackdown, children aged seven and younger are prohibited from selling papers.

1945 An increase in crime prompts a city social agency to study the rising problem of "unattached groups" of urban youths. Their subsequent report describes in lurid, first-person detail the street kids' affinity for loitering, playing craps, "relative open immorality (both heterosexual and homosexual)." The report concludes that "it is a serious matter that at a time when human resources are so greatly needed many persons cannot or will not restrain their anti-social tendencies and play a manful part in the present world crisis."

1949 In a *Saturday Night* article, parents complain that the influx of violent American crime comic books is "poisoning the minds" of our children. The House of Commons introduces a bill aimed at banning the comics and prosecuting their publishers. Legislators assure the nation that they are not targeting legitimate "funnies," and subsequently amend the Criminal Code to outlaw the printing, selling or distributing of crime comics unless the "public good was served" by their publication. The law is still on the books.

1977 Following the legalization of pinball machines by the federal government in 1976 — they were previously banned as "games of chance" — Metro officials move to regulate pinball establishments, limiting their hours and banning kids under the age of fourteen. Critics claim that the evil amusements lead to truancy, drunkenness and begging, but the Metro Licensing Commission rules that the city has no grounds to restrict access to the machines. A lawyer representing the owner of a pinball machine-operating lunch counter near Central Tech high school argues: "It'd be better having them play pinball machines than off in a car someplace smoking a marijuana cigarrette."

1987 The city at large becomes alarmed over reports of "swarming" — gangs of teens swooping down on their victims, usually other teens, demanding money or, in some cases, the victim's shoes. In one incident reported in the *Star*, twenty-four youths storm a Fran's restaurant and make off with "$20 to $25 worth of pastries." Metro councillor Norm Gardner expresses concern that this gang activity will sully the imminent Shriner's Convention, the biggest convention in the city's history. Police form a special undercover unit to deal with the crisis, then announce a month later that the problem has been defused.

1998 Squeegee kids — who are initially lauded in a *Globe and Mail* editorial as "traffic-dodging impresarios" with a plucky adherence to the tenets of capitalism — are now regarded as a serious threat to public safety. In mid-July, one squeegee kid is threatened with a gun by a motorist while another's dog is shot in the head by police. The *Globe*, lamenting its earlier charity, suggests licensing the kids as a way of controlling their activities and collecting taxes on their no-doubt sizeable earnings (Brearton, 1999: 2–3).

Most recently, these negative media-driven depictions have taken on racialized and gender-based overtones. Groups of youth, and particularly young (and black) males are perceived as gangs. In recent years, young women have been targeted for the same kind of treatment, with media hype about girl gangs.

In fact, where youth engage in delinquent or criminal behaviour, most of it is non-violent in nature. The creation and perpetuation of the image of violent youth by media reflects yet another way in which young people are mistreated. What is often neglected, and was partly addressed in Chapter 4, is that young people are more likely to be victims than perpetrators of violence.

This chapter will address youth deviance, crime, and the justice system. The role of youth as victims as well as perpetrators of crime will be explored. The main problem areas addressed are youth violence and youth gangs, including hate groups. The juvenile justice system and police behaviours will be approached critically.

Youth as Victims of Violence

In Chapter 4, we discussed the many ways in which young people are victimized in their families and by the authorities and agencies created to protect them. Additionally, youth are victimized by acquaintances and strangers, part of a general trend captured in Table. 7.1. Most violence against children and youth that is reported to the police is by acquaintances (fifty-two percent). An additional nineteen percent are violated by strangers. The majority of reported sexual assaults (forty-nine percent) is perpetrated by acquaintances with another fifteen percent by strangers. A similar pattern emerges in cases of physical assault, where fifty-three percent of perpetrators are acquaintances and one fifth are strangers. In cases of violence against children and youth by acquaintances and strangers, males tend to be more likely victims of violence than females. The exception is the higher reported sexual victimization of female children and youth by acquaintances (Statistics Canada, 2000a: 31–32). Excepting sexual victimization, male youth are victimized at higher rates than females (Paetch and Bertrand, 1999).

When examining the violent acts committed against children and youth by family members, acquaintances, and strangers, what is significant is that children and youth under eighteen years of age form sixty percent of all sexual assault victims and one fifth of physical assault victims. Most youth victims (fifty-three percent) of sexual assault are in the age category 12–17, and this age group also accounts for three quarters of victims of physical assault (Statistics Canada,

Table 7.1. Type of assault by age group of victim, 1999[1,2]

Type of Assault	Total Victims No.	Total %	Total Child & Youth (<18) %	Total Adult (18+) %	Age Breakdown as a Proportion of Total Children and Youth (under 18)			
					Total %	<3 %	3-11 %	12-17 %
Sexual Assault - Total	10,805	100	60	40	100	2	45	53
Aggravated Sexual Assault	95	100	39	61	100	3	43	54
Sexual Assault With a Weapon	202	100	27	73	100	-	17	83
Sexual Assault	9,073	100	57	43	100	2	43	55
Other Sexual Crimes[3]	1,435	100	85	15	100	2	57	40
Physical Assault - Total	94,095	100	20	80	100	2	22	76
Aggravated Assault	1,298	100	13	87	100	16	6	77
Assault with weapon/Causing bodily harm	19,423	100	19	81	100	2	20	78
Common Assault	69,542	100	21	79	100	2	22	76
Discharge Firearm With Intent	79	100	29	71	100	-	17	83
Assault Against Peace-Public Officer	2,567	100	-	100	-	-	-	-
Other Assaults[4]	1,186	100	14	86	100	9	23	68
Assault - Total	104,900	100	24	76	100	2	28	70

Percentages may not total 100% due to rounding. - Nil or zero.
[1] Data are not nationally representative. Data are based on a sample of 164 police departments, representing 46% of the national volume of crime in 1999.
[2] Includes only cases where age is known.
[3] The UCR2 Survey groups other sexual crimes including sexual interference, sexual touching, sexual exploitation, incest, etc., into one category. Most of these are directed at children.
[4] The UCR2 Survey groups other assault, including unlawfully causing bodily harm and criminal negligence causing bodily harm, etc., into one category.
Source: Statistics Canada, Canadian Centre for Justice Statistics, Incident-based Uniform Crime Reporting (UCR2) Survey (from Family Violence in Canada: A Statistical Profile 2000, Catalogue no. 85-224, p.32)

2000b: 31–32). Studies show that high-school-aged males are more likely to be victims of physical violence than females, while females are more likely to be sexually assaulted (Ryan et al., 1993; in Paetch and Bertrand, 1999: 352). Thus, youth are brutalized in disproportionate numbers compared with their proportion of the total population.

Youth as Perpetrators of Violence and Crime

Teenagers and young adults make up a disproportionately large share of persons accused of crime in Canada. It is estimated that three percent of Canadian youth are involved with the youth justice system (National Crime Prevention Council of Canada, 1996). As seen in Table 7.2, youth are disproportionately responsible for criminal acts. For example, while just over one fifth of violent crime in 1992 was attributed to youth aged 18–24, they only form ten percent of the general population. The percentages for those aged 25–34 are thirty-three and seventeen percent, respectively. Those in the age group thirty-four and over form two-thirds of the population but just thirty-two percent of violent incidents (Hung and Lipinski, 1995). In 1994, one fifth of crimes were committed by people aged twelve to seventeen (Kuryllowicz, 1996: 20–23).

However, in a startling contrast with the popular image and fears about youth violence against adults, in 1998, only two percent of victims of youth violence were adults aged fifty-five and over. Youths tend to victimize others in their own age group who are known to them, with approximately sixty percent of the victims being acquaintances and approximately half of youth being victims of other youth (Savoie, 1999; also see Paetch and Bertrand, 1999: 352). Adolescent males are responsible for one fifth of sexual assaults against adolescents and adults and between thirty and fifty percent of sexual assaults against children (Shields, 1995).

Nevertheless fears persist about a rise in youth violence. In fact, Canadian statistics indicate that youth violent crime rates increased in the early 1990s, but declined between 1994 and 1997, with an overall 1.9 percent increase over the 1990s

Table 7.2. Distribution Of Youths And Adults Charged By Major Crime Category, Canada, 1998

		Persons Charged	
		Youths 12 to 17 years	Adults 18 years and over
Violent Crimes	Number	22,145	113,127
	% of total Criminal Code	21	30
Property Crimes	Number	54,047	140,639
	% of total Criminal Code	51	37
Other Criminal Code Offences	Number	30,792	127,674
	% of total Criminal Code	29	33
Total Criminal Code [1]	**Number**	**106,984**	**381,440**
	% of total Criminal Code	**100**	**100**

[1] Excluding traffic offences
Note: Percentage may not add to 100% due to rounding
Source: Statistics Canada, Canadian Centre for Justice Statistics, Uniform Crime Reporting Survey (from Juristat, Catalogue no. 85-002, Vol. 19, No. 13, p.4.)

(Jaffe and Baker, 1999: 22–23; *Law Now*, 1996; Kuryllowicz, 1996: 20–23). As other types of crime showed a decrease in the 1990s, there was an increase in crimes involving violence (*Law Now*, 1996). However, despite the significant increase in the violent crime rate among youth since the mid-1980s (Hung and Lipinski, 1995), more adults than teens commit violent crime (Kuryllowicz, 1996: 20–23). In 1992, youth violent offences accounted for fourteen percent of all youth crime, while twenty-four percent of adult offences involved violence (Hung and Lipinski, 1995).

Although violent youth crime rates have declined recently, there has been an increase of seventy-seven percent in the last decade, compared with a six percent increase for adults (Savoie, 1999). In 1997, violent offences accounted for eighteen percent of all charges against youth. There was a 102 percent increase in violent crimes between 1987 and 1997. However, some question whether these are the result of actual increases in criminal violence by youth or an increase in reporting, due to changing public attitudes. Aggressive zero tolerance policies in schools, for example, lead to the police being called more frequently rather than the schools dealing with incidents themselves (Stevenson et al., 2000: 222–223).

As indicated in Table 7.3, the most common violent crimes by youth are assaults and robberies. Adults, on the other hand, are more likely to commit or attempt murder (Hung and Lipinski, 1995). Homicides by young offenders are relatively rare. Only under ten percent of all homicides are committed by youth, and this type of crime accounts for less than one percent of youth court cases in 1996–97 (Jaffe and Baker, 1999: 22–23). There were a total of 611 victims of youth homicide between 1961 and 1983 (Meloff and Silverman, 1992). Homicides by youth aged 12–17 have remained relatively stable between 1986 and 1997, with fifty-four youths charged with homicide in 1997 (Stevenson et al., 2000: 223).

Meloff and Silverman (1992) report that, of the 611 victims of homicide by youth between 1961 and 1983, the largest group among victims were acquaintances (thirty-five percent), followed by strangers (31.5 percent), other family members (19.5 percent), and parents (14 percent). The younger the age of the perpetrator, the more likely the victim is a parent or other family member, rather than an acquaintance or stranger. Among youth fifteen years of age and over, homicides are more likely to involve a stranger and be committed in the course of another crime. Native youth are more likely to kill a family member than non-Native youth. Generally, homicides by youth are intraracial, meaning, for example, that Caucasians kill Caucasians.

In comparison to adults, youth offenders are more likely to commit property- and drug-related crime than adults. Most

Table 7.3. Persons Charged[1] by Age, Selected Incidents, 1997

	Age Group	
	Adults %	Youths (12-17) %
Homicide[2]	88	12
Attempted murder	91	9
Assaults	86	14
Sexual assaults	84	16
Other sexual offences	86	14
Abduction	97	3
Robbery	62	38
Violent crime—Total	84	16
Breaking and entering	60	40
Motor vehicle theft	57	43
Fraud	93	7
Theft over $5000	80	20
Theft $5000 and under	71	29
Property crime—Total	71	29
Mischief	66	34
Arson	57	43
Prostitution	96	4
Offensive weapons	79	21
Criminal Code—Total	77	23
Impaired driving	...	...
Cocaine—Possession	96	4
Cocaine—Trafficking	96	4
Cannabis—Possession	82	18
Cannabis—Trafficking	85	15

[1] Represents all persons charged in Canada, Uniform Crime Reporting Survey, Canadian Centre for Justice Statistics.
[2] Homicide Survey, CCJS.
... Figures not available.
Source: Adapted from Statistics Canada (1995), Juristat, Cat. No. 85-002, p. 19 from Bell, 1999, p.64.

(fifty-eight percent) youth crimes in 1994 were property crimes and drug-related offences, compared with thirty-eight percent of crimes committed by adults (Kuryllowicz, 1996: 20–23; see also Hung and Lipinski, 1995).

In fact, as seen in Figure 7.1, most youth crimes are property crimes, theft being the most common. In 1997, nearly half of youths who were charged were involved in property crimes, including theft and breaking and entering (Stevenson et al., 2000: 222–223). About one in five offences involves violence. A small percentage involves serious injury or the use of a weapon (*Law Now*, 1996: 12; Stevenson et al., 2000: 222).

Figure 7.1. Youth Court Cases by Offense Category, Canada, 1986-87 and 1996-97

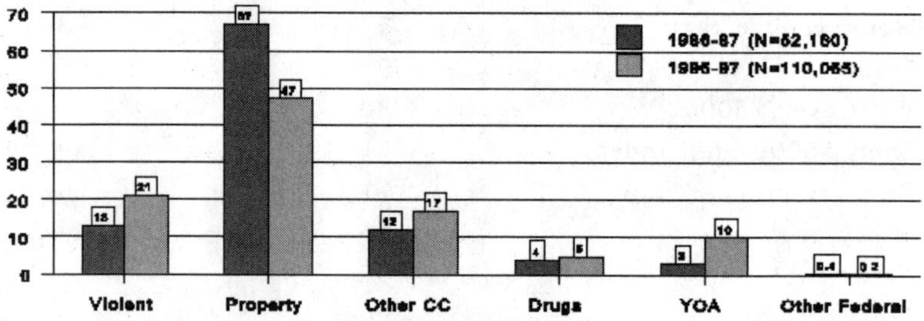

Source: Adapted from de Souza (1995); Statistics Canada (1998: xiii) from Bell, 1999, p. 43.

Contrary to the popular image of large numbers of youth engaging in sporadic delinquent behaviour at a spur of the moment, a lot of youth crime is committed by "repeat or persistent" offenders. For example, in 1996–97, approximately forty percent of convictions involved repeat offenders (Jaffe and Baker, 1999: 24; Stevenson et al., 2000: 224). Among this group, twenty-one percent had one prior conviction, ten percent had two, and eleven percent had three or more prior convictions (Stevenson et al., 2000: 224). This recidivism is particularly apparent among youth sex offenders. If young sexually aggressive males do not get treatment, they can be expected to commit an average of 380 sexual crimes in their lifetime (Shields, 1995).

Gender and Youth Crime

According to Statistics Canada (1999), most crimes are committed by adult males. In every age group, males far outnumber females in all crime categories. Males also engage in a wider variety of delinquent behaviours than females (Paetch and Bertrand, 1999). In 1992, eighty percent of youth crime was committed by males, with little change since 1986 (Hung and Lipinski, 1995).

The types of crimes that young males and females commit are similar, with theft under $5,000 being the most common offence for both. After that, for boys in 2000, it was breaking and entering, and common assault, while common assault and failure to appear in court were the next in line for girls (Stevenson et al., 2000: 223–224).

Despite statistics to the contrary (see Table 7.4), there is a persistent myth about the dramatically increasing crime, violence, and gang activity among young women (Pate, 1999). Males account for approximately eighty percent of all the violent crime caseload; they dominate at all age levels and are more likely to be repeat offenders (Jaffe and Baker, 1999: 23; Stevenson et al., 2000: 223). Girls account for a fraction of youth crime. However, there has been a dramatic increase in the number of violent crimes committed by girls, by 128 percent from 1986 to 1994 (Kuryllowicz, 1996: 20–23), while the violent crime rate of young males increased by sixty-five percent. There has also been an increase in the adult female violent crime rate by forty-seven percent, compared with a two percent increase for men. However, the violent crime rate of female youth is still only one third of the rate of male youth. Further, male youths tend to commit more serious violence, such as robbery and major assault, while most female youth commit common assault. Female offenders tend to be younger than male youths, with peak years at 14–15, while young males peak at around 16–17 (Savoie, 1999; Stevenson et al., 2000: 223; Jaffe and Baker, 1999: 23).

Table 7.4. Comparison Of Male And Female Violent Crime for Youths and Adults, Canada, 1998

	Youths 12 to 17 years		Adults 18 years and over	
	Male	Female	Male	Female
		%		
Homicide	0.3	0.0	0.4	0.4
Attempted Murder	0.4	0.1	0.5	0.4
Aggravated Sexual Assault	0.0	0.0	0.1	0.0
Sexual Assault with Weapon	0.2	0.0	0.2	0.0
Sexual Assault	8.2	0.8	7.7	0.8
Common Assault	45.9	67.3	59.6	64.9
Assault with weapon/causing bodily harm	19.7	16.0	16.9	20.1
Aggravated Assault	1.5	1.1	1.5	1.6
Abduction	0.0	0.0	0.1	0.6
Robbery	18.5	9.2	5.8	3.4
Other Violent Crimes	5.2	5.4	7.0	7.7
Crimes of Violence - Total	**100**	**100**	**100**	**100**
Number of Persons Charged With Violent Crimes	16,493	5,652	97,490	15,637

Source: Statistics Canada, Canadian Centre for Justice Statistics, Uniform Crime Reporting Survey (from Juristat, Catalogue no. 85-002, Vol. 19, No. 13, p.5.)

Only eleven percent of all youth who kill are females. When females kill, the victims are more likely to be male and more likely to be a family member (Meloff and Silverman, 1992). Most of the situations in which young women have been charged for violent crimes involve either defenses against attackers or offences that have been reclassified as serious offences because of the zero tolerance approach (Pate, 1999: 41).

Race, Ethnicity, and Youth Crime

Some race and ethnic minorities have distinct patterns of criminal and delinquent behaviour. For example, North American youth of Chinese descent tend to have lower than average rates of delinquency. Among this ethnic group, acculturation was found to be strongly correlated with increasing delinquency, while adherence to Chinese culture was found to lower delinquency (Wong, 1999).

On the other hand, some race minorities have more than their share of brushes with the police and the legal system. Canadian Centre for Justice Statistics (1997/98) confirms a widely reported phenomenon of Aboriginal youth being disproportionately represented at all levels of the criminal justice system. The marginalization of the Aboriginal populations puts them in a position of both living in high-risk communities where poverty, substance abuse, and violence are common. These communities are more visible and subject to more police presence, reflected in higher arrest rates.

A group particularly targeted for negative stereotyping as criminals and delinquents is black youth. Studies and official government reports done in Toronto in the 1980s and 1990s show that black males are more likely to be subjected to police harassment, mistaken identity, arbitrary arrests, and harsher penalties in the criminal justice system. Relations between police and the black community are tense. There is an element of suspicion directed at black people, and there is a particular "criminalization of young, black, working-class males." The context of this are the streets and other public spaces, where "just hanging out" by Black youths gets interpreted as "inappropriate" and a threat (James, 1998: 159–161).

In his interview and focus group study of fifty black youth (thirty male and twenty female) in six Ontario cities (Toronto, Ottawa, London, Windsor, Hamilton, and Amherstburg), James (1998) documents some of their encounters with the police. Many had experienced being stopped and questioned by police. They saw that this was because of their skin colour, clothing, and hairstyle, all of which carried negative stereotypical connotations. Some comments (James, 1998: 166) included:

> They drive by. They don't glimpse your clothes, they glimpse your colour. That's the first thing they look at. If they judge the clothes so much why don't they go and stop those white boys that are wearing those same things like us?
>
> There is a stereotype of Blacks — baggy pants, flashy jewellery, baseball caps, flashy colours, and so on. All Black people dress like this are [seen] as pimps or drug leaders. White people dress like this too, [but are] not seen as pimps, etc.

They also noted that they are more likely to be stopped because they looked like a suspect. Descriptions of black suspects are not as extensive as those of whites, leaving more room for misinterpretation, particularly when white officers seem to think that all blacks look alike. They are also more likely to be perceived as immigrants or outsiders. Among these groups, Somalis and Jamaicans are particularly targeted for the worst of negative stereotyping. Based on these views, any black youth standing around would be seen to be up to no good. For example, when white youth stand outside a store, they are seen to be window-shopping, while black youth are seen to be loitering (James, 1998: 166–168).

James also found that social class and gender differences overlap with consideration of race. The perception that black people are poor means that if one is wearing good clothes or walks in a wealthier neighbourhood, they are more likely to be questioned or harassed. Although both young black males and females seem to fall under suspicion, the girls tend to be treated less harshly by the police. However, there was a perception that both males and females get the same kind of harassment in malls and schools. (James, 1998: 166–167, 169–171).

Why do Youth Engage in Criminal Behaviour?

> If you were interested in creating a criminal you would have a pretty good chance if you took a young person from a seriously troubled home, put them into a series of foster and group homes, changed their primary worker on a regular basis, let them run away from "home" at an early age, allowed them to drop out of school and enabled them to develop a drug and/or alcohol addiction. Your chances would improve if, somewhere in their lonely and painful existence, they had been sexually, physically, or emotionally abused. If in those few instances that they sought for help, you would ensure that there were no accessible services, that the workers they encountered were rushed and overwhelmed by heavy caseloads, and that they would be seen first and foremost as trouble rather than troubled, is it surprising then that these young people would become perpetrators or victims of crime? (Youth voice, National Crime Prevention Council, 1997: 1)

There is a long list of reasons for criminal behaviour in general, and for youth offending in particular, ranging from psychopathology to personality traits to factors related to social class, family life, educational and occupational achievements, and interpersonal problems (Carrigan, 1998: 280–281; National Crime Prevention Council, 1996; also see Stevenson et al., 2000: 225; Shields, 1995).

It is true, and illustrated in the quote in the beginning of this chapter, that there are some teens and youth who have embraced the view of young people as violent and get satisfaction out of violent behaviour. On one hand, Peter Howard's statement could be read as typical bravado from someone on his way to becoming a hardened criminal. Howard's statement also reflects how important it is to feel powerful amidst larger forces that always seem to put you down.

For those individuals who don't have the capacity to keep on trying other pursuits, violence can be a way of temporarily reclaiming the strength they feel is rightfully theirs.

Aside from the small proportion of any violent individuals who are diagnosed with a psychopathology, such as a sociopathic personality, most violent behaviour can be explained by the negative social, economic, and political circumstances one is embedded in. Thus, parental physical and/or sexual abuse are major factors contributing to youth involvement in criminal activities (National Crime Prevention Council, 2000: 4). A typical juvenile offender's background consists of having been a repeat victim as a child (National Crime Prevention Council, 1996). Childhood abuse or witnessing of abuse lead to the kind of traumatization that can lead to violent and criminal behaviours (Jaffe and Baker, 1999: 24–25; Stevenson et al., 2000: 225).

A youth's involvement in a dysfunctional family setting with poor parenting and substance use/abuse is also acknowledged as a major factor (National Crime Prevention Council, 2000: 4; National Crime Prevention Council, 1996; also see Stevenson et al., 2000: 225). For example, a study by Correctional Service Canada (1999) found adult criminal activity linked to teenage substance abuse in three ways. First, teenage drug use led to higher conviction rates for property crimes than for non-drug users. Second, teenage regular alcohol use was linked to higher rates of conviction for all types of crimes than for irregular or non-users of alcohol. Third, there was a wider variety of crime convictions for those convicts who had high levels of both drug and alcohol use as teenagers.

Other major factors that related to youth crime are linked to poverty and inadequate living conditions (*Law Now,* 1996; also see Stevenson et al., 2000: 225). It must be noted that poverty itself does not cause delinquency. However, poverty may be associated with factors that can put youth at risk for delinquency, including family violence. Studies indicate that as income levels decrease, the rates of family dysfunction and parental depression increase. In addition, children's school readiness decreases, which can then lead to low achievement, school dropouts, and delinquency (Jaffe and Baker, 1999: 24–

25; Stevenson et al., 2000: 225; LeBlanc, Vallieres and McDuff, 1993). So, as child poverty increases, so does the chance of juvenile delinquency (Jaffe and Baker, 1999: 24–25; Stevenson et al., 2000: 225). Because of the link with poverty, youth in single-parent families are more likely to become delinquent (Stevenson et al., 2000: 226).

A 1997 report by the Canadian Centre for Justice Studies found that one of the key indicators for youth becoming involved in criminal activity is a lack of legitimate means of earning money (Stephenson, et al., 1997, 21). With a high unemployment rate added to other pressures such as growing up in a lone-parent family, lacking adequate social bonds, belonging to a gang, dropping out of school, physical and sexual abuse, television violence, and poor parenting (Stevenson et al., 2000), many youth end up participating in criminal activity. The strong link between economic factors and youth delinquent behaviour gains support from studies (reported in Chapter 3) that street youth who have a legitimate means of earning money (such as squeegeing) are less likely than other youth to engage in criminal behaviour, including drug use and theft.

More generally, an attachment or social bond to different institutions, including school and work, and peers, can help reduce criminal behaviour. If youth fall outside of the institutional support mechanisms, they are more likely to be attracted by alternative norms and values that contribute to a delinquent lifestyle. For instance, dropping out of school is linked to youth crime in that these youth are more likely to be unemployed and marginalized, and thus more likely to engage in anti-social activities (Stevenson et al., 2000: 225–226; also see Shields, 1995). With the worsening of the youth job market, there are concerns that marginalization will lead to more young people becoming alienated from society (Hartnagel, 1998: 436).

Peers, Gangs, and Delinquent Subcultures

As seen in previous chapters, peers provide youth with validation and social bonds if the adult world is seen to be of no help. Several studies demonstrate that peers are one of the strongest predictors of deviance and delinquence among youth. For example, Brownfield and Thompson (1991) report results consistent with social learning theory, in that peer involvement in delinquence was strongly and positively associated with self-reported delinquency. Further, Wong (1999) reports that association with delinquent peers was positively related to delinquency among Chinese-Canadian youth.

Some of the peer links can lead to an establishment of delinquent subcultures. In a study of 962 junior and senior high school students Paetch and Bertrand (1999) found that over half of the students admitted to having engaged in some form of delinquency in the past year. Interestingly, there was a link between being victimized and engaging in delinquent acts. Students who reported being victimized were also more likely to engage in delinquency, and vice versa.

Although individual acts or random group acts of delinquency exist, there is a quantitative leap toward youth gang activity. Gangs can be conceptualized as more permanent groupings with criminal intent, and as such they are relatively rare. Meanwhile, attention to youth gang activity by adults tends to be cyclical, and one of those increased interest cycles began in the 1990s (Smandych, 2001: 281–283; Gordon, 2001: 253–254).

Several Canadian studies from the 1990s point to a pattern of gang membership. Most are male with an average age of nineteen. The race and ethnic composition of gang membership depends on the geographic area one is looking at. For example, Gordon (1993, in Gordon, 2001: 250–251) reports that gangs in British Columbia tend to have mostly Caucasian membership, with the Asians being the next largest group. Very few members are East Indian, Hispanic, Aboriginal, or black. It has been noted that, although they tend to be small in numbers, street gangs in specific locations are "composed disproportionately of individuals from particular ethnic minorities" (Gordon, 2001: 259), and from among immigrant groups. For instance, in the Greater Vancouver Area Gang Study, visible minority members formed three quarters of all gang membership, with the Vietnamese as the largest single group. In comparison, in Toronto there is a disproportionate representation of Caribbean, Hispanic, and Portuguese populations in gangs (Gordon, 2001: 259–260).

These results reflect the links between ethnicity, immigration status, and socioeconomic status in the formation of street gangs. When these combine with limited language competency and a lack of marketable skills to produce a variety of economic vulnerabilities, including poverty, family disintegration, a lack of supportive community networks, and the lack of rewarding employment" (Gordon, 2001: 260), the end result is that street gangs are formed that seek illegal ways for dealing with these problems.

Skinheads and Hate Groups

One of the youth delinquent subgroups that has been subjected to much study, particularly by journalists, special-interest groups, or law enforcement agencies, are skinheads. These pseudo-scientific accounts depict skinheads variously as neo-Nazis, who are likened to terrorists, and misunderstood youth, who are alienated from a society which has rejected them. Some of these explorations point to the wide variety of skinhead groups and their diverse politics and the variety of backgrounds these youth come from (Khanna, 1999; Baron, 1997), ranging from stable middle-class homes to dysfunctional and abusive family environments. In recent academic studies, a similar trend prevails. Added to this, there is a more recent trend to examine skinheads as disaffected working-class youth. This approach is criticized for its lack of attention to the negative features of skinhead culture, including crime and violence (Baron, 1997).

There are an estimated 1,000 skinheads in Canada (Khanna, 1999: 18). In a rare Canadian ethnographic study, Baron (1997) interviewed a group of fourteen homeless Edmonton male skinheads, aged 15–22. They came from mixed social class backgrounds, but only three were from intact families. This supports findings of other studies suggesting conflict and tensions leading to a parental break-up are linked to some youths becoming "vulnerable to the influence of delinquent peers." The youths in this study had been subject to physical or sexual victimization in their families, mostly by their male guardians. These experiences left them filled with hatred and wanting revenge on their parents. The school environment, with its authority structure and requirements for order, was equally oppressive, and they got into serious problems due to nonconformist and violent behaviour. The average education level was grade nine, and only one member of the group interviewed had his high school diploma. Consequently, their connection to the labour market was tenuous, and all were unemployed at the time of the study. Without means to support themselves, they ended up on the streets where their anger and aggressions are evident in a large number of one-on-one fights resulting in serious injuries. Violence became a subculture with a code of retributive justice, where they expected to settle the score if harmed by another, or come to the aid of a comrade in a fight to show loyalty to the group. Robbery and drugs are also part of the life of skinheads. Most of the male youth interviewed were involved in drug trafficking, and all were heavy users of drugs and alcohol.

One of the major concerns about skinhead groups has to do with neo-Nazi political views. In this particular study, the youth were not involved in, nor did they display, "a great deal of racially motivated behaviour." Most of the youth reported no political views or agenda, but there were six extreme racists among them who were willing to use violence to achieve political change. Although there is a small core group compelled toward the neo-Nazi skinhead image, Baron (1997) does not believe this group is cohesive enough to be attracted to right-wing extremist organizations. Instead, they are "street crime" skinheads, more interested in crime and violence than organized political activity.

Nevertheless, there is increasing concern over the potential involvement of youth in racist and anti-Semitic hate groups. According to Khanna (1999: ii-6), the little research done so far indicates that organized hate groups recruit youth in schools and universities and through the Internet. There are at least thirty-two web sites that directly target children and youth. Though perpetrators of hateful acts against minorities come from diverse and varied backgrounds, the majority are males in their twenties. Khanna (1999: ii) notes that the prime target groups for these recruiters are "lonely, marginalized youth seeking a sense of identity, or angry young people who are seeking a solution to the problems they are facing."

Interestingly, in this case as well as in other cases of crime, youth tend to be viewed as more likely perpetrators than victims of hate crime. We discussed earlier (Chapter 2) that lesbian and gay youth tend to be subjected to harassment and violence in schools and in communities. However, hate crimes tend to be one of the most underreported, and youth are particularly unlikely to turn to the police in these cases. Youth tend not to report hate crimes to the police because they are uncertain about the degree of seriousness that warrants reporting, and they resist getting involved in the justice system. In schools, youth feel that they have little support and that they get blamed even before the perpetrator does. Students don't feel that adults take malicious incidents seriously enough. Instead, adults tend to minimize the acts and their consequences as nuisances or "childish pranks" that do not warrant serious punishment. Students also report that their peer group and the fear of potential retaliation lead them to deal with the incidents themselves rather than report them to adult authorities. Meanwhile, they suffer serious consequences to their "self-esteem, school performance, and sense of safety and security" (Khanna, 1999: 21–27).

Moral Panics, the Police, and Juvenile Law

Despite evidence to the contrary, most people seem to "know" that there is a lot of youth crime, particularly the violent kind, and that we need to do something about it because the current laws are "too lenient." In fact, studies show that the public's understanding of youth crime and justice systems is inaccurate and that most people's opinions are based on misinformation and sensationalism from the media. Public views tend to correlate youth crime with violent crime, contrary to what crime statistics actually tell us (Sprott, 1996; Jaffe and Baker, 1999: 22–23). For example, Sprott (1996: 271) found that while "most (ninety-four percent) of the stories about youth crime appearing in a sample of Toronto newspapers involved cases of violence," youth court statistics indicated "that fewer than a quarter of youth cases in Ontario involved violence." These widely prevalent "moral panics" over crime create an image of youth as out of control and feed negative stereotypes of bad youth (Schissel, 1997, in Bell, 1999: 31).

An important feature of the Canadian youth crime scene is that while the youth crime rate itself has remained relatively stable, there has been a dramatic increase in the youth incarceration rate, which is significantly higher than for adults (Jaffe and Baker, 1999: 23). Further, in comparison with adults (see Table 7.5), average youth custody sentences are twenty-two percent longer, and youth, unlike adults, are not eligible for parole after one third of their sentence (*Law Now*, 1996: 12).

The trend in sentencing seems to contradict the spirit of the Young Offenders Act. To put it briefly (Cuddington, 1995):

> The Young Offenders Act is based on the premise that youths should be held responsible for their illegal actions, but that young people have special needs as they develop and mature. Therefore, the Act creates a youth justice system *separate* from the adult system (emphasis in original).

Since being enacted in 1982, and in response to the public perception that it was too lenient, the federal Young Offenders Act (YOA) has been amended three times: in 1986, 1992, and 1995. The 1992 amendment lengthened the maximum sentence for murder from three to five years and eased the transfer from juvenile to adult court. The 1995 amendment extended the sentence for first degree murder to ten years and made it the defense attorney's responsibility to argue grounds for keeping sixteen- and seventeen-year-old offenders in the juvenile justice system rather than have them transferred to adult court. The toughening of the YOA means that incarceration is increasingly seen as the best solution to

**Table 7.5. Custody length for adult and
youth offenders, Canada 1998/99**

		Single charge cases	
		1 month or less	Greater than 1 month
Theft Under $5000	Adult	62	38
	Youth	42	58
Failure to Appear	Adult	78	22
	Youth	48	52
Minor Assault	Adult	57	43
	Youth	35	65
Break and Enter	Adult	20	80
	Youth	17	83
Property Damage/Mischief	Adult	71	29
	Youth	37	63
Possession (CDSA)	Adult	80	20
	Youth	55	45
Assault Weapon/Bodily Harm	Adult	37	63
	Youth	28	72
Possession of Stolen Property	Adult	46	54
	Youth	26	74
Robbery	Adult	14	86
	Youth	19	81

Source: Adult Criminal Court Survey, Youth Court Survey, Canadian
Centre for Justice Statistics, Statistics Canada (from Juristat
Catalogue no. 85-002, Vol. 20, No.7 p. 11.)

youth crime, rather than custodial sentences (Jaffe and Baker,
1999: 23).

Criticism of the "tough line" or "boot camp" approach to
young offenders is simply that this approach focuses on
individual-level solutions rather than linking juvenile
offending to the significant structural problems outlined above.
Overall criticism is summarized as follows (Jaffe and Baker,
1999: 23):

...the focus of legislative solutions has been misguided and has placed the emphasis on increasing the severity of consequences to crime rather than solutions aimed at preventing the development of criminal behaviour and changing persistent offending patterns.

The recently proposed Bill C-68 would repeal the YOA and replace it with the Youth Criminal Justice Act, aimed at both steering youth away from the juvenile justice system and more serious punishments for youth convicted of serious crimes, or for repeat offenders (Pate, 1999: 42).

This is already provided under the YOA. There were increased arrests and charges of youth, as a result of Criminal Code changes that hardened the approach of police and courts toward young offenders (Bell, 1999: 28–29). While the rates of police charging youth increased by twenty-one percent after the introduction of the Young Offenders Act (YOA) in 1984, the numbers of crimes committed remained the same (*Law Now*, 1996).

According to Carrington (1999), there was a seven percent increase in police-reported youth crime from the 1980s to the 1990s. At the same time, there was a twenty-seven percent jump in the rate of young persons charged by police, a "drop in the use of police discretion." In other words, the YOA seems to have led to changes in police practices in four provinces and one territory, because while there was no jump in the proportions of youth apprehended, there was a jump in the numbers charged. Carrington (1999: 25) concludes that "there is no basis in fact for public concern about increased levels of youth crime or the supposed failure of the YOA to control youth crime."

In these times of government cost-cutting, we should also note that youth incarceration is a costly alternative. For example, it costs on average $237 per day to keep a young offender in secure custody in Ontario. Open custody (halfway houses and other supervised facilities) cost on average $167 per day. Meanwhile, cost of community supervision is approximately one sixth of this cost (*Law Now*, 1996: 12).

Community supervision falls under alternative measures under the Young Offenders Act (1985) for offenders 12–17 years of age who would otherwise proceed to court. Instead, they are dealt with through non-judicial community-based alternatives. There were 33,000 of these cases in 1997/98 across Canada, excluding British Columbia. Participation rates are highest in the Prairies and lowest in Ontario. Most (seventy percent) participants have been charged with property-related offences, the majority of these being theft under $5,000. Only eight percent were charged with violent offences. Cases of common assault, mischief, other property offences (arson, possession of stolen goods), and other Criminal Code offences (such as disturbing the peace) accounted for seven percent each of the crimes. Community service is the most likely (twenty-two percent) alternative measure, like helping out in a non-profit community agency for a specified number of hours. Other measures include apologizing to the victim either personally or in writing (eighteen percent). Another category of measures (thirteen percent) involves financial compensation to the victim, educational sessions, and essays or presentations related to the offence. The least frequently used measures were personal service (two percent) and counselling (one percent) (Canadian Centre for Justice Statistics, 1997/98).

The most likely offenders in these programs are males aged fifteen years or older. While only one fifth of youth charged and brought to court are female, they accounted for thirty-six percent of youth in alternative measures. Females in the justice system tend to be younger on average than the males. Aboriginal youth who form four percent of the youth population are likewise overrepresented in the programs at thirteen percent of all participants. The percentages are even higher in provinces such as Saskatchewan, where Aboriginal youth form over one third of the alternative measures cases, although they represent fifteen percent of the province's youth population (Canadian Centre for Justice Statistics, 1997/98).

Alternative measures make a lot of sense, particularly because there is no evidence of a deterrent effect on youth crime by long sentences. *Law Now* (1996: 12) points out that:

> there is no evidence that longer sentences deter young offenders from future crime. There is growing evidence,

however, that the type of social environment a young offender returns to will influence the likelihood of his or her returning to crime. Placing a young offender in an inappropriate (i.e., adult) corrections environment will likely reduce his or her likelihood of developing a normal life.

The consequences of the general pressure toward incarceration rather than rehabilitation are serious for young people. Echoing the influential arguments of Schlissel (1997) regarding moral panics over youth crime, Pate (1999: 40) notes that:

> Rather than adopt a "zero violence" approach, "zero tolerance" policies are resulting in ever-increasing numbers of disenfranchised youth being jettisoned out of schools and communities, and usually through, rather than into, a thinning social safety net. Rather than nurturing our youth, we are increasingly scapegoating and disposing of them as though they were expendable human refuse.

Conclusions

There are distinct patterns in relation to youth and criminal or violent behaviour. First, youth are generally more likely to be victims than perpetrators of violence. Second, youth crime is generally decreasing, and, third, it is less likely to be of violent nature than adult crime. Fourth, young women continue to account for a fraction of violent crime, despite media reports to the contrary. Fifth, as exemplified in the cases of Aboriginal and black youth, there is widespread age-specific racism in the legal system, including police and the courts. And finally, only a small minority of youth engage in criminal or violent gang activity. Although there is a need to take these instances seriously, we also need to pay attention to youth as victims of hate crime, not only as perpetrators.

We also need to pay more attention to the structural conditions that marginalize youth, in order to find proper solutions that do not rely solely on a boot camp mentality toward young offenders. Moral panics over youth crime and violence manifest the generally negative experiences of youth in the new millennium. Fears are well founded in that the more poverty and discrimination Canadians tolerate, the more likely it is that increasing numbers of youth will become victims of family violence, school estrangement, poor job prospects, and general community disintegration.

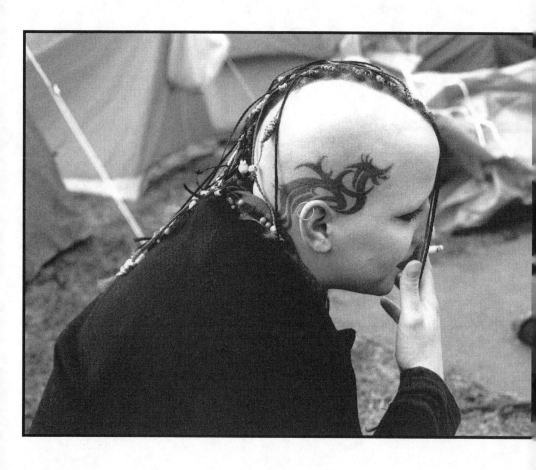

8 | Conclusions

[W]e need a revolution in the way we think about youth and
coming of age. (Côté and Allahar, 1994: 160)

So You say We Need a Revolution?

In western history, the second half of the twentieth century
can be identified as a period in which adolescents and youth
have been subjected to particular attention by the public,
academics, politicians, and policy-makers alike. Having
emerged from the ferment of the first few decades of that
century, adolescents and youth were identified as a population
in crisis. In 1968, the first comprehensive worldwide report
on youth was presented to the UNESCO General Conference.
Its concerns related to the political mobilization of youth in
North America and Western Europe. This large-scale collective
activism of the baby boom cohort (those born 1946–1959) in
western society was relatively short-lived. Soon enough, it was
replaced by the anxiety-ridden 1970s and 1980s and a focus
on young people's prospects for survival in school, work, and
community (UNESCO, 1981: 13–20). These issues continue to
preoccupy studies of subsequent cohorts of youth, identified
as "Generation-X" (or the "echo" generation, born between
1960–1966), the "baby-bust" (born 1967–1979), and most

recently, "Generation-Y" (or "echo boomers," born between 1980–1995) (Bourette, 1999).

Although issues related to youth have been highlighted in Canada throughout the twentieth century (e.g. Ambrose, 1991), there has been a particularly active period of government attention from the 1980s onwards (Special Senate Committee on Youth, 1986; Marquardt, 1998: 4; Human Resources Development Canada, 1999a). Currently, the National Longitudinal Survey on Children and Youth is attempting to address the issues and problems in the lives of the youngest of the population. A similar increase in attention to the condition of young people has been observed among academics. For example, Gfellener and Hundleby (1990: 133) found in a sample of twelve relevant journals from 1980 to 1987, "a fifty percent increase in publications on adolescents by Canadian authors."

This recent attention is well deserved, considering the multiple problem areas outlined in this book that indicate that the state of crisis among youth continues and has possibly deepened. Some of the major areas under scrutiny and selected policy options have been identified in the preceding chapters. In this final chapter, I will both summarize the issues and policies arising from the preceding pages and put them in the general context of Canadian social forces.

The main conclusion to be drawn from the range of adversity facing youth today is that most of their problems have deep roots in general inequities prevailing in society, based on social class, gender, race, and ethnicity. Notably, young age itself is a basis of inequality linked with these other forms, and specifically with the main features of living under capitalism. Youth is a liability in societies where one's livelihood depends on the amount of wages earned. Youth are made to feel their state of dependency on others. The fates of adolescents and youth, more so than those of most adults in working-age groups, are tied to the level of success of those who they live with. Thus, families are the primary setting that can either provide youth with opportunities or seriously hinder their chances. At the same time, the prolonged education they are subjected to prevents them from participating in the labour force fully. However, there is a high likelihood that young people will work in jobs where their education is not utilized. Because of the links between social class, gender, race, and ethnicity, the problems of youth multiply as the number of relatively powerless categories they belong to are added. Thus, whether through their families or on their own and among their peers, young people's lives are governed both by social institutions in which their position is that of powerlessness and marginalization.

Family Life

Most adolescents and youth live in families where their emotional and material needs are met. However, there is a significant proportion whose chances of making it in the world are seriously hampered by a multitude of problems, some of which are a reflection of the wider social forces in which families are embedded. Social class differences are manifested most starkly in the high proportion of families who live in poverty. Economic conditions of families are also indicative of overlapping of social class with gender, ethnic, and racial inequality, as it is more likely to find female-headed and minority families among those living in economically stressed circumstances. Such inequities have dire consequences for children and youth who get a precarious start to life in a society where those with material and cultural capital fare better in competition. At particular risk are Aboriginal populations, where centuries of colonialism have created a crisis situation. Further, the phenomenon of young people leaving home later, or returning home to reside with their parents as young adults, is both a sign of worsening economic conditions and a wake-up call to policy makers to take steps toward helping youth who face particular risks in getting established.

Inside families, young people are faced with the misuse of parental power. This power is rooted in the economic capabilities of adults over youth and the presumed superiority of knowledge and experience based on age. Although most people would acknowledge that youth need guidance, in some families the power parents hold over their children can be exhibited in aggressive and destructive ways. Youth are subjected to a range of abusive acts and neglect in their families. Consequently, their mental health suffers, and they risk becoming castaway or throwaway kids on the streets, involved in a precarious life that offers little hope.

As discussed in Chapter 4, what makes the plight of young people at risk even worse is that young people put in the care of the state sometimes find a replication of the problems and abuse experienced in their families. Youth in state care also find it difficult to make a transition to normal life (Martin, 1996). This shows one of the fundamental flaws of programs that target specific populations. When a segment of the population is subjected to a program, it is assumed to be this population (in this case, traumatized youth) that is need of treatment, while the symptoms (systemic inequalities that create the problems in the first place) are ignored. A more systematic approach is needed, one that focuses on creating better opportunities for all families. This includes wide-ranging policies, including income equalization through taxation and social policies, that help all segments of the population achieve an acceptable standard of living for an advanced and affluent industrial society.

Education and Employment

The education system likewise reflects systemic barriers to those in minority positions. There is ongoing concern over high dropout rates. Research tells us that the best predictors of dropping out are being from a lower socio-economic status, usually accompanied by visible minority status, or being female. Getting a post-secondary degree is becoming more difficult, with rising tuition and debt loads of post-secondary students. Students without means are solving this problem by holding a job to finance their education or dropping to part-time studies. It is left to the individual students to amass debt while funding cuts to post-secondary education lead to staggering increases in tuition, forcing students into serious debt even before they get a start in their working careers (Marquardt, 1998: 116).

Youth in general have higher unemployment rates than adult Canadians. Although these trends are sometimes blamed on the sizes of the different cohorts of youth in competition over jobs, most of the blame lies in the higher sensitivity of youth labour markets to economic fluctuations. Youth tend to work in the service sector, where they provide a flexible pool of casual labourers who can be pulled in and pushed out of work, depending on the vagaries of the market. The high incidence of casual, particularly part-time, work among youth is a sign of their expendability and precarious position.

These trends in the youth labour market are actively supported and endorsed by the Canadian government. Official policies are founded on a two-prong approach which, on the one hand, aims at creating good jobs with corresponding quality control mechanisms in education. Transitions to work are facilitated by programs that combine schooling with workplace experience. The problem is that, overall, the opportunities given to students come at a cost of low wages, while short-term employment does not necessarily result in permanent jobs. On the other hand, there is an aim to expand the low-wage work sector. The problem with this element of Canadian employment policy is that the enticements offered to employers serve to deteriorate both the wages and the social safety net of the work force, as there is pressure to lower the minimum wage and cut employers' UI premiums and pension plan contributions.

Aside from these general difficulties, the fates of youth also depend on the social category they represent. Inside the education system itself, there is an institutionalization of inequalities, reflected in the "hidden curriculum," which provides selected minority groups, particularly blacks, Aboriginal and immigrant youth, and women, with a qualitatively different experience from the mainstream. Youth from disadvantaged backgrounds continue to fall between the cracks and are caught in an intergenerational cycle of higher chances of dropping out of education with consequent low-wage employment or unemployment and attendant poverty. Of particular concern lately are youth from single-parent families, who are much more likely to live in poverty than their counterparts in two-income families.

The gender segregation in education is mirrored in the labour force experience of young people. Young women and men continue to be streamed to different areas of work, with an associated wage gap. Education and work environments alike reflect male domination in society in general, as particularly young women are subjected to sexual harassment. Meanwhile, not enough has been done to assist either female or minority youth in their educational or employment experiences.

Young People's Relationships

Being a young parent has not always been problematic, but in Canada we are creating circumstances in which it is impossible for young women to raise children without state assistance. These women get stigmatized while they are in a difficult situation where they cannot make enough money from wages, are forced into dependency on the state, and the fathers of the children are absent and not held accountable for their actions.

In addition to illustrating patriarchal oppression of young women, both by the individual men they are involved with, and society at large, the example of teenage pregnancy also illustrates how economically difficult it is for young couples to create a family unit. This is also seen in the increasing numbers of young people who choose to either delay marriage or live common-law. Young people are living in a semi-independent state for a longer time, extending their education and delaying economic sustainability, putting their personal lives on hold. Thus, supporting a family is difficult for all youth and may partly explain, though not excuse, the rate at which young males neglect their responsibilities toward their dependents. Couple relationships generally mirror the stresses they are subject to in a capitalist and patriarchal society. These overlapping power relationships manifest themselves in the lives of young couples in the unequal division of household labour, traditional expectations that stress women's role in adjusting their wage work patterns to fit family and child care needs, and in an extreme form in the abuse of females by their male partners.

Thus, forming relationships grounded on sexuality and romance is more complicated than even a couple of decades ago. Even with an increased acceptance of homosexuality and bisexuality, youth who come out still face serious problems, including abuse from their families and friends alike. While the sexuality of young people is more accepted today, it poses its own problems. In addition to teenage pregnancy, there is fear over sexually transmitted diseases, especially AIDS. Both issues raise concerns over the heightened risk of specific youth populations. As discussed in Chapter 4, information and services are more readily available in more affluent areas, while those in the less well-to-do areas fare a lot worse, with the noted overlap with social class and minority group status.

Criminalizing Youth

Gender and social class distinctions are manifested in separate youth cultures among males and females of different social echelons. Additionally, there are distinct youth cultures based on race or ethnicity. What unites all of youth is the extensive invasion of media and advertising where youth create their own identity and culture. Mass media perpetuate divisions among youth that follow different trends, while creating an atmosphere of relentless consumerism. This is seen in the countless youth fads in the twentieth century, and also in the newest twenty-first century youth trend: raves. Raves began as an authentic youth phenomenon but have been gradually targeted for consumerism, including clothes, CDs, and other goods. In their ugliest manifestation, business interests invade young people's lives in the form of a range of drugs, including tobacco, alcohol, and other state-altering substances. Ironically, drug use among youth is turned against them. Youth are targeted for state control mechanisms and policing, instead of concentrating effort on catching criminals who make the destruction of youthful bodies and minds their business.

Similar patterns of criminalizing youth are seen in other areas. Some youth are pushed to the fringes of society and can be found in the informal work sector, such as squeegeeing. This legitimate attempt to make a living without engaging in crime has been hampered by legislation banning this type of activity, with the anticipated result that more youth will become involved in other illegal activities. That this law-and-order or boot-camp approach is not working is also seen in the juvenile justice system where harsher measures push young people further and further from any chance of establishing a normal life, and instead push them to the fringes of society.

The tendency to blame youthful victims and create moral panic over their behaviour is also noticeable in the areas of youth crime and violence. Although youth are more likely to be victims than perpetrators of violence, media images of youth run amok persist, and politicians are jumping on the bandwagon of boot camps and other increasingly harsh tactics to deal with a crisis that has little bearing in reality. Here, too, social class, gender, ethnic, and racial inequalities persist, with images of increased violence and gang behaviour among young women and black youth.

What proponents of law and order measures ignore are the true causes of youth criminal and violent behaviour: poverty and marginalization, with associated ill effects on family life. Thus, tougher measures further alienate young people already dissociated from social bonds that might help engage them in more constructive ways. In the face of their marginalized position, one of the most dangerous manifestations of youth alienation is the existence of hate groups. The misdirected hate of young people against other more powerless groups in society is understandable in the light of a general ambience of competition in the capitalist economy. Youth are more likely to adopt a "zero-sum" concept of distribution of social goods, in which anything that others get is something taken away from "me" or "us." Media fuel this fire with misrepresentations of minority groups and equity programs. No wonder then that some youth are lashing out.

However, youth are also finding ways of resisting these trends. Their interest in politics is taking a different form from their parents or other adults, and it is understandable that they would have inherent suspicion toward adult-led organizations and institutions. Instead, they opt for types of resistance that involve their peers. As indicated in the previous chapters, examples of these can be found in schools, workplaces, communities, and larger society. This does not mean that all types of youth group activity can be seen as protest, but that more attention needs to be paid to groups and events organized by and led by young people themselves.

What is the Real Problem and What Can be Done About it?

The main trends in Canadian policy have been captured under the labels of liberal, and most recently, neo-liberal approaches to the welfare state (Marquardt, 1998: 110–111). Generally speaking, what holds up this type of system is the view that individuals and their families, instead of the state, are ultimately responsible for their well-being. The welfare state is only seen as a final resort, in cases where there are individual failures or a lack of familial supports (Pupo, 1994: 128; Chappell, 1997: 10–13). These principles have become more entrenched from the 1990s onward, an era that is variously called neo-conservative or neo-liberal (Pulkingham and Ternowetsky, 1996).

This philosophy contains two main premises. First, it is assumed that families will look after their adolescents and youth, that the family is a private institution, and that state policies should not apply to it. In reality, state has a great deal to do with families, mainly because families are not always in a position to look after their members, and it is left to the state to deal with the costs. Due to the widening gap between haves and have-nots, there are more young people in need of assistance, and it is all the more convenient for the state to make families or the private sector responsible for costs (Mitchell and Gee, 1996: 68–69; Brodie, 1996: 22–23).

The second major assumption embedded in the politics from teh 1990s onward is the idea that state responses are only required whenever there is a specific problem. Such a problem-centred approach means that policies related to youth have been developed in a piecemeal fashion with separate policies that relate to, for example, youth in education, employment, the justice system, and vague family policies that apply to young people in general (see Chappell, 1997: 233–258).

A major dilemma in social policy related to youth is the targeting of specific groups as recipients of specialized services. For example, youth policies and programs typically target teen mothers, Aboriginal youth, black youth, or young criminals. Group-specific measures are meant to respond to a specific need and are arguably necessary to bring much required help to segments in a crisis situation.

However, the end result of these programs is the extensive stigmatization of the populations in question (Chappell, 1997: 13). Through ideologically laden media coverage, the public gets an impression that the problems are not the result of a lack of help, but with the specific populations themselves. Negative stereotypes prevail: teenage mothers are amoral girls from poverty-stricken and ignorant families, black youth are naturally prone to crime, Aboriginal youth are lazy kids who cannot handle their alcohol, and street youth are thugs who need to be sent to boot camps. However, targeting these groups is likely to fail because they remain isolated from the rest of the community, while specialized programs offer little in the form of solutions to a bad situation. Thus, we have high rates of recidivism among incarcerated juvenile offenders, and poverty-stricken teenage mothers or street youth, or Aboriginal youth who are unable to break away from the cycle of poverty.

Ineffectiveness of existing policy measures alone should be a warning sign to decision-makers that things are simply not working. Ironically, in these times when politicians and the public are concerned with fiscal accountability, the failure of the numerous targeted programs has produced waste countable in billions of dollars. Problems continue and the targeted groups continue to be vilified for their lack of progress.

Targeting obscures the real source of the problems. When a society is fundamentally ruled by inequalities, we need to systematically attack those inequalities in order for any relief policy to be effective.

An Integrated Life-Course Approach to Policies Related to Youth

There are a growing number of voices that call for a more integrated approach to social policy. One such proposal is for programs related to youth to take a life-course perspective, including both youth and adult service delivery systems that must be coordinated so consensus can be reached across programs and their goals. This is important because, first, what happens earlier in a person's life influences the form their later lives will take. Second, the same structural limitations based on social class, gender, race, ethnicity, sexual orientation, ability, and rural/urban differences exert their influence across an individual's life span (Hiebert and Thomlison, 1996: 56–57; Copeland, Armitage, and Rutman, 1996: 272–273; McAlpine, Grindstaff, and Sorenson, 1996: 311).

An integrated approach to youth proposes important links between generations and between different segments of society. Whereas most approaches put emphasis on the notions of independence and self-support based on salaried employment, Galaway and Hudson (1996: xix) ask a crucially important question:

> ...isn't adulthood more than [independence]? Are we really seeking independence or is interdependence a more appropriate concept? Interdependence would imply the ability to function in a community — both to receive benefits and to contribute to the well-being of others.

Interdependence rather than dependence as a guiding principle of policy formation would consider youth simultaneously in the "roles of income earner, parent, and home manager," as well as take responsibility over the general well-being of communities and neighbourhoods (Galaway and Hudson, 1996: xix; see also McDaniel, 1997). In other words, to succeed youth need to be better integrated in all aspects of society, rather than isolated from adult institutions, so their skills and capabilities are emphasized, and they can take a measure of control over their own lives.

A more cohesive approach is evident in some specific policies that would integrate juvenile offenders into their communities and make them accountable and responsible to their neighbours for their actions. It is more integrative than those that emphasize long-term isolation in juvenile detention centres, where they have little chance of future adjustment. It would also support and strengthen those policies that aid the transition from school to work. Programs in this area require a system of checks and balances to ensure that youth are not exploited while they are combining schooling with a job.

The most difficult aspect of life-course programs is working with marginalized youth populations. Special school-based, work-based, or community-based programs will continue to fail unless there is more of an effort to address the real needs of young people and adopt their issues into the mainstream, rather than expect an unrealistc uniformity of youth needs, dictated by a privileged adult population. This is a larger project, which requires coordination between generations, between families, communities, and different levels of government. Ultimately, what we are talking about are general and universal programs to make it possible for all members of society to have equitable access to different areas of social life.

To be successful, policies must account for the wide range of transitions that youth make on their way to adulthood, related to education, employment, families, and relationships with their peers. Looker and Lowe (1996: 139) argue that the definition of success must be broadened to help young people understand that fulfilment is not solely linked to economic status and participation in the full-time labour force. There are linkages between the different transitions to adulthood, transitions between school and work, out of the parental home, to post-secondary institutions, and those involving marriage and parenting. A program designed to deal with one transition is unlikely to be effective if it ignores the relevance of other transitions. Family and community ties are important to the transitions of young people. Government programs should help to nurture support and resources available from families and community and provide active backup in communities where naturally occurring supports are inadequate. Efforts should be made to ensure that programs are not concentrated solely in urban centres, ignoring the needs of youth in rural and remote areas. It is important for youth to feel that they belong and are in control of their lives; intervention programs should build on the skills that young people have, rather than focusing on their academic, social, physical, or psychological inadequacies.

Sources

Adams, Mary Louise. 1997. *The Trouble with Normal: Postwar Youth and the Making of Heterosexuality*. Toronto: University of Toronto Press.

Addelson, Kathryn Pyne. 1999. How Should We Live? Some Reflections on Procreation. In *Teen Pregnancy and Parenting: Social and Ethical Issues*. James Wong and David Checkland eds. Toronto: University of Toronto Press.

African Heritage Educators' Network and the Ontario Women's Directorate. 1996. *Succeeding Young Sisters: A Guide to the Development of After-School Encouragement and Mentoring Programs for Young Black Women*. Toronto: African Educator's Network and the Ontario Women's Directorate.

Akers, J., Jones, R. and D. Coyl. 1998. Adolescent Friendships Pairs: Similarities in identity development, behaviors, attitudes, and intentions. *Journal of Adolescent Research* 13 (2): 175–195.

Allahar, Anton L. and James E. Côté. 1998. *Richer & Poorer: The Structure of Inequality in Canada*. Toronto: Lorimer.

Ambert, Anne-Marie. 1992. *The Effect of Children on Parents*. Binghamton, NY: The Haworth Press.

Ambert, Anne-Marie. 1997. *Parents, Children and Adolescents: Interactive Relationships and Development in Context*. Binghamton, N.Y.:The Haworth Press.

Ambrose, Linda M. 1991. Collecting Youth Opinion: The Research of the Canadian Youth Commission, 1943–1945. In *Dimensions of Childhood: Essays on the History of Children and Youth in Canada*, Russell Smandych, Gordon Dodds and Alvin Esau eds. University of Manitoba: Legal Research Institute of the University of Manitoba.

Anderson, Stephen A. and Ronald M. Sabatelli. 1999. *Family Interaction: A Multigenerational Developmental Perspective.* 2nd edition. Toronto: Allyn & Bacon.

Anisef, Paul. 1994. *Learning and Sociological Profiles of Canadian High School Students.* Lewiston/Queenston/ Lampeter: The Edwin Mellen Press.

Anisef, Paul and Kenise Murphy Kilbride. 2000. *The Needs of Newcomer Youth and the Emerging "Best Practices" to Meet Those Needs.* Toronto: Joint Centre of Excellence for Research on Immigration and Settlement.

Anisef, Paul, Gottfried Paasche and Anton H. Turrittin. 1980. *Is the Die Cast? Educational Achievements and Work Destinations of Ontario Youth: A six-year follow-up of the Critical juncture High School Students.* Toronto: Ministry of Colleges and Universities, Ontario.

Archambault, Richard and Louis Grignon. 1999. Decline in Youth Participation in Canada in the 1990s: Structural or Cyclical? *Canadian Business Economics* 7 (2): 71–87.

Arruda, Antonio Filomena. 1993. Expanding the View: Growing up in Portuguese-Canadian Families, 1962–1980. *Canadian Ethnic Studies* 25 (3): 8–25.

Association of Canadian Community Colleges. 1996. *Youth Task Force.* April. http//:199.71.68.106/english/advocacy/ gov_relations/youth.htm

Axelrod, Paul and John G. Reid. 1987. *Youth, University and Canadian Society: Essays in the Social History of Higher Education.* Kingston: McGill-Queen's University Press.

Bailey, Sue. 1999. Graduates Under Increasing Pressure to Pay Back Soaring Student Loans. *The Globe and Mail*, November 8: A7.

Baker, Maureen. 1989. *Families in Canadian Society: An Introduction.* Toronto: McGraw-Hill Ryerson Limited.

Baker, Maureen. 1996a. Introduction to Family Studies: Cultural Variations and Family Trends. In *Families: Changing Trends in Canada.* Third Edition, Maureen Baker ed. Toronto: McGraw-Hill Ryerson Limited.

Baker, Maureen. 1996b. The Future of Family Life. In *Families: Changing Trends in Canada.* Third Edition, Maureen Baker ed. Toronto: McGraw-Hill Ryerson Limited.

Baker, Maureen and Janet Dryden. 1993. *Families in Canadian Society.* Second Edition. Toronto: McGraw-Hill Ryerson Limited.

Barber, John. 1999. Innu People Devastated by Latest Teen Suicide. *The Globe and Mail*, November 11: A9.

Baron, Stephen W. 1997. Canadian Male Street Skinheads: Street Gang or Street Terrorist? *The Canadian Review of Sociology and Anthropology*, 34 (1): 125–154.

Baron, Stephen W. 1999. Street Youths and Substance Abuse: The Role of Background, Street Lifestyle, and Economic Factors. *Youth & Society* 31 (1): 3–26.

Beaumont, Sherry L. 1996. Adolescent Girls' Perceptions of Conversations with Mothers and Friends. *Journal of Adolescent Research* 11 (3): 325–340.

Bell, Sandra J. 1999. *Young Offenders and Juvenile Justice a Century After the Fact.* Toronto: International Thomson Publishing Company.

Belle, Marilyn and Kevin McQuillan. 2000. Births Outside Marriage: A Growing Alternative. *Canadian Social Trends. Vol. 3.* Toronto: Thompson Educational Publishing, Inc.

Belyea, Susan and Karen Dubinsky. 1994. "Don't Judge us too Quickly": Writing About Teenage Girls and Sex. In *Sex in Schools. Canadian Education & Sexual Regulation,* Susan Prentice ed. Toronto: Our Schools/Ourselves.

Bethune, Brian. 2000. Inquiry Into The Agony of Ecstasy. *Maclean's* 113 (17): 41.

Bibby, Reginald W. 2001. *Canada's Teens: Today, Yesterday, and Tomorrow.* Toronto: Stoddart.

Blanchflower, D. and R. Freeman. 1998. Why youth unemployment will be hard to reduce. *Policy Options Politiques* 3, April: 3–7.

Bloomfield, Elizabeth and G.T. Bloomfield. 1991. *Canadian Women in Workshops, Mills, and Factories: The Evidence of the 1871 Census Manuscripts.* University of Guelph: Department of Geography.

Bolter, Andrew. 1999. Squeegee Law Overlooks Real Problem. *The London Free Press* December 2: A13.

Bourette, Susan. 1999. Lowering the Boom on GenX — Again. *The Globe and Mail* January 25: A1, A19.

Boyd, Monica and Doug Norris. 2000. The Crowded Nest: Young Adults at Home. *Canadian Social Trends. Vol. 3.* Toronto: Thompson Educational Publishing, Inc.

Bradbury, Bettina. 1993. Women and the History of Their Work in Canada: Some Recent Books. *Journal of Canadian Studies/ Revue d'etudes canadiennes* 28 (3): 159–178.

Bradbury, Bettina. 1996. The Social and Economic Origins of Contemporary Families. In *Families: Changing Trends in Canada.* Third Edition, Maureen Baker ed. Toronto: McGraw-Hill Ryerson Limited.

Brake, Michael. 1985. *Comparative Youth Culture: The Sociology of Youth Cultures and Youth Subcultures in America, Britain and Canada.* London, U.K.: Routledge & Kegan.

Brearton, Steve. 1999. Youth Hostile. *Toronto Life* 33 (1): 2–3

Brodie, Janine. 1996. Canadian Women, Changing State Forms, and Public Policy. In *Women and Canadian Public Policy,* Janine Brodie ed. Toronto: Harcourt Brace & Company, Canada.

Brown, Carolyn Joyce. 1990. Generation X. Youth in the 1980s Were Unemployed, Under-Employed, Marginalized and Poor. *Perception* 14 (2): 62–65.

Brownfield, David and Kevin Thompson. 1991. Attachment to Peers and Delinquent Behaviour. *Canadian Journal of Criminology* 33 (1): 45–60.

Burrows, M. and L. Olsen. 1998. A Holistic Peer Education Program to Reduce STD Infection Among Transient Young Adults in a Resort Community. *The Canadian Journal of Human Sexuality* 7(4): 365–370.

Calliste, Agnes. 1996. Black Families in Canada: Exploring the Interconnections of Race, Class and Gender. In *Voices: Essays on Canadian Families*, Marion Lynn ed. Toronto: Nelson Canada.

The Cambridge Reporter. 2000. Lawyers set to Challenge Ontario's Squeegee Ban. February 2: 5A.

Cameron, Sandy. 2000. *Poverty. A Student Learning Resource.* Vancouver: End Legislated Poverty. www.bctf.bc.ca/lessonsaid/online/la2030.htm

Canadian Centre for Justice Statistics. 1997/98. *Alternative Measures for Youth in Canada 1997/98.* qsilver.queensu.ca./rcjnet/research/youth.html

Canadian Centre on Substance Abuse. 1999. *Canadian Profile 1999 — Special Populations: Highlights.*

Canadian Council on Social Development. 1998. *The Progress of Canada's Children: Focus on Youth.* Ottawa: Canadian Council on Social Development.

Canadian Council on Social Development. 2000. *Immigrant Youth in Canada.* Ottawa: Canadian Council on Social Development.

The Canadian Press. 2000. 10,000 Ravers Pack Toronto City Square To Protest Rave Ban. August 1.

Caragata, Lea. 1999. The Construction of Teen Parenting and the Decline of Adoption. In *Teen Pregnancy and Parenting: Social and Ethical Issues,* James Wong and David Checkland eds. Toronto: University of Toronto Press.

Carrigan, D. Owen. 1998. *Juvenile Delinquency in Canada: A History.* Concord, ON: Irwin Publishing.

Carrington, Peter J. 1999. Trends in Youth Crime in Canada, 1977–1996. *Canadian Journal of Criminology* 41 (1): 1–32.

Chappell, Rosalie. 1997. *Social Welfare in Canadian Society.* Toronto: ITP Nelson.

Charity, Patty. 2000. Raves: A Vehicle To Gender Equality. Unpublished Term Paper, SOC603 — Sociology of Gender. Toronto: Ryerson Polytechnic University.

Cheney, Peter. 1999. Judge Lays Blame for Reserve Suicides. *The Globe and Mail*, September 22: A3.

Chimbos, Peter D. 1980. The Greek-Canadian Family: Tradition and Change. In *Canadian Families: Ethnic Variations*, K. Ishwaran ed. Toronto: McGraw-Hill Ryerson.

Christensen, Carole Pigler and Morton Weinfeld. 1993. The Black Family in Canada: A Preliminary Exploration of Family Patterns and Inequality. *Canadian Ethnic Studies* 25(3): 26–44.

Chui, Tina. 1999. Canada's Population: Charting Into the 21st Century. *Canadian Social Trends. Volume 3.* Toronto: Thompson Educational Publishing, Inc.

Church, Elizabeth. 1996. Kinship and Stepfamilies. In *Voices: Essays on Canadian Families*, edited by Marion Lynn. Toronto: Nelson Canada.

Clark, Andrew. 1999. How Teens Got The Power: Gen Y Has the Cash, the Cool — And a Burgeoning Consumer Culture. *Maclean's* 112 (12): 42.

Clark, Susan. 1999. What do we know about unmarried mothers? In *Teen Pregnancy and Parenting: Social and Ethical Issues*, James Wong and David Checkland eds. Toronto: University of Toronto Press.

Cochrane, Mongrieff. 1988. Addressing Youth and Family Vulnerability: Empowerment in an Ecological Context. *Canadian Journal of Public Health Supplement* 79 November/ December: S10–S16.

Connolly, Jennifer, Wendy Craig, Adele Goldberg and Debra Pepler. 1999. Conceptions of Cross-Sex Friendships and Romantic Relationships in Early Adolescence. *Journal of Youth and Adolescence* 28 (4): 481–494.

Conway, John F. 1993. *The Canadian Family in Crisis.* Second edition. Toronto: James Lorimer & Company Ltd.

Copeland, Brenda, Andrew Armitage and Deborah Rutman. 1996. Preparation for Responsible Community Living. In

Youth in Transition: Perspectives on Research and Policy, Burt Galaway and Joe Hudson eds. Toronto: Thompson Educational Publishing, Inc.

Corak, Miles. 1999. Long term prospects of the young. *Canadian Economic Observer* January. Ottawa, Ontario: Minister of Industry.

Corbeil, Jean-Pierre. 2000. Sport Participation in Canada. *Canadian Social Trends. Volume 3.* Toronto: Thompson Educational Publishing, Inc.

Correctional Service Canada. 1999. *Substance Use by Adolescents and Subsequent Adult Criminal Activity.* scc.ca/text/pblct/forum/e033/e033f.shtm

Côté, James E. and Anton L. Allahar. 1994. *Generation on Hold: Coming of Age in the Late Twentieth Century.* Toronto: Stoddart.

Council of Ministers of Education, Canada (CMEC). 1999. *A Report on Public Expectations of Post-secondary Education in Canada.* Toronto: Council of Ministers of Education, Canada.

Cox, Kevin. 2000. Innu to Show Video of Gas-Sniffers in Agony. *The Globe and Mail*, November 25: A7.

Crago, Anna-Louise. 1996. Queer and Young and So Much Else. *Canadian Woman Studies* 16 (2): 15–17.

Cuddington, Lynn. 1995. Young Offenders: A Correctional Policy Perspective. *Safety Dignity and Respect for All* 7 (1). Correctional Service Canada. www.csc-scc.ca/text/pblct/forum/e07/e071e.shtm

Currie, D. 1999. *"Girl Talk": Adolescent Magazines and Their Readers.* Toronto: University of Toronto Press.

Daly, Conway. 1999. Dialogue Sought to Prevent Suicides by Quebec Teenagers. *The Globe and Mail*, September 10: A7.

Danesi, Marcel. 1994. *Cool: The Signs and Meanings of Adolescence.* Toronto: University of Toronto Press.

Davies, Gwendolyn. 1995. Private Education for Women in Early Nova Scotia: 1784–1894. *Atlantis* 20 (1): 9–19.

Davies, Linda, Margaret McKinnon and Prue Rains. 1999. 'On My Own': A New Discourse of Dependence and Independence from Teen Mothers. In *Teen Pregnancy and Parenting: Social and Ethical Issues*, James Wong and David Checkland eds. Toronto: University of Toronto Press.

Davies, Scott. 1994. In Search of Resistance and Rebellion Among High School Dropouts. *The Canadian Journal of Sociology* 19 (1): 331–350.

Davies, Scott and Neil Guppy. 1998. Race and Canadian Education. In *Racism and Social Inequality in Canada: Concepts, Controversies and Strategies of Resistance*, Vic Satzewitch ed. Toronto: Thompson Educational Publishing, Inc.

Dei, George J. Sefa. 1993. Narrative Discourses of Black/African-Canadian Parents and the Canadian Public School System. *Canadian Ethnic Studies* 25 (3): 45–66.

DeKeseredy, Walter S. 1996. Patterns of Family Violence. In *Families: Changing Trends in Canada.* Third Edition, Maureen Baker ed. Toronto: McGraw-Hill Ryerson Limited.

Dhruvarajan, Vanaja. 1996. Hindu Indo-Canadian Families. In *Voices: Essays on Canadian Families,* Marion Lynn ed. Toronto: Nelson Canada.

Dowd, James J. 1981. Age and Inequality: A Critique of the Age Stratification Model. *Human Development* 24: 157–171.

Duffy, Anne and Julianne Momirov. 1997. *Family Violence: A Canadian Introduction.* Toronto: James Lorimer & Company, Publishers.

Duncan, Steve. 2000. *Is there a Generation Gap?* Montana State University, Communication Services. www.montana.edu/wwwpb/home/gap.html.

Dupont, Claudine. 2000. Unrebellious Youth: Old Assumptions About Marketing to the Young Don't Work with the Screenagers. *Marketing* 105 (1): 20.

Durham, M. 1999. Girls, Media, and the Negotiation of Sexuality: A Study of Race, Class, and Gender in Adolescent Peer Groups. *Journalism and Mass Communication Quarterly* 76 (2): 193–200.

Eaton, Jonathan. 1997. Labour's Love Lost? *The Toronto Star*, September 1: E1.

Education Today. 1996. Post-Schooling Employment. *Education Today* 8 (1): 5.

Elton, Sarah and Steve Brearton. 1997. Youth and Work. *This Magazine* 31 (1): 4–5.

Ferguson, Sue. 2000. Wired Teens: A New Study Documents the Embraces of the Internet by Canadian Kids — And Lifts the Veil on How They Use It. *Maclean's* 113 (22): 38.

Fine, Sean. 1999. Teenage Daughters Still Find Dad Distant. *The Globe and Mail*, October 11: A1, A6.

Fine, Sean. 2000. University Fee Hikes Slowing: Statscan. *The Globe and Mail*, August 29: A8.

Fiske, Jo-Anne and Rose Johnny. 1996. The Nedut'en Family: Yesterday and Today. In *Voices: Essays on Canadian Families*, Marion Lynn ed. Toronto: Nelson Canada.

Fitzgerald, Michael D. 1995. Homeless Youths and The Child Welfare System: Implications for Policy and Service. *Child Welfare* 74 (3): 717–731.

Frank, Blye. 1994. Queer Selves/Queer in Schools: Young Men and Sexualities. In *Sex in Schools: Canadian Education & Sexual Regulation*, Susan Prentice ed. Toronto: Our Schools/Ourselves.

Frank, Jeffrey. 2000. 15 Years of AIDS in Canada. *Canadian Social Trends. Volume 3.* Toronto: Thompson Educational Publishing, Inc.

Frederick, Judith A. and Monica Boyd. 1998. The Impact of Family Structure on High School Completion. *Canadian Social Trends* 48 (Spring): 12–14.

Freeze, Colin. 1999. Teen Dies in a Dough-Making Machine. *The Globe and Mail*, September 27: A8.

Fuligni, Andrew J. 1997. The Academic Achievement of Adolescents from Immigrant Families: The Roles of Family Background, Attitudes, and Behavior. *Child Development* 68 (2): 351–363.

Gabor, Peter, Steven Thibodeau and Santanita Manychief. 1996. Taking Flight? The Transition Experiences of Native Youth. In *Youth in Transition: Perspectives on Research and Policy,* Burt Galaway and Joe Hudson eds. Toronto: Thompson Educational Publishing, Inc.

Gaetz, Stephen, Bill O'Grady and Bryan Vaillaincourt. 1999. *Making Money: The Shout Clinic Report on Homeless Youth and Employment*. Toronto: Central Toronto Community Health Centres.

Galambos, Nancy L. and Giselle C. Kolaric. 1994. Canada. In *International Handbook of Adolescence*, Klaus Hurrelmann ed. Westport, Connecticut: Greenwood Press.

Galt, Virginia. 1999a. "I Can't Afford it Any More. I'm 20 Grand in Debt." *The Globe and Mail*, December 13: A16.

Galt, Virginia. 1999b. Fighting "Poor" Label Earns Parkdale Kids Special Recognition. *The Globe and Mail*, November 15: A7.

Gerbner, George. 1998. Who Is Shooting Whom? The Content and the Context of Media Violence. In *Bang Bang Shoot Shoot: Essays on Guns and Popular Culture*, Murray Pomerance and John Sakeris eds. Toronto: Media Studies Working Group.

Gerbner, George. 1995. Casting And Fate: Women and Minorities on Television Drama, Game Shows, and News. In *Communication, Cultures, and Community*, E. Hollander, C. van der Linden and P. Rutten eds. The Netherlands: Bohn Stafleu van Logham.

Gfellner, Barbara M. and John D. Hundleby. 1990. The Status of Canadian Research on Adolescence: 1980–1987. *Canadian Psychology* 31 (2): 132–137.

Giese, Rachel. 1999. Anger of Today's Youth is In-Your-Face Reality. *The Toronto Star*, July 29. www.thestar.ca/thestar/back_issue...90729

The Globe and Mail. 1999. More Students Burdened by Loans, Study Finds. July 31: A2.

Goldstein, Jay and Alexander Segall. 1991. Ethnic Intermarriage and Ethnic Identity. In *Continuity and Change in Marriage and Family*, Jean E. Veevers ed. Toronto: Holt, Reinhart & Winston Canada.

Gordon, Daphne. 2000. Glow Sticks All the Rave. *The Toronto Star*, June 17: R14.

Government of Canada. 1998. *Tobacco and Health: Government Responses*. December.

Graydon, Shari. 1997. *Round Table Report on the Portrayal of Young Women in the Media.* Vancouver: Status of Women Canada.

Grinder, Robert E. 1973. *Adolescence.* Toronto: John Wiley & Sons.

Guttman, Julius and Mary Alice. 1991. Issues in the Career Development of Adolescent Females: Implications for Educational and Guidance Practices. *Guidance & Counselling* 6 (3): 59–75.

The Hamilton Spectator. 1995. Workers at 3 Hortons Stores Vote to Join Union. *The Hamilton Spectator*, March 9: C3.

Hampson, K. 1996. Authenticity, Music, Television. In *Pictures of a Generation on Hold: Selected Papers*, Murray Pomerance and John Sakeris eds. Toronto, Canada: Media Studies Working Group.

Hargrove, Buzz. 2000. Dying to Work: We Should Protect Our Young. *The Globe and Mail,* July 19: A11.

Hartnagel, Timothy F. 1998. Labour-Market Problems and Crime in the Transition from School to Work. *The Canadian Review of Sociology and Anthropology* 35 (3): 435–460.

Health and Welfare Canada. 1992. Research Update. *Health Promotion* 31 (2): 16–7.

Health Canada. 2000. *Examining Youth Smoking and Relapse Prevention: A Review of the Literature.* www.hc-sc.gc.ca/hppb/tobaccoreduct

Henry, Frances and Carol Tator. 1994. Racism and the University. *Canadian Ethnic Studies* 26 (3): 74–91.

Hewitt, D., G. Vinje and P. MacNeil. 1995. Young Canadians' Alcohol and Other Drug Use: Increasing Our Understanding. Health Canada: *Horizons Three.*

Hiebert, Bryan and Barbara Thomlison. 1996. Facilitating Transitions to Adulthood: Research and Policy Implications. In *Youth in Transition: Perspectives on Research and Policy*, Burt Galaway and Joe Hudson eds. Toronto: Thompson Educational Publishing, Inc.

Hill, Donna. Ed. 1981. *A Black Man's Toronto 1914–1980: The Reminiscences of Harry Cairey.* Toronto: The Multicultural History Society of Ontario.

Hobart, Charles. 1996. Intimacy and Family Life: Sexuality, Cohabitation, and Marriage. In *Families: Changing Trends in Canada.* Third Edition, Maureen Baker ed. Toronto: McGraw-Hill Ryerson Limited.

Holmes, Janelle and Eliane Leslau Silverman. 1992. *We're Here, Listen to Us! A Survey of Young Women in Canada.* Ottawa: Canadian Advisory Council on the Status of Women.

Howe, Nina and William M. Bukowski. 1996. What are Children and How do They Become Adults? Childrearing and Socialization. *Families: Changing Trends in Canada.* Third Edition, Maureen Baker ed. Toronto: McGraw-Hill Ryerson Limited.

Hudon, Raymond, Bernard Fournier, Louis Métivier, with the assistance of Benoît-Paul Hébert. 1991. To What Extent Are Today's Young People Interested in Politics? Inquiries Among 16- to 24- Year-Olds. In *Youth in Canadian Politics: Participation and Involvement. Volume 8 of the Research Studies*, Kathy Megyery ed. Royal Commission on Electoral Reform and Party Financing and Canada Communication Group. Toronto and Oxford: Dundurn Press.

Human Resources Development Canada. 1999a. Developments. *National Longitudinal Survey of Children and Youth,* 4 (1).

Human Resources Development Canada. 1999b. Post-Secondary education in Canada: Still a good investment. *Applied Research Bulletin,* 5 (1), 12–13.

Human Resources Development Canada. 1999c. Dropping Out and Working While Studying. *Applied Research Bulletin* 5 (1): 17–19.

Hung, Kwing and Stan Lipinski. 1995. *Questions and Answers on Youth and Justice.* Correctional Service Canada. www.csc-scc.ca/text/pblct/forum/e07/e071b.shtm

Irvine, Martha. 1997. Young and Unionizing. *The Toronto Star,* August 18: E3.

Isajiw, Wsevolod W. 1999. *Understanding Diversity: Ethnicity and Race in the Canadian Context.* Toronto: Thompson Educational Publishing, Inc.

Jaffe, Peter G. and Linda L. Baker. 1999. Why Changing the YOA Does Not Impact Youth Crime: Developing Effective Prevention Programs for Children and Adolescents. *Canadian Psychology* 40 (1): 22–29.

James, Carl E. 1998. "Up to no good": Black on the Streets and Encountering Police. In *Racism and Social Inequality in Canada: Concepts, Controversies and Strategies of Resistance,* Vic Satzewitch ed. Toronto: Thompson Educational Publishing, Inc.

James, Carl E. 1999. *Seeing Ourselves: Exploring Race, Ethnicity and Culture.* 2nd Edition. Toronto: Thompson Educational Publishing, Inc.

James, Carl, E. 1990. *Making it: Black Youth, Racism and Career Aspirations in a Big City.* Toronto: Mosaic Press.

Jennings, Philip. 1998. School Enrolment and the Declining Youth Participation Rate. *Policy Options Politiques,* April: 10–14.

Johnson, Holly. 1996. *Dangerous Domains: Violence Against Women in Canada.* Toronto: Nelson Canada.

Kalbach, Madeline A. 2000. Ethnicity and the Altar. In *Perspectives on Ethnicity in Canada: A Reader,* Madeline A. Kalbach, Warren E. Kalbach eds. Toronto: Harcourt Canada.

Kaufman, Miriam. 1999. Day-to-Day Ethical issues in the Care of Young Parents and Their Children. In *Teen Pregnancy and Parenting: Social and Ethical Issues,* James Wong and David Checkland eds. Toronto: University of Toronto Press.

Kearney-Cooke, A. 1999. Gender Differences and Self Esteem. *The Journal of Gender-Specific Medicine* 2 (3): 46–52. http://www.mmhe.com/jgsm/articles/JGSM9906/Cooke.html

Kelly, Deirdre M. 1999. A Critical Feminist Perspective on Teen Pregnancy and Parenthood. In *Teen Pregnancy and Parenting: Social and Ethical Issues,* James Wong and David Checkland eds. Toronto: University of Toronto Press.

Kelly, Jennifer. 1998. *Under the Gaze: Learning to be Black in a White Society.* Halifax, NS: Fernwood.

Kelly, Karen, Linda Howatson-Leo and Warren Clark. 2000. "I feel Overqualified for my Job...". *Canadian Social Trends. Volume 3.* Toronto: Thompson Educational Publishing, Inc.

Kendal, D., J. Murray and R. Linden. 1997. *Sociology in Our Times: First Canadian Edition.* Scarborough, Ontario: International Thomson Publishing.

Kerr, Alison. 1991. Pornography. *Canadian Woman Studies* 11 (4): 51

Kerr, Kevin B. 1997. *Youth Unemployment Trends.* Ottawa: Government of Canada, Depository Services Program, BP–448E.

Kerr, Kevin B. 1999. *Youth Unemployment in Canada.* Ottawa: Government of Canada, Depository Services Program, 82–4E.

King, Alan, Robert Perreault and Kevin Roeter. 1988. Results of an Ontario Secondary School Study. *Canadian Journal of Public Health Supplement* 79 (December): S46–47.

Khanna, Mala. 1999. *Hate/Bias Motivate Acts Perpetrated By and Against Youth: A Research Overview.* Ottawa: Canadian Heritage.

Kingsmill, Suzanne and Benjamin Schlesinger. 1998. *The Family Squeeze: Surviving the Sandwich Generation.* Toronto: University of Toronto Press.

Kingston, J. 2000. Ecstasy Kills. Mom, 21, Was At Rave Club. *The Toronto Sun,* June 28: 10.

The Kitchener-Waterloo Record. 1998. Women Signing Up for Unions Faster Than Men, Report Says. *The Kitchener-Waterloo Record,* September 4: F5.

Klein, Naomi. 1997. British Activists Have Already McWon. *The Toronto Star,* June 9: A17.

Kolaric, Giselle C. and Nancy L. Galambos. 1995. Face-to-Face Interactions in Unacquainted Female-Male Adolescent Dyads: How do Girls and Boys Behave? *Journal of Early Adolescence* 15 (3): 363–382.

Koller, Marvin R. *Families: A Multigenerational Approach.* Toronto: McGraw Hill.

Kunz, J. L., and L. Hanvey, 2000. *Cultural Diversity: Immigrant Youth in Canada.* Ottawa: Canadian Council on Social Development.

Kuryllowicz, Kara. 1996. Youth Crime: Behind the Stats. *What! A Magazine* 10 (1): 20–23.

Larkin, June. 1994. *Sexual Harassment: High School Girls Speak Out.* Toronto: Second Story Press.

Law Now. 1996. Youth Crime — What Do We Know? *Law Now* 21 (1): 12.

LeBlanc, Marc, Evelyne Vallieres and Pierre McDuff. 1993. The Prediction of Males' Adolescent and Adult Offending from School Experience. *Canadian Journal of Criminology* 35 (1): 459–478.

Lenskyj, Helen. 1990. Beyond Plumbing and Prevention: Feminist Approaches to Sex Education. *Gender & Education* 2 (2): 217–221.

Li, Peter S. 1988. *Ethnic Inequality in Class Society.* Toronto: Thompson Educational Publishing.

Links, Paul S. 1998. Suicide and Life: The Ultimate Juxtaposition. *Canadian Medical Association Journal* 158 (4): 524–516.

Livingstone, D. W. 1999. *The Education-Jobs Gap.* Toronto: Garamond Press.

Little, Bruce. 1998. Minimum-Wage Workers Disproportionately Young. *The Globe and Mail*, September 7: A3.

Looker, E. Dianne and Graham S. Lowe. 1996. The Transitions to Adult Roles: Youth Views and Policy Implications. In *Youth in Transition: Perspectives on Research and Policy*, Burt Galaway and Joe Hudson eds. Toronto: Thompson Educational Publishing, Inc.

Lowe, Graham S. and Harvey Krahn. 1994–5. *Job Related Education and Training Among Young Workers.* Kingston: Queen's University, School of Industrial Relations/Industrial

Relations Centre, Queen's Papers in Industrial Relations. Working Paper Series.

Lowe, Justin. 1990. Youth Environmental Movement Flourishing. *Earth Island Journal* 5 (4): 17–18.

Lynn, Marion and Eimear O'Neill. 1995. Families, Power, and Violence. In *Canadian Families: Diversity, Conflict and Change*, Nancy Mandell and Ann Duffy eds. Toronto: Harcourt Brace & Company, Canada.

MacKinnon, Mark. 2000a. Young Voters Feel Disaffected. *The Globe and Mail*, November 6: A1, A9.

MacKinnon, Mark. 2000b. Canadian Tobacco Firms After Young, Wigand Says. *The Globe and Mail*, May 31: A7.

MacKinnon, Mark. 2000c. Tobacco Sales Target Was Youth. *The Globe and Mail*, May 29: A1, A7.

Maclean's. 2000. Wild Ones Through The Ages: Some of the Youth Movements that Have Captivated Kids — And, In Most Cases, Scandalized Parents — Over the Past 80 Years. *Maclean's* 113 (4): 43–44.

Mandell, Nancy. 1988. The Child Question: Links Between Women and Children in the Family. In *Reconstructing the Canadian Family: Feminist Perspectives*, Nancy Mandell & Ann Duffy eds. Toronto: Butterworths.

Mandell, Nancy and Stewart Crysdale. 1993. Gender Tracks: Male-Female Perceptions of Home-School-Work Transitions. In *Transitions: Schooling and Employment in Canada*, Paul Anisef & Paul Axelrod eds. Thompson Educational Publishing, Inc.

Marquardt, Richard. 1998. *Enter At Your Own Risk: Canadian Youth and the Labour Market*. Toronto: Between the Lines.

Martin, Fay E. 1996. Tales of Transition: Leaving Public Care. In *Youth in Transition: Perspectives on Research and Policy*, Burt Galaway and Joe Hudson eds. Toronto: Thompson Educational Publishing, Inc.

Mathews, Frederick. 1996. *The Invisible Boy: Revisioning the Victimization of Male Children and Teens*. Ottawa: Health Canada.

Maxwell, Mary Percival and James D. Maxwell. 1994. Three Decades of Private School Females' Ambitions: Implications for Canadian Elites. *Canadian Review of Sociology and Anthropology* 31 (2): 137–167.

Maynard, Steven. 1997. "Horrible Temptations": Sex, Men, and Working-Class Male Youth in Urban Ontario, 1890–1935. *The Canadian Historical Review* 78 (2): 191–235.

Mayseless, Ofra and Hadas Wiseman. 1998. Adolescents' Relationships with Father, Mother, and Same-Sex Friend. *Journal of Adolescent Research* 13 (1): 101–124.

McAlpine, Donna D., Carl F. Grindstaff and Ann Marie Sorenson. 1996. Competence and Control in the Transition for Adolescence to Adulthood: A Longitudinal Study of Teenage Mothers. In *Youth in Transition: Perspectives on Research and Policy*, Burt Galaway and Joe Hudson eds. Toronto: Thompson Educational Publishing, Inc.

McCormick, Naomi and Clinton J. Jesser. 1991. The Courtship Game: Power in the Sexual Encounter. In *Continuity and Change in Marriage and Family*, Jean E. Veevers ed. Toronto: Holt, Reinhart & Winston Canada.

McCreary Centre Society. 1998. *Results from the Adolescent Health Survey.* Vancouver: McCreary Centre Society.

McDaniel, Susan. 1997. Intergenerational Transfers, Social Solidarity, and Social Policy: Unanswered Questions and Policy Challenges. *Canadian Public Policy Supplement 1997:* 1–21.

McIlroy, Anne. 1999. Illegal Sales of Cigarettes to Minors Rising, Study Finds. *The Globe and Mail*, June 23: A7.

McKay, Alexander & Philippa Holowaty. 1997. Sexual Health Education: A Study of Adolescents' Opinions, Self-Perceived Needs, and Current and Preferred Sources of Information. *The Canadian Journal of Human Sexuality* 6 (1): 29–38.

McKinley, E. Graham. 1996. In The Back Of Your Head: *Beverly Hills, 90210, Friends*, and the Discursive Construction of Identity. In *Pictures of a Generation on Hold: Selected Papers*, Murray Pomerance and John Sakeris eds. Toronto: Media Studies Working Group.

Meloff, William and Robert A. Silverman. 1992. Canadian Kids Who Kill. *Canadian Journal of Criminology* 34 (1): 15–34.

Miller, Crispen Mark. 1996. North American Youth and the Entertainment State. In *Pictures of a Generation on Hold: Selected Papers*, Murray Pomerance and John Sakeris eds. Toronto: Media Studies Working Group.

Mintz, Eric. 1993. Two Generations: The Political Attitudes of High School Students and their Parents. *International Journal of Canadian Studies/Revue internationale d'études canadiennes,* Special Issue, Winter: 59–71.

Mitchell, Barbara. 1998. Too Close for Comfort? Parental Assessments of "Boomerang Kid" Living Arrangements. *Canadian Journal of Sociology* 23 (1): 21–46.

Mitchell, Barbara A. and Ellen M. Gee. 1996. Young Adults Returning Home: Implications for Social Policy. In *Youth in Transition. Perspectives on Research and Policy*, Burt Galaway and Joe Hudson eds. Toronto: Thompson Educational Publishing, Inc.

Moss, Kirk. Everyday Racism. *Equality Today.* Toronto: Young People's Press. http//:www.equalitytoday.org/racism.html

Nakamura, Alice and Ging Wong. 1998. Rethinking our National Stay-in-School Rhetoric. *Policy Options Politique,* April: 7–10.

National Crime Prevention Council of Canada. 1996. *Is Youth Crime a Problem?* www.crime-prevention.org/ncpc/publications/children/family/introd_e.htm

National Crime Prevention Council. 2000. *Young People Say. Report from the Youth Consultation Initiative.* Ottawa: National Crime Prevention Council.

National Film Board. 1990. *Playing For Keeps: A Film About Teen Mothers.* Montreal: National Film Board.

National Film Board. 1992. *Speak it! From the Heart of Nova Scotia.* Halifax: National Film Board, Atlantic Centre.

National Film Board. 1994. *Children For Hire.* Montreal: National Film Board.

National Film Board. 1997. *All the Right Stuff.* Montreal: National Film Board.

Nelson, E.D. and Barrie W. Robinson. 1999. *Gender in Canada.* Scarborough, ON: Prentice Hall Allyn and Bacon Canada.

Nett, Emily M. 1993. *Canadian Families: Past and Present.* 2nd Edition. Toronto: Butterworths.

Noller, Patricia and Mary Anne Fitzpatrick. 1993. *Communication in Family Relationships.* New York: Prentice Hall.

Normand, Josée. 2000. Education of Women in Canada. *Canadian Social Trends. Volume 3.* Toronto: Thompson Educational Publishing, Inc.

O'Brien, Carol-Anne and Lorna Weir. 1995. Lesbians and Gay Men Inside and Outside Families. In *Canadian Families: Diversity, Conflict and Change*, Nancy Mandell and Ann Duffy eds. Toronto: Harcourt Brace & Company, Canada.

Oderkirk, Jillian. 2000. Marriage in Canada: Changing Beliefs and Behaviours 1600–1900. *Canadian Social Trends. Volume 3.* Toronto: Thompson Educational Publishing, Inc.

O'Donnell, Mike. 1985. *Age and Generation.* New York: Society Now.

Offer, Daniel and Judith Offer. 1972. Developmental Psychology of Youth. In *Youth: Problems and Approaches*, S.J. Samsie ed. Philadelphia: Lea & Febiger.

O'Grady, B., R. Bright and E. Cohen. 1998. Sub-Employment and Street Youths: An Analysis of the Impact of Squeegee Cleaning on Homeless Youths. *Security Journal* 11: 315–323.

Oh, Susan. 2000. Rave Fever: Raves are all the Rage, But Drugs are Casting a Pall Over Their Sunny Peace-And-Love Ethos. *Maclean's* 113 (17): 38.

O'Rand, Angela, M. 1990. Stratification and the Life Course. In *Handbook of Aging and the Social Sciences.* Third Edition. Academic Press, Inc.

Organization for Economic Co-Operation and Development (OECD). 1986. *Girls and Women in Education: A Cross-National Study of Sex Inequalities in Upbringing and in Schools and Colleges.* Paris: Organization for Economic Co-operation and Development.

Orton, Maureen Jessop. 1999. Changing High-Risk Policies to Reduce High-Risk Sexual Behaviours. In *Teen Pregnancy and Parenting: Social and Ethical Issues*, James Wong and David Checkland eds. Toronto: University of Toronto Press.

Otis, Joanne, Joseph Levy, Jean-Marc Samson, Francois Pilote and Annie Fugere. 1997. Gender Differences in Sexuality and Interpersonal Power Relations Among French-Speaking Young Adults from Quebec: A Province-Wide Study. *The Canadian Journal of Human Sexuality* 6 (1): 17–28.

Paetch, Joanne J. and Lorne D. Bertrand. 1999. Victimization and Delinquency Among Canadian Youth. *Adolescence* 34 (134): 351–367.

Pate, Kim. 1999. Young Women and Violent Offences: Myths and Realities. *Canadian Woman Studies* 19 (1&2): 39–43.

Paulson, Sharon E. and Cheryl L. Sputa. 1996. Patterns of Parenting During Adolescence: Perceptions of Adolescents and Parents. *Adolescence* 31 (122): 369–382.

Pearson, Patricia. 1993. Teenage Mutant Ninja Canadians? *Chatelaine* 66 (3): 72–75, 116.

Philp, Margaret. 2000. Young Workers Face High Risks. *The Globe and Mail*, July 10: A2.

Picot, Ganett and John Myles. 2000. Children in Low-Income Families. *Canadian Social Trends. Volume 3.* Toronto: Thompson Educational Publishing, Inc.

Pizanias, Caterina. 1996. Greek Families in Canada: Fragile Truths, Fragmented Stories. In *Voices: Essays on Canadian Families,* Marion Lynn ed. Toronto: Nelson International Thompson Publishing, Inc.

Price, Lisa S. 1989. *Patterns of Violence in the Lives of Girls and Women: A Reading Guide.* Vancouver: Women's Research Centre.

The Progressive Conservative Party of Ontario. 1999. *PC Blueprint.* Toronto: PC Party of Ontario.

Pulkingham, Jane and Gordon Ternowetsky, eds. 1996. *Remaking Canadian Social Policy: Social Security in the Late 1990s.* Halifax: Fernwood Publishing.

Pupo, Norene. 1994. Dissecting the Role of the State. In *Canadian Society: Understanding and Surviving in the 1990s*, Dan Glenday and Ann Duffy eds. Toronto: McClelland & Stewart.

Puxley, Chinta. 2000. Squeegee Law Shows Harris is Out of Touch. *The Hamilton Spectator*, August 2.

Raychaba, Brian. 1993. *"Pain...Lots of Pain": Family Violence and Abuse in the Lives of Young People in Care*. Ottawa: National Youth Care Network.

Read, Deborah. 1996. The Young and the Jobless. *The Globe and Mail Report on Business Magazine*, April: 117–119.

Reynolds, Cecilia. 1998. The Educational System. In *Feminist Issues: Race, Class, and Sexuality*. Second Edition, Nancy Mandell ed. Scarborough, ON: Prentice Hall Allyn and Bacon Canada.

Rhynard, Jill, and Marlene Krebs. 1997. Sexual Assault in Dating Relationships. *Journal of School Health* 67 (3): 89–97.

Richardson, C. James. 1996. Divorce and Remarriage. In *Families: Changing Trends in Canada*. Third Edition, Maureen Baker ed. Toronto: McGraw-Hill Ryerson Limited.

Rosenthal, Carolyn J. 1987. Aging and Intergenerational Relations in Canada. In *Aging in Canada*. Second Edition, Victor Marshall ed. Toronto: Fitzhenry and Whiteside, 311–341.

Savoie, Josée. 1999. Youth Vilolent Crime. *Juristat*. Canadian Centre for Justice Statistics, Statistics Canada — Catalogue No. 85-002-XPE, 19 (13).

Schissel, Bernard. 1997. *Blaming Children: Youth Crime, Moral Panics and the Politics of Hate*. Halifax: Fernwood Publishing.

Sears, H. A. and V.H. Armstrong. 1998. A Prospective Study of Adolescents' Self-Reported Depressive Symptoms: Are Risk Behaviours a Stronger Predictor Than Anxiety Symptoms? *Journal of Behavioural Science* 30 (4): 225–233.

Seltzer, Vivian Center. 1989. *The Psychosocial Worlds of the Adolescent: Public and Private*. Toronto: Wiley & Sons.

Sharpe, Donald and Janelle K. Taylor. 1999. An Examination of Variables from a Social-Developmental Model to Explain

Physical and Psychological Dating Violence. *Canadian Journal of Behavioural Science* 31 (3): 165–175.

Sheremata, Davis. 1999. A Break for Working Girls. *Western Report* 14 (4): 25.

Sherwood, Jane. 1993. Teaching Tolerance. *Canada & the World* 59 (2): 22–24.

Shields, Ian W. 1995. Young Sex Offenders: A Comparison with a Control Group of Non-Sex Offenders. *Safety Dignity and Respect for All* 7 (1). Correctional Service Canada. www.csc-scc.ca/text/pblct/forum/e07/e071e.shtm

Silcott, Mireille. 2000. Built For Speed: In the Rave Scene, Ecstasy is no Longer the Drug of Choice. Which is not Good News. *Saturday Night* 115 (6): 16

Silcott, M. 2000. Raves Roots. *The Toronto Star*, February 19: M1.

Single, E., A. Maclennan and P. MacNeil. 1994. Alcohol and Other Drug Use in Canada. *Horizons.*

Sippola, Lorrie K. 1999. Getting to Know the "Other": The Characteristics and Developmental Significance of Other-Sex Relationships in Adolescence. *Journal of Youth and Adolescence* 28 (4): 407–418.

Spears, John. 1999. Mayor's Program Called Attack on Poor. *The Toronto Star*, August 4. www.thestar.ca/thestar/back_issue...990804.

Sprott, Jane B. 1996. Understanding Public Views of Youth Crime and the Youth Justice System. *Canadian Journal of Criminology* 38 (3): 271–290.

Stanleigh, Sean. 2000. Peaceful Rave Rally Was A Seminal Event: Youth Accented Positive Vibes to City Politicians. *The Toronto Star*, April 8: B4.

Statistics Canada. Secondary School Graduates, 1991–1996. Catalogue no. 81-229-XIB.

Statistics Canada, 1990–1997. Enrolment in Elementary and Secondary Schools, 1990–1997. Catalogue no. 81-229-XIB.

Statistics Canada. 1993–1997. Community College Postsecondary Enrolment, 1993–1997. Catalogue no. 81-229-XIB.

Statistics Canada. 1993–1998. University Enrolment, Full-time and Part-Time, by Sex, 1993-1998. CANSIM, cross-classified tables 00580701, 00580702.

Statistics Canada. 1996. Immigrant Population by Place of Birth and Period of Immigration, 1996 Census, Nation Tables. www.statcan.ca/english/Pgdb/People/Population/demo25a.htm

Statistics Canada. 1998a. 1996 Census: Education, Mobility and Migration. *The Daily*, April 14.

Statistics Canada. 1998b. Multiple Risk Behaviour in Teenagers and Young Adults, 1994/95. *The Daily*, October 29.

Statistics Canada. 1998c. Participation Rates and Unemployment Rates By Age and Sex. www.statcan.ca/english/Pgbd/People/Labour/labor23a.htm

Statistics Canada. 1999a. Labour Force Characteristics By Age and Sex. www.statcan.ca/english/pgdb/People/Labour/labour20a.htm

Statistics Canada. 1999b. Labour Force Participation Rates. www.statcan.ca/english/Pgdb/People/Labour05.htm

Statistics Canada. 1999c. Marriages. *The Daily*, October 28.

Statistics Canada. 1999d. Population 15 Years and Over by Sex, Age Groups and Labour Force Activity, for Canada, Provinces and Territories, 1981–1996 Censuses (20% Sample Data). Nation Series, Catalogue No. 93F0027XDB96001.

Statistics Canada. 1999e. Selected Notifiable Diseases. Catalogue No. 82F0075XCB.

Statistics Canada. 1999f. Youths and Adults Charged in Criminal Incidents, Criminal Code and Federal Statutes, by Sex. CANSIM, Matrices 2198 and 2199.

Statistics Canada. 1999g. Youths and the Labour Market, 1998–99. *Labour Force Update* 3 (4).

Statistics Canada. 2000a. *Average Hours per week of Television Watching*. Ottawa: Statistics Canada, Catalogue no. 87F0006XIB.

Statistics Canada. 2000b. *Family Violence in Canada: A Statistical Profile 2000*. Ottawa: Canadian Centre for Justice Statistics. Catalogue No. 85-224-XIE.

Statistics Canada. 2000c. *Labour Force Survey*. April.

Stevenson, Kathryn, Jennifer Tufts, Dianne Hendrick and Melanie Kowalski. 2000. Youth and Crime. *Canadian Social Trends. Volume 3*. Toronto: Thompson Educational Publishing, Inc.

Stewart, Doug. 1998. High School Rules: Recognizing High Schools as Cultural Centres Leads to a Better Understanding of Teens. *Marketing Magazine*, November 2: 26.

Strange, Carolyn. 1995. *Toronto's Girls Problem: The Perils and Pleasures of the City, 1880–1930*. Toronto: University of Toronto Press.

Strange, Carolyn. 1997. Sin or Salvation? Protecting Toronto's Working Girls. *The Beaver* 77 (3): 8–13.

Synge, Jane. 1979. The Transition From School to Work: Growing Up Working Class in Early 20th Century Hamilton, Ontario. In *Childhood and Adolescence in Canada*, K. Ishwaran ed. Toronto: McGraw-Hill Ryerson Limited.

Tait, Heather. 2000. Educational Achievement of Young Aboriginal Adults. In *Canadian Social Trends. Volume 3*. Toronto: Thompson Educational Publishing, Inc.

Tait, Heather. 1999. Educational Achievement of Young Aboriginal Adults. *Canadian Social Trends* Spring, No. 52: 6–10.

Talaga, Tanya. 2000. Ecstasy Use May Cause Depression: Study. *The Toronto Star*, July 25: A15.

Tanner, Julian. 1990. Reluctant rebels: A case study of Edmonton High School Drop-Outs. *The Canadian Review of Sociology and Anthropology* 27 (1): 74–94.

Taylor, Peter Shawn. 1997. Getting the Drop on Dropouts. *Canadian Business* 70 (13): 22–24.

Thiessen, Victor and E. Dianne Looker. 1993. Generation, Gender and Class Perspectives on Work. *International Journal of Canadian Studies/Revue Internationale d'etudes canadiennes*, Special Issue, Winter: 35–45.

Thomson, Colin A. 1979. *Blacks in Deep Snow: Black Pioneers in Canada*. Don Mills, ON: James Dent & Sons (Canada) Limited.

The Toronto Star. 2000a. Challenge to the Safe Streets Act. *The Toronto Star*, June 14: B4.

The Toronto Star. 2000b. Making Raves Safe. *The Toronto Star*, June 3: K6

The Toronto Star. 2000c. Right Decision On Raves. *The Toronto Star*, August 6: A12.

Turcotte, Pierre and Alain Belanger. 2000. Moving in Together: The Formation of First Common-Law Unions. In *Canadian Social Trends. Volume 3*. Toronto: Thompson Educational Publishing, Inc.

UNESCO. 1981. *Youth in the 1980s*. Paris: United Nations Educational, Scientific and Cultural Organization.

Vanier Institute of the Family. 2000. *Profiling Canada's Families II*. Nepean, ON: The Vanier Institute of the Family.

Van deer Veen, Wilma. 1994. Young People and the Environment: A Comparative Analysis of Young Environmentalists and Decision-Makers in Australia and Canada. *Youth Studies* 13 (4): 24–30.

Van Roosmalen, E. and H. Krahn. 1996. Boundaries of Youth. *Youth and Society* 28 (1): 36–45.

Van Wert, Bob. 1997. Change your Future: Transition Programs for Minority Youth. *Guidance and Counselling* 13 (1): 16–18.

Varpalotai, Aniko. 1996. Canadian Girls in Transition to Womanhood. In *Youth in Transition: Perspectives on Research and Policy*, Burt Galaway and Joe Hudson eds. Toronto: Thompson Educational Publishing, Inc.

Vertinsky, P. 1989. Substance Abuse Prevention Programs: The State of the Art in School Health. *Health Promotion* 27 (4): 8–14.

Wackett, J. 1998. A Theory-Based Initiative to Reduce the Rates of Chlamydia Trachomitis Infection Among Young Adults in the Yukon. *The Canadian Journal of Human Sexuality* 7 (4): 347–370.

Wade, Terrance J. and Augustine Brannigan. 1998. The Genesis of Adolescent Risk-Taking: Pathways Through Family, School and Peers. *The Canadian Journal of Sociology* 23 (1): 1–20.

Wadhera, Surinder and Wayne J. Millar. 1997. Teenage Pregnancies, 1974 to 1994. Statistics Canada, *Health Reports* 9 (3): 9–17.

Waldie, Paul. 1993. Kids at Work: Recession is Forcing More Canadian Children to Become Partial Family Breadwinners. *The Financial Post*, June 19: S18.

Walker, James W. St. G. 1985. *Racial Discrimination in Canada: The Black Experience.* Ottawa: Canadian Historical Association. Historical Booklet No. 41.

Wall, Julie, Katherine Covell and Peter D. MacIntyre. 1999. Implications of Social Supports for Adolescents' Education and Career Aspirations. *Canadian Journal of Behavioural Science* 31 (2): 63–71.

Webber, Marlene. 1991. *Street Kids: The Tragedy of Canada's Runaways.* Toronto: University of Toronto Press.

Willms, J. Douglas. 1997. Literacy Skills of Canadian Youth. Ottawa: Statistics Canada, Catalogue No. 89-552-MPE, no. 1.

Willms, J. Douglas. 1999. *Inequalities in Literary Skills Among Youth in Canada and the United States.* Ottawa: Statistics Canada, Human Resources Development Canada.

Winks, Robin W. 1997. *The Blacks in Canada: A History.* Second Edition. Montreal & Kingston: McGill-Queen's University Press.

Wong, James and David Checkland, eds. 1999. *Teen Pregnancy and Parenting: Social and Ethical Issues.* University of Toronto Press.

Wong, Siu Kwong. 1999. Acculturation, Peer Relation, and Delinquent Behaviour of Chinese-Canadian Youth. *Adolescence* 34 (133): 107–119.

Wood, Darryl, and Curt Taylor Griffiths. 1996. The Lost Generation: Inuit Youth in Transition to Adulthood. In *Youth in Transition: Perspectives on Research and Policy*, Burt Galaway and Joe Hudson eds. Toronto: Thompson Educational Publishing, Inc.

Wotherspoon, Terry. 1998. *The Sociology of Education in Canada: Critical Perspectives.* Toronto: Oxford University Press.

Zhao, John Z., Fernando Rajulton and Zenaida R. Ranavera. 1995. Leaving Parental Homes in Canada: Effects of Family Structure, Gender, and Culture. *Canadian Journal of Sociology* 20 (1): 31–50.

On April 22, 2001, Canada was host to the FTAA Summit Meeting in Quebec City. As thousands of activists gathered in peaceful protest, the authorities guarded a fence positioned between the delegates and the crowd. Toronto-based graphic designer and teacher, roB Breadner, captured the struggle of several young activists as they pushed toward the barrier and were confronted by police. After witnessing the violence, roB developed an "observer's lens" web site dedicated to showing the importance of the protests. It is from this site that many of the cover images are borrowed.

During the month of October, 2000, women from across Canada gathered to march on Parliament Hill in Ottawa. The event, sparked by women's groups, social activists, and the increasingly deeper cuts to social programs, provided a forum for young women to speak out against violence, poverty, and oppression. Rebecka Sheffield captured the spirit of the young protesters through a series of photographs. One of these images appears on the bottom right corner of the cover.